happier by degrees

happier by degrees

A College Reentry Guide for Women

PAM MENDELSOHN

 Ten Speed Press

1🕭

TEN SPEED PRESS
P O Box 7123
Berkeley, California 94707

Library of Congress Catalog Number: 79-19380
ISBN: 0-89815-161-9

Book Design by Nicola Mazzella
Cover Design by Brenton Beck, Fifth Street Design Associates

Library of Congress Cataloging in Publication Data

Mendelsohn, Pamela.
    Happier by degrees.
    Bibiography: p. 245
    1. Higher education of women—United States.
    2. Continuing Education—United States.
    3. Study, Method of—Handbooks, manuals, etc.
    I. Title
LC1756.M34   378.73   79-19380

Printed in the United States of America

10 9 8 7 6 5 4 3 2 1

To my daughter Rebekah for being so incredibly good-natured
and because she teaches me new things every day

To my parents, the late Stella and William Mendelsohn,
for their support and interest through thick and thin

To Peter Palmquist for understanding that the whole can be
greater than the sum of its parts

Contents

Preface

During the four years I spent in college fresh out of high school, I ran into exactly one "reentry" student. As it turned out, we were more or less the same age, *but* she was married, and that meant we were worlds apart. There was no doubt about it—she was definitely a novelty.

Things have really changed! If your image of today's college student involves only 19-year-old football players and bobby-soxed sorority sisters, you can label it way out-of-date. In 1983, according to the U.S. Census Bureau, more than one-third of the students on college campuses in the United States were over the age of 25, and 55 percent of them were women. In fact, people aged 35 and older constitute the fastest-growing student population on college campuses right now—and of this population, 2 out of every 3 are women!

Women who have never worked outside their homes, women who have been happily or unhappily employed for years, and women who have been contributing tremendous amounts of energy to volunteer work are all back in school. For most, the process of returning to a student life appears overwhelming—on any number of levels.

For example, applying to college straight out of high school may have been nerve-wracking, but at least there was a whole regiment of guidance counselors to tell you what you were supposed to do and when. Now you wonder where to begin. Are they serious about wanting to know the grades I got 20 years ago? Do I really have to take an aptitude test? How do I find out about financial aid?

One of the biggest stumbling blocks for the potential returnee is lack of confidence—will I be able to compete with these younger students? Can I actually get back into memorizing, test taking, term papers? Even more basic than that, will I really be able to juggle my life/my family life once I become a student?

In the spring of 1976, I began thinking about getting a master's degree in psychology. I had been out of undergraduate school ten years. A few encounters with the admissions people, financial aid, the psychology department, not to mention the incredible maze of parking lots, made me realize that what I needed was a good friend to go through the reentry process with me. Many of my high school and college friends were already back in school, but they were spread across the country. Besides, I soon discovered that *one* friend could not possibly fill the bill—I needed to talk with someone who could understand my anxieties about trying to find decent child care for my two-year-old daughter; someone else to help me draw up a checklist of everything I needed to gather in order to apply for graduate school; and an army of people who would not necessarily know all the answers but who would at least help me phrase the questions I needed to ask.

The months while I was being "processed" turned out to be fairly bewildering, and in retrospect I see many steps that could have been saved. Nevertheless, once school started, a support system presented itself. The campus child-care center had the reputation of being the best in the county; I felt great about having Rebekah there, as did she. Also, through the center, I made contact with other women who were trying to juggle the roles of mother and student.

I took a Psychology of Women course my first quarter and found quite a few returnees among my classmates—some who served as role models because they had been in school several quarters, and others who, like me, were just getting their academic feet wet.

A recurring question among the newly returned students was "Has anyone seen a book that speaks to the special needs of women returning to school?" We knew of good resource books on child care, on improving study habits, and on time-management techniques; but nothing which was directed specifically to our growing segment of the population.

My tentative idea of writing a resource-and-support book for women returning to school met with enthusiastic approval from my new colleagues. Everyone had a special piece of advice or an experience she wanted to share with potential returnees. After months of talking with every reentry student I could corner, and of reading everything I could find on the subject, I designed a questionnaire.

At that point I wrote to friends and selected directors of reentry programs across the country, asking if they would be willing to conduct interviews for the book. Altogether, 44 people contributed nearly 200 taped interviews with returning students and members of their families. Most of the student interviews lasted at least an hour, and each proved to be a veritable gold mine of information and support. For the purposes of this book, although the material in the interviews is reported as taped, the names have been changed.

Big question: how to organize the information so that it helps you add a student role to your life in the smoothest possible way. Chapters 1 and 2 will give you an idea of who is back in school and why. Chapters 3 through 10 explore ways to get beyond major psychological hurdles that might plague you along the reentry route.

If you have been away from the academic world for an extended period of time, you are bound to be unsure of your options. Chapters 11 through 14 will fill you in on differences between junior colleges, colleges, and universities; how to go through the admissions process; how to finance your education; and other essential factors you will need to consider.

If you need help in finding the right kind of child-care situation, turn to Chapter 15. Chapter 16 gives advice on how to renew or improve your study habits and how to attack the problem of incorporating study time into an already full schedule. Chapters 17 and 18 discuss the kinds of support systems that might be available at a school near you, and how you can slow down or speed up your schooling process, depending on your own distinct needs.

Where's it all leading? If you will be looking for work in a specific field, it is crucial that you do a thorough investigation of that field before and during your school days. Chapters 19 and 20 explain how to go about it and give general advice on the whole job-hunt process.

Why have so many women decided to add a student role to their already busy lives? Read on. And bon voyage!

Acknowledgments

When this book was just a free-floating idea in my mind, I had not the slightest inkling that so many people would become involved in giving it life.

I am grateful to the following for volunteering their time as interviewers of the reentry students and their families: Kit Basquin, Sarah Beacom, Wende Bowie, Pam Cellucci, Barbara Cousineau, Audrey Cross, Sondra Finegold, Cynthia FitzGerald, Julie Fulkerson, Barry Goode, Erica Goode, Natalie Graham, Doreen Hamilton, Patty Harvey, Ann Hinds, Lillabelle Holt, Lynn Johnson, Debbie Kaetz, Susan Kaetz, Merrily Kahn, Leo Klebanow, Sylvia Klebanow, Dorothy Krueger, Barbara Lafon, Judith Lerner, Migs Levy, Anne Malone, Susan Mendelsohn, Vivian Mitchel, Helen Munch, Laurie Parsons, Helen Ranney, Irene Rich, Roberta Rothman, Eleanor Sears, Norma Spodak, Laurie Steig, Mary Sullivan, Carolyn Wells, Susan Wheelock, Ann Whetstone, and Carol Whitley. Charlotte Goode and the late William Mendelsohn interviewed half of Long Island and Connecticut, respectively! Their support and commitment were really a source of inspiration to me.

Although I have met very few of the returning students and those in their families who took the time to have their experiences and advice recorded, I feel as if I know them. They would never believe the number of times I have replayed their taped voices! It is their enthusiasm and ideas that are the real core of this book.

Two friends were especially important as "midwives" to this book. Dr. Adele Clarke of the University of California, San Francisco, encouraged me to go back to school in the first place, then planted the idea for this book. Dr. Margaret McKoane, who headed the reentry program at California State University, Sacramento until her retirement and was a founding member of the California Advocates for Re-entry Education, provided unending inspiration.

Two excellent books have been very helpful to me: Elinor Lenz and Marjorie Hansen Shaevitz's *So You Want to Go Back to School* and Eileen Gray's *Everywoman's Guide to College.* (Sadly, both these books are out of print. However, they can be found in libraries and used book stores.) In addition, the products of extensive research done through the University of Michigan's Center for Continuing Education of Women and the Project on the Status and Education of Women have been especially motivating and valuable. I was also able to take advantage of the National Association for Women Deans, Administrators, and Counselors' *Journal*, which has been committed to publishing fine articles about reentry for over 20 years.

Many people associated with Humboldt State University in Arcata, California, have been very supportive. Drs. Warren Carlson and Susan Frances, members of my master's project committee, were very important resources. I am deeply indebted to the entire staff of the campus Children's Center. The superb care that Rebekah received there for three years freed me to concentrate on my school work and then the book.

Other people who have given generously of their time include: Ruth Hernandez of the U.S. Department of Labor Solicitor's Office; Annie Hart and Helen Davis of the U.S. Department of Labor Women's Bureau; Maureen Matheson of the College Entrance Examination Board; and Ellen Anderson of the Clairol Scholarship Program. My editor, George Young, has mastered the art of combining good solid advice with lots of moral support. His comments and encouragement during the updating of this book were helpful beyond words.

Finally, there is my daughter Rebekah and my companion Peter Palmquist. These two have lived through the research, the writing process, and the updating and claim to be none the worse for wear. I don't really know how to thank them for their encouragement, patience, affection, and persistent optimism.

Chapter 1

Who Is Back in School and Why

Do any of the following situations that are oringing women back to school strike a familiar chord?

• You have advanced as far as you possibly can in your career only to find that what prevents you from taking the next step is a few courses or an additional degree.

• You have had it with the kind of demoralization that comes from working long hours for low pay in a variety of unpleasant settings. You are seeking work that offers more security and better possibilities of economic advancement.

• Your training has been on the back burner for many years while you concentrated on other areas of your life. On close examination you find that your credentials are out-of-date or no longer in a field that interests you.

• You have spent many years working inside your home and for charitable organizations and discover—for financial, emotional, or intellectual reasons—that you need to do something else even though you're not sure what it is.

The backgrounds of women returning to school are so diversified that it is hard to come up with a realistic composite image of them.

1

A "reentry woman" can be generally defined as *anyone* who has been out of school long enough to feel uncomfortable about being on a college campus. A 19-year-old mother of a 2-year-old child fits the category of "reentry student," as does a 65-year-old woman who decides that she wants to study American literature.

At Connecticut College in New London, the women and men involved with the Return To College Program in 1985 ranged in age from 25 to 70, with the majority clustered in their late 20s and 30s. In the same year at the University of California in Santa Cruz, 192 students age 25 and over were just starting to get their academic feet wet. Of these, 47 percent were between the ages of 25 and 30, 40 percent were 31 to 40, and 13 percent were over 40.

Many women who return to school head their own households, and are back in school to find a career that will provide financial support. At Mount Holyoke College in South Hadley, Massachusetts, for example, one-third of the reentry students are divorced, and all but one of these divorced women have children. The University of Michigan's Center for Continuing Education of Women has seen a dramatic change in the family structure of the women who come for career and educational counseling. In 1965, 79 percent of the women coming to the Center were married, and 88 percent had children. In 1982, only 39 percent were married, and only 45 percent had children.

Why do women leave school in the first place? Why did you? In 1976, 35 percent of the returning students at the University of Michigan had completed a bachelor's degree before leaving the academic world the first time. Some had gone off in search of a job while others got married and became homemakers. Many of the housewives later felt intimidated by or unqualified for paying jobs and devoted their energy to volunteer work. Twenty-six percent of the University of Michigan returnees were gathering credits toward a college degree when they interrupted their education. The reasons for stopping were many: marriage, pregnancy, financial difficulties, lack of clearly defined goals, boredom, a good job possibility, or bad grades. Women who dropped out of college in order to marry often went to work to support their husband through school.

Twenty-four percent of the 1976 University of Michigan returnees and 60 percent of the 71 reentry students entering Mount Holyoke in 1985 stopped their studies after graduating from high school. Some reentry students say that their parents have actively discouraged them from continuing their education. Parents may feel that a "career" is unnecessary for a daughter who might soon be married or could be self-supporting without the additional expense of a college education. Other high school graduates have been unable to finance a college education. Marriage, motherhood, lack of interest, wanting to become financially independent are all reasons why women do not continue their education directly after high school.

Returning students discover that their motivation for being in college is often very different from their earlier experience. Goals are now much more clearly defined, and the decision to attend school is theirs alone—no pressure from family and friends as there was the first time. "I was there because everyone expected me to be there" and "It never dawned on me to do anything else" are typical reasons returnees give for their first stint in college. "I was just passing through looking for an MRS (as in Mr. and . . .) degree" is another frequently mentioned incentive from "the old days." Nearly every woman back in school will tell you that it is hard to juggle school responsibilities with other major commitments. But most of them will also tell you that they get a lot more done on campus now than they used to because they are determined not to be distracted from their goals.

Why the return to school? When the women interviewed for this book were asked to rank their reasons for returning to school, 36 percent said that their major reason for being there was to prepare for employment. Another 29 percent said they were fulfilling a need or desire for education or achievement. Other reasons were also mentioned: 19 percent wanted to facilitate personal growth, 10 percent were in school for the stimulation, and 5 percent said they thought school would help them to become more independent. The College Board surveyed 2,000 Americans age 25 and over who had gone back to school, to find out what had brought them there. The catalyst, according to 56 percent, was a career transition; according to 29 percent, it was transitions in their family and leisure life—divorce, children leaving home, retirement, etc. In *Americans in Transition*, Carol Aslanian and Henry Brickell point out that 80 percent of adults who return to school do so because their lives are changing.

PREPARING FOR EMPLOYMENT—A MAJOR INCENTIVE

Women are entering the labor market in droves! According to the Women's Bureau of the United States Department of Labor, by 1984, 64 percent of all American women ages 18 to 64 years old were working or looking for work. Women were holding 44 percent of all the jobs in the United States. In 1984, 60 percent of women with children under the age of 18 were in the labor force. In fact, 52 percent of all mothers with preschool children were labor-force participants. Forty-eight percent of women with children age three and under were either working or looking for work.

Why the dramatic increase in the number of working women? The reasons are many. More and more married couples are finding that they cannot maintain even a moderate standard of living without two wage earners in the family. In fact, almost half the children who lived in two-parent families in 1984 had both an employed mother and father. The Family Economics Research Group of the U.S. Department of Agriculture reports that children born in 1985 into a family of moderate income (defined as $35,000 or more annual income) living in an urban area will cost $146,175 at June 1985 prices by their eighteenth birthdays! That's *before* college! And as of September 1985, the average price of a new house, nationwide, reached $103,600. Two wage-earner families are becoming a necessity even if you live modestly.

The number of families headed by a woman increased by more than 84 percent between 1970 and 1984. In fact, one out of every five families is maintained by a woman. According to a Census Bureau report, children born in the 1980s have a 45 percent likelihood that their parents will divorce. Promised alimony and child support tend not to materialize, and women who may or may not have the skills enter the labor market as sole provider for their family.

Women who do not have to work for financial reasons are just as motivated to pursue a job or career. The survey done for this book showed that 42 percent of the returnees who did not need to work for financial reasons still planned to do so. Some feel unfulfilled being "just" housewives, especially once their children enter school or leave home. Others feel a special need for the kind of intellectual challenge that many careers provide. Still others have decided that working is the best insurance policy they could possibly have—they have observed the dramatic change in life-style as the husbands of friends unexpectedly die, leave, or get laid off from work. Also, women who have logged in endless hours of volunteer work decide that they should be paid for their expertise. Work *can* be enjoyable—according to a 1983 *New York Times* poll, 58 percent of American working women would rather work than stay home even if they didn't have to.

Many of the women entering the labor force today have made

the decision that a college education will open the door to more fulfilling or better-paying work. In fact, according to the Women's Bureau, U.S. Department of Labor, the median annual income of women age 25 and over who had completed four years of college and were working full-time in 1984 was $20,257 ($25,076 for those with five or more years of college) while female high school graduates in the same age group had a median income of $14,569. At least, there is the hope that a college education will narrow the difference between what men and women earn—for every $6.40 a woman makes, a man earns $10.00!

According to the Bureau of Labor Statistics, in 1982 unemployment for college graduates was 5.6 percent, while nearly three times that many high school graduates were out of work. A 1983–84 survey of 6,621 Michigan State University graduates is very encouraging. *Just three months after graduation*, only 8.53 percent were unemployed; 16.66 percent were going on to graduate school, and the rest were employed. The average annual *starting* salary for students with bachelor's degrees was $18,934; for those with master's degrees, $22,937; and with Ph.Ds, $25,441.

Returning to school may mean having to give up a well-paying job, financial security, most of your free time. If being in school will mean changing your life-style dramatically, realize that you will probably periodically question your decision to resume your studies. "Will it have been worth it?" is a very common question that eats at the morale of reentry students. Will this degree, these courses really lead you where you want to go?

A study by Gleason Ewing shows that more than three-quarters of her sample of reentry women students felt their college experience had been worthwhile insofar as it expanded their employment opportunities. In addition, 96 percent of these women felt that school had been worth it in terms of their own personal development. So be prepared to doubt it from time to time, but chances aren't bad that you'll consider your school experience a good investment of your time.

COLLEGES' RECEPTIVITY—THEN AND NOW

If you decide to return to school, you can be almost certain that you will be more warmly received on campus than reentry students were 20 years ago. What was it like for a woman who made the decision to return to school in the 1960s? For one thing, few academic settings took her seriously. It was automatically assumed that you were a matron who was dabbling in enrichment courses—that is, if you weren't mistaken for a member of the faculty or staff. College administrators seemed completely oblivious to the special needs that older students might have as they tried to juggle their home life and/or job plus school.

Financial aid was almost unheard-of for part-time students. Campus child care was essentially nonexistent. If you were worried about rusty study habits, few schools were equipped to help. Finding classes that were scheduled at realistic times was a monumental challenge. School simply was not geared to meet the needs of people committed to working long hours either inside or outside their home.

Only a handful of colleges in the early 1960s saw that support systems and special programs were needed for returning students. The Radcliffe Institute for Independent Study, Sarah Lawrence College, and the Universities of Minnesota, Wisconsin, and Michigan were some of the pioneers in the field of continuing education for women. Private foundations such as Carnegie and Kellogg also saw the need and provided financial assistance to several of these schools. As late as 1968, however, there were still fewer than 100 colleges which mentioned that they provided special help to older students.

Women who returned to school prior to the 1970s would be very surprised by the dramatic changes now taking place on campuses across the country. Many schools have an office specifically geared to help students who have interrupted their education. If not, you can almost always locate a campus facility that serves reentry students as one of its functions. Good on-campus resources include the counseling office, career development center, admissions office, women's studies department, women's center, office of continuing education, and special student services office. One of these may be particularly committed to meeting the needs of students who are resuming their studies.

The image of the dabbling matron has definitely fallen by the wayside. Younger students no longer take it for granted that if you are over the age of 30, you are staff, faculty, or somebody's mother. Professors often assume that you will be a good student *because* of the skills that you have gained through life experience.

College administrators have become deeply concerned about a sharp decrease in enrollment among younger students. According to the Carnegie Council on Policy Studies in Higher Education, a

23 percent decline in the traditional college-bound group of 18 to 24 year-olds is expected by 1997. In addition, more and more young students are "stopping out" at some point during their college years. Some universities have reported stop-out rates as high as 56 percent! Returning students are being looked to as the group that might be able to fill in the various enrollment gaps. Because of this, administrators are becoming much more responsive to the special needs of older students.

Late-afternoon, evening, and weekend classes, plus the increasing receptivity of college administrators to earning academic credit through standardized testing, all make it easier for you to combine school with family and/or job responsibilities. Terrific campus child-care and preschool facilities are becoming much more common. Learning centers can help renew and improve your study habits. Changing admissions policies now take your life experience into consideration.

For the academic year 1984–85, more than five million students received more than $16 billion in various forms of student assistance for postsecondary education and training. An alarming $6.6 billion of student financial aid from the private sector has gone unused annually, in recent years Reentry students often assume that they are somehow *less* eligible for grants, loans, scholarships, and work-study opportunities than traditional age students. This simply is not so. In fact, there are even special scholarships and grants specifically designated for reentry students. Federal, state, and private resources of financial assistance definitely exist. It's a matter of tracking them down.

Should you return to school, you will meet many students with the same goals and needs as yours, who have decided that resuming their studies was the best way to get there. There will be others whose circumstances and reasons for being in school are worlds apart from your own. In fact, one of the many fringe benefits from being back in school is that it will give you the opportunity to explore the knowledge and experiences of a whole new set of people. Returnees often find their interactions with colleagues are as valuable as whatever else they set out to gain.

The trend definitely exists! According to the College Board's Office of Adult Learning Services, college campuses will have more students over the age of 25 than under the age of 25 by the year 2000.

Chapter 2

These Women Went
Back to School:
Fourteen Case Histories

Who are some of the returning women students you will meet on the college campus? What are their circumstances, their reasons for adding a student role to their life, the major problems that they faced? The women described in this chapter have completed the reentry process or are in its various stages. Even if your life-style is completely different from theirs, see if you notice any similarities between them and you.

> *"I knew I would soon be required to have a degree for the job I was already doing."*

Anna is a nurse who got her degree in 1945, and who had worked her way up to the position of supervisor of the operating room. "When the town hospital merged with the university medical school," she explains, "they made all kinds of changes in what the qualifications would be for supervisory jobs. I saw the handwriting on the wall—eventually they would require a B.S. degree for my job. My R.N. degree was worth three years of college, so I needed one more year."

In 1967, Anna took a year off from her job at the hospital and went back to school. Her main concern was that she was giving up a secure salary while she got her degree. The lack of income caused hardships; her husband's business was not doing well, and her father had recently come to live with them. "I wasn't really sure I needed the degree," Anna said, "and I had no one who could offer me any advice about it. Counseling services just weren't available."

Although her family supported her decision, some of her friends thought it was unwise. "They thought I was nuts to give up a secure job, and they wondered why I thought I'd be able to pass the courses after being out of school for so long."

She felt some concern about her study habits, especially since she had not been a good student the first time around. But now she found that she did well because of sheer determination. "I had a goal, and I had made a big commitment," she explained. "And I had learned a great deal through my job. But the first half of the first semester was really rough, believe me." She feels that she might not have made it through the year if she had not received special support from one of the deans and one of her teachers.

The big surprise for Anna was how much confidence she gained from getting the degree. Back at her old job, she no longer felt intimidated by the physicians or her colleagues. Six years later, she decided to return to school to earn a master's degree. She is now in charge of all the operating rooms at a major teaching hospital in New England. "When I went into nursing thirty-five years ago," she says, "I never thought I'd wind up with a secretary and an appointment book." Her substantial increase in salary was timely. Her husband suffered a stroke and is no longer able to work, but the salary she earns now is sufficient to provide well for her family.

"I want to be able to provide for my son and me."

Cathy is 29 and studying for a master's degree in psychology. She spent almost 10 years getting her bachelor's degree because she married during her first year of college, then left school and began working full-time in order to support her student husband. She earned most of her A.A. degree by taking one or two night classes each quarter. When her son was two years old, the marriage ended, and she decided to go to school full-time.

Being the head of a household and responsible for a child, I feel a very strong need to be able to support us. I wanted to have a job, a career, where I know I'd be okay financially. I had been a secretary at one time, and I knew I couldn't support us on that kind of salary. Going on welfare in order to return to school reinforces my feeling that I want to be financially independent, to always be able to take care of myself and my son.

Welfare, loans, federal grants, and a work-study position made it possible for Cathy to enroll in a California city college where tuition was free. Her major concern, over who would look after her child, was solved when she discovered that the college had an excellent day-care center, also free. "He was really well taken care of there," Cathy recalls.

Things got much more complicated after she moved to a different town so that she could get her master's degree. Her son was then ready for kindergarten. Locating a day-care center that would accept older children, and then getting him there, were two enormous problems. "I had no choice at all," Cathy said. "It's the only day-care center in town that accepts school-age children. It's just amazing that the elementary schools here don't offer any day care for the children of working and student mothers after the school day ends." She feels that her being in school has had no negative effect on her son. "He actually probably gets *more* attention from me than if I stayed home all day. And he's learned to be very constructive with his time."

Student mothers who are on welfare usually choose programs that will give them very marketable skills as soon as they graduate. Cathy investigated the school counselor program at the state university and found that almost all the recent graduates had found jobs in their field.

Cathy's life-style has changed quite a bit since she became a full-time student. She'd like some new clothes, a stereo, a few things beyond the bare necessities, but feels pleased that she is able to manage on a low budget. "It won't be like this forever, anyway." Although she has had to give up some material things, she feels that she has gained a great deal as well. "I've developed some of the most meaningful friendships I've ever had," she explained. "And I've gained so much self-confidence. I really feel as if I can attain the goals I've set for myself. You know, they told me I wasn't college material in high school!"

"I became really anxious to get out of that volunteer classification."

It had been 29 years since Gloria got her bachelor's degree in psychology. Back in 1971, she had been a volunteer counselor for a family planning agency.

I had some very strong feelings: This is a very important kind of counseling, I'd like to learn a lot more about it, and I ought to be getting paid. It's intriguing that there's nothing between the volunteer who doesn't get paid at all and the working person who does. Why isn't there some compromise? Why aren't volunteers paid to be trained, at least given some expense money, a token payment? A group of us at the family planning agency resented being in our own little class, complete with stereotypes. Somehow you aren't expected to be as dependable or capable as the paid personnel. The pregnancy counseling seemed like such a responsible position, and we felt that the only recognition was to be paid for it. In order to get a paying job doing the kind of counseling I wanted to do, I needed a master's degree.

When Gloria resumed her studies, her husband was preparing to retire and very much looking forward to their being able to do a lot of traveling. "I would have felt a lot better if she had done it five years earlier so that we could have retired together," he commented. Nevertheless, he supported her decision. "I could see she had had it with volunteer work. She felt she was licking envelopes while someone who was less qualified had the real responsibilities."

Gloria's two daughters, who were both away at college at the time, were also very supportive. However, two teenage sons who were still living at home were quite negative. "The superficial message from them was that going back to school was a dumb idea," she recalls. "How could I be a good counselor to someone else if I didn't take care of them the way I ought to? Believe me, I enjoyed missing dinner with them two nights a week!"

Another concern at first was that she would not be able to keep up with her younger classmates at the state university in Ohio where she had enrolled. "I was absolutely convinced I wasn't smart enough or capable enough." She was surprised to find that her colleagues at school were extremely supportive and really encouraged her to stick with her student role. Her first semester, she actually got as far as dropping two of her three courses before another student urged her to reconsider, and helped her go through the process of adding the courses. Her fears basically disappeared mid-semester when she saw that her work was comparable to that of her colleagues.

Gloria graduated with two master's degrees, one in rehabilitation counseling and the other in college counseling, maintaining a B+ average. Her job hunting was not typical. "I fell into a job as a college career counselor," she said. "The dean called me right before I finished school. I was interviewed and landed the job." She enjoyed career counseling for two years. Just when she was deciding to look for a different kind of job experience, she was called about her present job as community organizer for a free clinic.

"You can only go so far professionally without a college degree."

Lorraine had been away from school for 25 years when she enrolled as a freshman at a community college. "In high school," she recalled, "I fell madly in love with my husband and was only interested in getting married."

> I was working with a community organizer who was a college graduate. He was leaving the position and suggested that I apply for his job. He told me I was as good as he was if not better. I applied, went before the board, and the man whom they hired was a college graduate who knew nothing about the job at all. I had to take him around and show him all the things that I knew, and he was getting over twice as much money as I was. I felt really crushed that I didn't get that position. I didn't need it so much financially, but it was a matter of pride. I had done a good job, and to have him come in and get the job and I had to teach him, that really hurt.

Lorraine's husband encouraged her to go back to school and was supportive throughout her academic years.

The biggest problem for Lorraine was setting a schedule and sticking to it. She and her husband have nine children, the youngest of whom was in the second grade when Lorraine resumed her studies. "School was everything to me," she remarked, "but it was always secondary to my family." Between her freshman and sophomore years, she took off a year to care for her convalescing father-in-law, who had come to live with the family. "I was always wife first, then mother, and then student," she commented. "Sometimes class would run over, and I'd have to just get up and leave. And I have two elderly grandmothers, plus I do all the shopping and errands for my mother." She discovered from talking with other women on campus that role conflict is a common problem. Sharing her feelings about it really helped.

Before Lorraine returned to school, she had spent a great deal of her time doing household chores that other family members were perfectly capable of doing. She and her husband enrolled in a class in family management. "The teacher called the mother the number-one slave, the father the number-two slave, and the children the lords and masters," Lorraine remembers. "It really opened our eyes. We started having family meetings and posting daily, weekly, and seasonal chores on the refrigerator."

"I used to think I was a good mother when I did everything for my children," Lorraine said, "But this course taught me they need to learn independence and responsibility." She was astounded that her children accepted the new system so easily. "I suddenly had all this time to start thinking about myself for a change. I could never have made it through school without their cooperation and support."

After she received her A.A. degree, Lorraine was accepted through a resumed education program at a private university in her New England hometown. She qualified for financial aid and loans because her husband and *five* of their children were all either in college or recently graduated. She majored in sociology and maintained a B average. Scheduling classes around other responsibilities was always quite a feat. "I really did speed along. It isn't good to rush around like that, although it helped me to lose weight! If I had it to do over again, I'd take the last two years in three."

At the time she was interviewed, Lorraine had not yet found a job. But she had been elected director of the statewide association for retarded citizens—a real feather in her cap since that is the field she wants to work in. "College has given me the self-confidence I needed to feel on a par with any other professional in my field."

"I've always had a desire to learn in a college setting."

I've never doubted that my instincts were good, but I've lacked the basic knowledge to back up my opinions. I went back to school to learn the basics and to study what I want to study. I've always been curious and felt that school could provide me with some direction, some answers. I have no intentions of getting a job—I just want to take courses indefinitely.

Judith had not gone to college after graduating from high school in 1941 because she was convinced that she would not be able to do well enough. Thirty-three years later, her main worry was basically the same: "Would I be intelligent enough to grasp college work?"

Three years after resuming her studies at a college in New York, she was earning a B+ average and had much more confidence in her abilities. "I'm no longer afraid of the classroom," she said. "I feel on a par with anyone else in the class. I'm getting the background that I've always wanted." Her confidence affected all areas of her life. "I'll venture into things without the basic fear I had before. I'm so much more sure of myself."

The problem for Judith was that although her husband seemed happy at first about her decision to return to school, all did not go smoothly once classes actually started. "Whatever I had to do for school was fine as long as I did it when my husband wasn't home," she said. "He was proud that I was going, but he didn't want it to interfere with his time with me."

Resentment built up on both sides until finally there was an enormous argument. "I had always been available at his beck and call," Judith said. A family friend spoke to her husband and helped him to see how important school was to Judith. Thereafter Judith noticed a marked improvement in her husband's attitude. She, in turn, felt more understanding about his insecurities:

> In a way, it's a threat to a man. We were both high school graduates. He's really expanded a great deal since then, and I didn't all that much. He was off in the business world, and I was involved with apron strings. He never felt the lack the way I did. He's proud when I finish the crossword puzzle before he does, but he has to finish it before I do once in a while. My being more independent in my thinking than I used to be is very hard for him to get used to.

Judith went to a lot of trouble to schedule courses in ways that would cause the least amount of conflict with her husband. She never took classes at night, for example. She often studied between 3:00 A.M. and breakfast. The couple came to an understanding that might not be comfortable for everyone, but that was comfortable for them.

"My decision to return to school was part of a major overall life decision."

Florence was 26 years old when she spent her year back in school. A little young to be thought of as a reentry student? She *definitely* considered herself one.

> I had been living in New York City and working in film and television production since I graduated with my bachelor's degree. Even though I was establishing a name for myself, I didn't feel I could or

wanted to compete. The last few years, I free-lanced, and although I got jobs, I felt I wasn't getting what I needed out of my life situation. I wanted to move out of New York and change my career plans. I had always liked kids and decided to become a teacher. I made the decision to move to Boston and get a master's in education. I knew there were very few teaching jobs, but I was determined to land one of them.

Florence felt that her whole approach to college was different from the first time, and that having such clearly defined goals was an enormous help to her. "If you've been out of school for a while, you're at a great advantage over people who have not taken a break from school," she commented. "They have not had to cope with issues that people who have been out in the world have had to cope with. You gain extremely valuable skills through life experience."

Florence was unmarried and didn't have to worry about meshing her schedule with someone else's. "I had men in my life, but I coordinated my social life around my school obligations. My being in school didn't cause many problems for me in my relationships with men." Her parents were sympathetic, and gladly backed her financially for the school year. Family and friends can sometimes be incredulous that you would consider going to all the trouble if you already have a halfway decent job.

As it turned out, after going back to school specifically to become an elementary school teacher, Florence could not find a job in that field. Instead, she became a curriculum coordinator for an education program that brings together inner-city and suburban children. Although this was not her goal, she was enjoying her job and felt that her training had been a great help to her. "I lived through the fears and the worries about whether or not the year would have been worth it, and it definitely was."

"I've wanted to do something intellectually stimulating for such a long time."

I was becoming more and more aware that being at home, doing volunteer work at the children's schools, taking craft and exercise classes was getting stale and very unsatisfying. I've always wanted to go to college but was unable to do it fifteen years ago because of financial difficulties. Now I have a voracious appetite to learn anything and everything that I can.

Susan's major problem was learning how to study again and coordinating her study time with her other major commitments. "After so many years of not using my brain in this way, having to focus all my energies like this is very exhausting," she said. "And it's hard to find time to study because of all the demands that a family and house can make."

For Susan the reentry process was made easier by a course especially designed to help mature women decide what they want to do. The community college she attends in Maryland has an excellent learning skills center and offers a wide variety of personal development courses.

As a freshman, Susan saw her desire for a stimulating environment fulfilled in many ways. "I'm much happier with myself, my husband, and my children. I feel vibrant and alive."

"Being in school has brought me close to my children," she said. "It's given us an important common bond." Susan felt that her relationship with her husband had also benefited. "We have a lot more to talk about, and I'm no longer taking my frustrations out on him." Her husband agreed: "I have peace of mind knowing that she's happier. We have less time together, but the overall positive effects are very important to her and therefore very important to me."

Although Susan had no need to work for financial reasons, she did plan to find a job or establish a career after she left school. She felt that working would help her to maintain her sense of well-being.

"My husband is ill and wants me to be able to take care of the family when it becomes necessary."

Carla graduated from high school in 1943. She often had to work with her family in the fields. "My people just didn't pursue a formal education," she explained. "I was the only one who graduated from high school. The only time I got to go to school was when there weren't any crops."

The desire to go to college had always been there, but "opportunity and finances" had not. In 1975, a community college was built near her home in Arkansas, and Carla went to help her son register. "When I called my husband to tell him," she remembered, "he told me to go back and register myself because he was sending us both.

"We consider my being in school a family project," she said.

"My husband is disabled, and we almost lost him twice in the summer of seventy-three. After that, he began to point out to me that I should go back to school. He knew I had always wanted to. The whole family is very proud of me."

Carla's major concern was her study habits. "I had no confidence," she said. "It took me quite some time to learn how to study, but I had a lot of encouragement and help from the people at school. Those I didn't even know gained an interest in me. Counselors, students, and instructors have all offered their time and advice."

Both Carla and her son feel that they have established a very special relationship because of their shared college experience. They commute to school together and even study with each other for exams. Her husband is very proud of both of them, and Carla feels that there were some fringe benefits for him that he hadn't counted on. "He left school in the sixth grade, but he's such a smart man. My being in school," Carla said, "has given him the opportunity to learn more, too. He's very interested in history, and he's learning as much as I am from these courses."

Carla's goal was definite—she had always wanted to be an elementary school teacher. During World War II, while her husband was overseas, she taught school for a few years. She has been a volunteer at her church's preschool program for 18 years. She completed her A.A. degree in two years and then transferred to a four-year college, where she was earning credits toward a degree in education.

"I'm in school because I really need to feel as if I'm accomplishing something."

Donna's first son was born just 10 days after she graduated from a California university with a bachelor's degree in genetics. She had wanted to go right on for a master's degree in the same field. "I went to apply, and the man took one look at me, very pregnant at the time, and it was obvious that they wouldn't consider me," she remembers. "At another school the adviser came right out and said that they didn't want a bored housewife in the department. It didn't seem to matter that I had been a very good student in the field." On top of that, her husband did not want her to mix early motherhood with studenting. So she stayed home.

When her firstborn was three years old, she spent a year getting her teaching credentials, discovered that she was dissatisfied, and dropped out. When she recently went back to school, it was because of the feeling, as she put it, that she'd been a dilettante far too long.

> I need to be able to say that I have a skill, that I've learned something and can do it well. Also, a personal crisis started brewing about the time my second son was born. He was a very difficult baby, and I didn't go anywhere or do anything for a long time. I had no freedom, and I realized that I no longer had any personal goals. At age thirty, I wondered what I would do with myself when I grew up. I began hoping for something that would become more than it is when you interact with it, something to get excited about.

When it dawned on her that she had the abilities it took to become an architect, she applied for admission into a master's program. "I figured I didn't have a chance in the world of being admitted," she remarked. "I've had no academic background in the field, and hardly any practical experience—just an intense interest." She got in.

After she had applied, but before she was accepted, her marriage ended, so she had the additional problem of heading a household for the first time. An equitable financial settlement was made, but being able to support her family became more of a concern to Donna. She had worked for her parents' company and knew she could count on a job there if school didn't work out. "I feel this is my last chance," she said. "If I fail, I'm back working for my parents. There's no way I can really be self-sufficient without additional training. I can't even type."

"In order to get any kind of employment that earns well, I need a college education."

Tracy was twenty-eight, a sophomore at a community college in Massachusetts. Her husband was also a student, and they had an eight-year-old son. Tracy, like many of her friends, had had her fill of unchallenging jobs that pay next to nothing and lead nowhere. She stopped her education after graduating from high school. "I had been conditioned all through my high school years to think that I was a failure. I would never have made it in college right after high school." Some of her friends went directly on to college, but most of them quit because they were eager to get out into "the real world." At that time the connection between uninteresting required courses and a good job seemed extremely remote. Now,

Tracy is amazed to see how many of her old high school friends are in classes with her.

> For nine or ten years, I've been doing jobs like tending bar, waitressing, filing, being a chambermaid, things like that, and I was just sick of it. I knew I had more potential somewhere, and I was determined to explore it. I was sick of not having any money, and I had been feeling unfulfilled since high school. It's important to me to be able to provide for my son's college education. It's going to take money to give him the things I want him to have.

Tracy and her husband decided that being poor for a few years (a $4,000 income the year before) would be worth it if the credentials they gathered ultimately earned them better salaries and more interesting work. In the meantime, a good part of their income came from federal grant money and work/study funds.

Tracy and her husband had as little time together as they did money, but she believed that their involvement with school had helped to improve their relationship. "Whenever we do have time together, we have a lot more to offer each other," she explained. "I feel as if we're really growing."

How did her son adjust? "I think I neglected him at first because I wanted so badly to do well," Tracy said. "Things are much better now. I think he is really proud of me, and I feel great about providing him with such a good role model. When I was in grammar school, I hated to study, but when he sees me study he grabs a book, too."

Initially, she had serious doubts that she would be able to keep up with her classmates. She recalled: "I found myself spending all my available time on schoolwork at first. I was really obsessed with proving to myself that I could do well." A straight-A student, she could now allow herself to be a little more relaxed about her study habits. Self-confidence has accompanied the good grades. "I'm not afraid to speak out in class anymore. I feel I have a lot to offer."

Tracy's career goal is still developing. When she first went back to school, she chose the human services program because it looked like the easiest program in the catalog. "It didn't require SAT's, a specific high school average, or anything else," she explained. Before the first semester was over, however, she realized that she would not be getting the necessary course work to apply toward a bachelor's degree, so she switched to liberal arts. Her interests are mainly in the social sciences, and she hopes to become involved in research.

"School seemed like a good alternative when my marriage was breaking up."

When I got divorced, I really needed to do something with myself. I decided to study business because I felt it could help me personally as well as to get a job ultimately. I needed to be on top of all the things that came up since I was in charge of a household now. That's really what gave me the impetus to go back.

Although Mary had earned a bachelor's degree in history ten years earlier, and had experience as a nursery school teacher, awareness of her past accomplishments did nothing to boost her confidence when she first resumed her studies. "The sheer mechanics of getting admitted and registering for classes seemed overwhelming," she recalls. "Finding a parking space, getting to the right classroom, making sure I had the right book, paying my fees on time—it was all very difficult for me then. I felt like a complete incompetent." She was convinced she was going to fail. "I was so frightened that I couldn't slow my mind down long enough to absorb the material." One of her professors encouraged her to explore her fears instead of allowing them to paralyze her. "Identifying the fear really helped me," Mary explained. "I wasn't even aware that other people had the same feelings until I started reading and talking about it."

Mary was concerned at first about how her having become a student would affect her three children, ages eleven, ten, and six, but she felt that they had benefited greatly from it. "I'm so much happier, and it's good for them to see me like this," she said. "They see that I think learning is fun and exciting. My son's grades have completely turned around since I became a student."

Mary was majoring in accounting, and although she did not need to work to support her family, she intended to pursue a career as a financial consultant.

"I wanted a career, a position of responsibility, absolute certainty that I could provide for all of us."

Tamara was divorced, with six children ranging from thirteen to three, when she went back to school. It meant that she had to give up her job, move to a place where she had never been before, and go on welfare.

When I graduated from the community college in 1955, I got married and thought I was going to live happily ever after. I majored in fine arts because I love to draw and paint. I was still in the frame of mind that when you got married, your husband supported you. Well, my ex-husband did not take care of us. He didn't have a strong sense of responsibility; he never worked. So I worked as a teacher's aide. It was a frustrating job because I realized I would do a lot of things differently if I were a teacher. At that point I heard about ITEP [Indian Teacher Education Program] and applied. I was accepted back in sixty-nine, and that's how I got my teaching credentials. Kate was only three then, and I really put a lot of energy into finding the right person to look after her. The others were all in school already, but it was hard for them to leave their friends. I was keenly aware of that.

After receiving her teaching credentials, Tamara found a job as a community college counselor in an area where there is a large Native American population. "I feel that I'm in a good position to help. It's a major adjustment to go to college, and I'm always available for counseling," Tamara said. "I've made it a point to become an expert on financial aid because most of the Native Americans here don't have any money, so in order to get them here you have to figure out a financial aid program for them."

In 1977 Tamara was back in school again, this time to earn a master's degree in psychology, which she believed might at some point be required for her job. She was a full-time student, mother of seven, and working full-time.

"I'm doing this because I don't want to be hassled by a licensing bureau, a credentials committee, or anyone at any institution I work for," she explained. "I'm getting this master's degree so that no one can say I don't have a master's degree. I will get more money, do the same work, and have peace of mind.

"Believe it or not, I feel much freer than I did when I was a student in 1955," she declared. "I can provide for us well, I love my job, and my children are very supportive." In fact, the person most supportive of Tamara's student role was Kate at age 11.

"I might work after graduation, but school is basically a personal growing experience for me."

Connie had finished three years of college before she interrupted her education. When asked what her major was then, she replied, "Skiing and men." Thirteen years later, she said,

I kind of slid into returning to school. I was feeling restless, and a friend encouraged me to go to the women's resource center at the university to take an interest test. I took the test and had a counseling session afterward. I almost fell over. What came out loud and clear was nursing. I had totally forgotten about my interest in nursing, and all of a sudden it made a lot of sense. I've started taking the courses for an R.N. degree, but I still don't want to be held to it. I'm not promising anyone that I'll finish. It just feels as if I'm doing something constructive with my time, and it's purely for me. It's made life complicated, but it feels great!

As the mother of two children, ages eight and ten, Connie found that her biggest problem was arranging study time without feeling guilty. Nevertheless, she found that the quality of her time with her children greatly improved. "I'm really glad to see them when I get home, and I have a lot more patience."

It took Connie's husband a while to adjust to her being in school. There were arguments about doing things around the house. "My duties at home haven't changed," Connie said, "yet I'm doing twice as much as I was. I told him recently he should share more in the housework, and he asked why." Even so, Connie felt that being in school improved their relationship. "He's much more interested in me as *me* now, not just as his wife. And I think he's beginning to see that I work really hard all day, too." Her husband agreed that their relationship had gotten better. "The fact that she can relate to other people outside of the household and has different experiences to bring home makes her more interesting," he said. "I don't see any negative effects for us as a couple. Everything doesn't get done the way it used to, but *she's* the one who feels bad about that."

Having finished her first stint in school with a D+ average, Connie was concerned about whether or not she would do well in her courses at the community college. As it turned out, she had a straight-A average! And her whole approach to school had changed. "I'm interested now. I don't want to cut classes because I really don't want to miss anything," she explained. "I'm not working for grades. It's information I'm after, and I really want to understand it." Connie's plans after the A.A. degree in nursing are undecided. She might go to work, since the extra income would be helpful to her family. Or she might take the courses she needs for a bachelor's degree. "I know I'll want to do something once I'm finished with this degree, but I'm not sure what yet."

"Without the work of caring for my children, I knew I'd be without a job."

Ruth's return to school was precipitated by a slowly forming sense of crisis.

> When I graduated from high school in 1935, I expected and aspired to get married, be a wife and mother, and be taken care of for the rest of my life. I had no desire for a career—it never even crossed my mind. Thirty-seven years later, all my children were leaving home, and I knew I would lose my major role of being a mother. I knew I'd be facing the empty-nest syndrome. A person is defined in our society by what he or she does, so I had to find something to do with my life. I wanted to become independent, psychologically and financially. I couldn't face the rest of my life not knowing what I was going to do with myself.

Her oldest daughter was involved with the women's liberation movement. They had many serious discussions, and Ruth joined a consciousness-raising group. "I became aware that other women were experiencing the same feelings. I realized that there wasn't anything particularly wrong with me, that women had been misled by not being encouraged to develop their own potential as individuals."

Ruth's husband and three daughters all supported her decision to return to school. Her husband commented, "She's always been extremely capable but she's never believed it. School has given her confidence in her abilities, and she's a much happier person."

Ruth first thought she would become an elementary school teacher, but then decided that this might be too draining, physically and emotionally, and switched to social work.

Initially, she was concerned about whether she would be able to pass her courses and how she would fit in with the other students. A solid B student, she was surprised that she could handle the academic work so well. "I find that I can speak out with confidence and that all college teachers aren't as intelligent as I thought they were." She also discovered that she could relate to and interact with a variety of people. "I feel really good about that."

Ruth received her bachelor's degree just as her oldest daughter, also a reentry student, was receiving a master's degree in the same field. The next step for both was to begin looking for a job—one in Connecticut and the other in Ohio.

Chapter 3

Can I Make It Academically?

If you're thinking about going back to college, there are several hurdles that will have to be cleared before you make a decision. One question that troubles many women is: Will I be able to make it academically, after all these years? The women whose experiences are described in the previous chapter should give some clues. Anna, who had not been a good student when she got her nursing degree in 1945, did well the second time round—out of sheer determination. Lorraine, with nine children and heavy family responsibilities, maintained a B average. Tracy, who through high school had been conditioned to think of herself as a failure, got straight A's. So did Connie, a D+ student in her first try at college. Collectively, the women who were surveyed for this book had a grade-point average equal to an A—. And one-third of these same women listed fear of failure as a primary concern!

Other research has been just as encouraging. One project showed that women 40 years old and over did an average of 10 percentile points better than their classmates between 18 and 25. They earned more A's, an equal number of B's and C's, and fewer D's and F's than the younger women. The conclusions of Irma Halfter, who conducted the research, are unmistakable: Absence from formal education for ten years or more has no discernible adverse effect. K. Clements, who conducted another project, came to similar conclusions: Women over 40 do better than those between the ages of 18 and 25. And at the University of Michigan, where female reentry students were surveyed in 1972, 91 percent were earning grades equal to or better than their earlier record.

One reason older students do so well is that they are generally so thoroughly goal oriented. Tracy, who wound up with a 4.0 G.P.A.,* remembers that she "never got good grades in high school because any excuse would do to get away from my studies. I discipline myself really well now. I enjoy studying because I know where it will get me." A California woman working toward a master's degree in counseling, with a 3.9 G.P.A., described herself as a "robot student" the first time she went to college. Now, she said, "I'm excited by the reading and writing. I really love being in school, and I feel motivated to do well."

When Gloria entered graduate school at the age of 50, she listed fear of failure as her major concern. Now, having finished with a 3.7 G.P.A., she says: "You certainly don't deteriorate with age! In fact, being older, you can take yourself more seriously and you have more experience to draw on. Having been a mom of five kids and having a busy household really taught me a lot about planning my time. I learned to be very efficient."

One older undergraduate, a junior with a 3.8 G.P.A., confessed: "I knew zilch about Plato and Nathaniel Hawthorne, and I was convinced that you had to in order to fit in. As it turns out, I knew more than most people just because I was older and had experience and had done some reading. No one else in the philosophy class knew anything about Plato either."

There is a subtler way in which life experience can help. You are probably committed to such a number of responsibilities, as an adult with a family or an outside career or both, that schoolwork may actually feel like a *vacation* from your heavier responsibilities! In much of what you do with your life, it is impossible to measure your progress. Who can be sure she is doing a good job as a mother? You *can* measure your progress as a student, and the immediate feedback may come as a relief. Although 10 years ago you would have disliked being judged on what you had learned, by now you will probably welcome these judgments as concrete indicators of how you are doing in one realm of your life.

---

* In the grade-point average system, 4.0 is a high A, 3.0 is a B, and 2.0 is a C.

Nevertheless, fear of failure does haunt many women—including any number of straight A's who didn't tell a soul they were back in school until they could be sure they weren't going to flunk out—women who were convinced, as one so graphically put it, that their "brain cells have rotted from disuse."

Tension usually reaches an all-time high just before the first exam. One woman who had been out of school for 10 years remembers: "I studied so hard for that first exam. I got a 68, and was absolutely panic-stricken. I thought, What am I doing here? When the teacher put the grades on the board, the maximum you could have gotten was 71. I had gotten my first A!"

Another woman, a junior in geology, studied three hours a night for a week before her first exam. "When I got home," she recalls, "I was practically in tears. I was convinced that I had flunked. It turns out I got a 97, the highest grade in the class. My first thought was that he must have confused my paper with someone else's or that maybe he had missed my mistakes."

Many women who return to school discover that it is a long time before they stop feeling incredulous about doing so well. The comment of one woman is typical: "Sometimes when I hear myself in class, I do a double take: was that *me* who said that?"

Knowing that other women have experienced such misgivings, and done so well, is one source of comfort and encouragement. Another is to talk to women who have resumed their studies. Finding them ought not to be difficult. If you begin inquiring, you are bound to discover a friend who has a friend who has gone back to school, or that one of your children has a classmate whose mother is a student. If there is a reentry or continuing education center at the college or university nearest you, then you are really in luck. You're quite likely to find that some staff members there are older students themselves. With older students now being actively recruited in many places, your questions will probably be well received.

The following suggestions are ways that other reentry students used to cut down on anxiety:

• *Make your reentry a gradual process.* It doesn't have to be a nosedive into being a full-time student. Take one course to see how you feel about being in an academic environment. If that course goes well, take two the next quarter. Unless your career is on the line and it is crucial to get done with school as quickly as possible, begin by taking only courses that you are fairly sure you will like.

Self-development courses and courses through the women's studies department could be especially valuable to you. These courses often emphasize many of the issues that you are facing as a returning student—lack of confidence in your ability for one. If you honestly are petrified with fear that you are going to flunk, then audit the class so that you can remove any and all worry about grades.

• *Establish a support system.* Explain your apprehension to your family and friends, and let them know that you could use their support. Join a support group on campus. Knowing that you are not alone with your anxieties can be very comforting. At the same time, look for role models—women on campus who feel comfortable about being good students. It's more than likely that they, too, were initially concerned about their academic ability. Talk with these women about their transition from anxiety to confidence. Ask them for advice.

• *Become familiar with the campus atmosphere.* A lot of your anxiety has to do with the strangeness of the academic environment after so many years away. Spending time on campus before classes actually begin will probably help you to be less nervous once they do. Talk with people. Gather together all the questions that float through your mind in the middle of the night and ask them.

• *You don't have to be a perfect student.* The only person who is really pressuring you to get straight A's is *you*! As one returnee remarked, "We don't have to take our grades home to Mommy." When you are struggling with your papers, keep it in mind that it is not necessary to hand in material that is ready to be published. No one is expecting you to be perfect.

• *Try to relax.* If you approach your exams, papers, and texts in a really anxious state, you won't do nearly as well as you would if you were calmer. It takes a certain rise in tension to be able to learn, but if you are *too* tense, your mind will be so busy sorting out the anxiety that it won't be able to handle the new material.

• *When you approach something difficult, look back on your past accomplishments.* Look to your successes in other areas. Do you consider yourself successful at home or at your job? These roles require a lot of hard work. If you can succeed at them, you can do it with school as well. Once you are back in school and have a few academic successes in your repertoire, use them to fall back on when you are presented with a challenge. For example, if you are anxious about writing a paper, reread one you wrote that you feel good about.

• *Be sure to take one course guaranteed to be enjoyable each quarter.* If you are planning to get a bachelor's degree, you will have to take quite a few required courses that you might not otherwise select. Arrange your schedule so that you can count on at least one course that you *know* you'll enjoy. Many returning students take a physical education class each quarter and say that these classes do wonders for their moods. If you have a favorite teacher, take a class from him or her. If you like small discussion groups and hear of a class that relies heavily on them, sign up. It's very reassuring to have a class you can count on enjoying.

• *Spend time working on your study habits.* If you are worried about whether or not you can remember how to study, find out whether the campus has a learning center. If so, it will probably offer workshops to help you bone up on your reading skills, library research, term paper organization, preparation and taking of exams, and general study skills. A composition course can really help you to feel better about approaching term papers. (For details, see the chapter on improving your study habits.)

• *Explore your fear of failure.* Why are you so afraid of failing? What specifically is it that you feel you will be a failure at? How closely is your fear of failure associated with a fear of success? In 1968 Dr. Martina S. Horner, president of Radcliffe College, studied achievement motivation among college students and found that 65 percent of the women (as opposed to 10 percent of the men) demonstrated a definite "motive to avoid success." Do you feel that succeeding in college will interfere with being a good mother or a good wife? Does being successful mean that you must become "unfeminine"? What is "feminine" behavior? An article in a recent issue of a popular family magazine ended with: "There is no stronger drive than that of a woman to become pregnant." If you have finished with that drive, never had it at all, or want to combine it with several other strong drives, how does that statement make you feel as far as defining success and failure?

Which is most threatening, success or failure—or are the two bound tightly together? It can help alleviate some of the confusion and ambivalence to read about why success is so threatening to women. (See Appendix D, Section 7 for some suggestions.) And it can help to know that other women are having the same feelings. Discuss these fears with other people in a supportive situation. If there is a Psychology of Women course offered, try to schedule it in because it usually includes a segment on fear of success as part of the curriculum.

Anyone who is having reservations about her abilities will probably appreciate the process that Gloria went through after being out of school 29 years:

> I decided that I would take three courses. There was a horrendous registration process which involved four different buildings and took hours. I went to the first three classes, went home, and absolutely panicked. I didn't sleep a wink all night! I thought: My God, what have I gotten myself into? I can't possibly do this. I decided in the middle of the night to drop two of the three courses and did that over the weekend. The next Wednesday, I went to the one remaining class and ran into a graduate student in her late twenties. She said: "Come on, you can do it. Take ————'s class, he's a great teacher." She helped me add the course again. What a sweet gal, a total stranger! She really bolstered me up. And as soon as I got the first midterm and paper back, I knew I could handle it.

Chapter 4

How Being a Student Affects Family Life

Are you feeling guilty already about spending less time with your family once school begins? Are you having a hard time imagining how you will combine your family and school commitments? Are you hoping that your student role will have little or no effect on your family? You are right on course! Concern about how to combine being a family person and a student is foremost for women (especially mothers) considering a return to school.

Certainly, the pressures of time, the fact that there is such an amazing lack of time, takes its toll on everyone involved with you. However, *do not overlook the glorious positive effects that being in school can have on your family life.* Many returnees have said that they are glad to be in school *if only* because of the good changes they have seen for all members of their family.

ARE STUDENT MOTHERS BETTER MOTHERS? MOST THINK THEY ARE!

Women who initially hope that their return to school will not harm their children discover that significant changes do, in fact, occur. To their surprise, they find that being a student mother can mean many fringe benefits for their children. In talking with student mothers, it will be common for you to hear them expound at length about how their relationship with their children has improved since they resumed their studies. The following are some of the reasons why.

"I'm a better mother because I feel so much better about myself."

So many women discover that being in school makes them feel happier—you can almost count on it as a bonus. Your new satisfaction about how you are spending your time is bound to affect your relationship with your family. As one mother of four comments:

> Your children will benefit from having a mother who is interested, who is aware, who is doing, who is learning. My children have a much better mother because I am accomplishing, because I'm proud of the fact that I'm in school. When I wasn't feeling as good about myself, I wasn't as good a mother as I am now.

"I feel that I'm a really good role model for my children."

Providing a good role model is another definite plus that student mothers mention when they discuss benefits from being in school. Returning student mothers feel great about knocking down stereotyped ideas their children have about what women, adults, and students are supposed to be like.

The whole idea of women as only housewives can be quickly dispelled, not by long discussions, but through simple observation. A family where everyone in the house assumes the title of homemaker and everyone is considered a learner becomes a much easier picture to paint when you are actually living it. One California woman who is studying to get her law degree feels that her role as a student sets a fine example for her ten- and seven-year-old son and daughter. She says:

> My kids see that women can do other things. They don't necessarily have to be just housewives. It's good for kids to know that there's a partnership operating in a family, that the father doesn't automatically go out and make the money, that the mother doesn't automatically stay home and clean. Unfortunately, a lot of their friends have mothers who stay home, and my kids wonder if they're being deprived. I'm really honest with them. I say: "Hey, I was the cookie chairperson this year for scouts, and I take bunches of kids to the park and store, too."

Women who take courses in women's studies find that their teenage daughters are very receptive to the topics covered in class—the changing role of women, discrimination against women in the job market, etc. As *your* awareness and attitudes change, so do those of your children. As you become educated on these issues, so will they.

Student mothers who have been in the role of homemaker for many years often say that how their children relate to them changes considerably. It is easy for children to expect that their mother's main function is to serve them if her primary role is one of homemaker. When the new role is added, so too is a new attitude. One mother whose children are seven and eleven years old remarks: "Your children will benefit because they'll see that their mother isn't just this person who exists to wait on them hand and foot. They'll learn that you're a real human being." Children watch with interest as their mothers approach and tackle something they really believe in.

Mothers seem especially concerned about having their daughters understand that it is possible to lead a self-sufficient life. One mother of six has been elected to political office and been extremely influential in her community. Nevertheless, she says that she has always felt inferior without a college education. She says:

> I've never felt I could strike out on my own if I ever wanted to. I've always felt that I *have* to remain someone's mother and someone's wife. No matter how qualified you are or how smart, if you don't have the degree, you just can't get a good job. I really want my girls to stay in school so they will have the freedom to not be tied in if they don't want to be.

An increased enthusiasm about school is a common occurrence among the children of women who are themselves involved with their studies. Many mothers and their children study together or even compare notes. A mother of 10, for example, mentions that her 13-year-old daughter not only props herself up alongside her on the bed to study, but that she has adopted her study habits as well. Another mother smiled with amusement when she was asked whether her return to school was benefiting her children. "In fact," she said, "my daughter came in from San Diego a few weeks ago and went back with one of my papers and my whole notebook. Some benefit!"

Actually, term papers can flow both ways. A mother of 15 (all

10 college-agers have continued their studies) mentions that her oldest daughter helped her with term papers when she first became a student. Other student mothers will tell you that they study for exams with their children, taking turns asking each other questions.

Having a mother for a student can definitely serve to focus your children on their education. You may find that having gone back yourself will motivate your children who are in their late twenties and thirties to return to school as well. And your younger children will find college much more accessible than they did before. A thirty-five-year-old freshman says that her two children, ages seven and ten, are now indicating an interest in going on to college. "I wish I had had a model when I was younger," she comments.

Even children who are just learning to read try to model their mother's behavior. One mother comments: "When I was in grammar school, I never wanted to study. But when my seven-year-old sees me studying, he takes out a book, too."

A drastic improvement in grades is a logical consequence of an increased interest in school. One student mother stated that her 11-year-old son was very intrigued by seeing her enjoy the learning process so much. "We study together now," she said, "and his grades have completely turned around."

"It's great—I'm just too busy to smother her with attention!"

Children of women who have returned to school become more self-reliant and take on more responsibility, according to their student mothers. In fact, over 70 percent of the women surveyed for this book reported that their children were more independent.

One parenting task that many women find particularly difficult is the encouragement of self-reliance. If you succeed, you are suddenly out of a job, and that can be very threatening. Becoming involved with school can serve as an outlet for some of the energy that goes into "providing" for your children. One mother, in discussing her relationship with her 15-year-old daughter, said:

She's grown up quite a bit and gotten very independent. She was used to having mommy chauffeur her around a lot. Now she gets out the bus maps and plots her routes so that she doesn't have to be dependent on me. I've always done too much for my children. Going back to school gives you something else to be perfect at, another outlet for you to prove your self-worth.

Parents who themselves might have been conditioned to feel that children should not be required to share in household responsibilities may be reluctant to ask their children for help initially. The mother of three children, ages two, four, and seven, in Oklahoma remembers that before she went back to school she would stop everything to get her children a drink of water or a cookie. "They've gained so much independence since I started school," she added. "I have them help me do things now that I would never have thought of asking them to do before—simply because I *need* the help. That's a real benefit to them."

"It's not the quantity of time spent, it's the quality."

Women who worry about spending less time with their children are usually relieved to discover that the time they do spend seems more satisfying for both mother and children. There is a great motivation to make the most of the time that is available. A statement such as "I see more of my child now than if I were home with him all day" makes perfect sense to a student mother.

If you are seeing less of your children, you make an effort to give all of your attention when you do have time together. You find that you do in fact have enough time together because it is better quality time. Connie's children were eight and ten years old when she enrolled in nursing school. She comments:

> When I was with them all the time we didn't really interact. Now I'm glad to see them when I get home from school. It's nice to be able to get involved with what they've been doing, and I have much more patience. This summer when I was home playing supermom it was awful. We all hated it. If I'm busy doing my thing, and they're busy doing their thing, we're much happier.

"My being in school has brought me so much closer to my children."

The kind of bond that often forms between mother and child once they have school in common can be really quite extraordinary. It may have to do with a rapidly developed empathy for anyone else involved in the learning process. Or the generation gap can narrow considerably when you start taking your younger colleagues seriously. Whatever the reason, many student mothers and their children mention that they feel a lot closer to each other.

When you return to school, the pressures that your children are up against become a lot more real to you—worrying about tests, papers, where it's all leading—the very same things that are pressuring you. There is definitely a link created when all of you share in the joys and frustrations of academic life.

Mary's children, ages eleven, ten, and six, go with her at the end of each quarter to pick up her grades. If she does well, they say: "Gee, Mom, when you studied that Tuesday night before the test when you couldn't give us dinner, that's okay, it was worth it." If she doesn't do so well, they say: "Why aren't you studying, Mother? You should stop running errands and let us do them while you get your studying done."

Another woman whose children were 13 and 17 when she went back to school says that the return is bound to make you and your children feel less removed from each other. "It has really given me a greater understanding of their pressures," she stated. "You can't really comprehend how much energy can go into a homework assignment until it's a reality for you, too."

THE DRAWBACKS

By far the biggest stumbling block when it comes to how your involvement with school affects your children will be that there simply is less *time* to be together. The protests from your children may be mild or furious, depending on how well their needs are being met at any given time. The next chapter is devoted to the reactions children have to their student mothers and suggestions for how to get beyond the problematic ones.

What about long-term effects? As you have seen, many returnees attribute their children's interest in college to being involved with a mother who is excited about learning. But what about long-term negative effects from having a mother who isn't home a lot of the time?

Studies on how children are affected by having a mother who works are very encouraging. According to an article by Lois Wladis Hoffman, who did an extensive review of research on the subject, children of working mothers have a more positive view of female competence. They usually have higher career aspirations and somewhat higher motivation to achieve as well. In one study cited by Hoffman, the adolescent daughters of working women were more likely to name their mother as the person they most admired than were the daughters of nonworking mothers.

Attitudes about working and nonworking women are definitely changing. In 1970, nearly half the women in a Virginia Slims poll felt that career mothers were worse mothers than their nonworking counterparts. However, in 1983, a *New York Times* poll showed that only 25 percent of working and nonworking women still felt that way.

MANY STUDENTS FEEL THEIR MARRIAGES BENEFIT

Are you worried that your student role might cause friction between you and your husband? *All* change causes a certain amount of strain, especially when it involves time and energy being spent on other things.

In a survey done at the University of Michigan, however, only 2.5 percent of the women said that returning to school resulted in an unhappy or divided family. Durchholz and O'Connor's study, involving University of Cincinnati students, reported that over three-quarters of the married women felt their husband's attitude about the student role was favorable or very favorable. (While this is encouraging, it is important to keep in mind that many women may never have gotten to the point of actually becoming students because of resisting husbands.)

Support from your spouse *is* important. The more support you receive, the more likely you are to return to college, stay there, and enjoy it. The odds are in your favor that your husband will be supportive. Over two-thirds of the married women interviewed for this book reported that their husbands gave them the most support for their role as a student. In Astin, Leland, and Katz's study, 65 percent of the women characterized their husbands as very supportive of their return to school, and of those, 42 percent said their marital relations had improved as a result of their student role.

Most women don't expect that their marriages will improve when they go back to school. Yet this is often one of the reported special bonuses of being a student. The following are some of the reasons that reentry women gave for improved relationships with their husbands.

"It's good for both of us that I'm happier."

Most people during the months (years?) before they finally make a decision involving major life changes feel quite restless and frustrated. You may be feeling that a change needs to be made, but you are unsure of which direction to take or what the outcome will be. Often a person who is in the throes of making a decision like this is not the most pleasant to be around. Once the decision has been made to return to school, you may feel some relief. But then there are many practical matters that need to be dealt with in addition to your anxieties about many of the very things that are discussed in this and subsequent chapters.

The fact is, however, that most returning students, once submerged in their student role, love school! A University of Michigan study reported that 85 percent of the women in their survey said they enjoyed school very much. Because you are spending time on something that is really important to you, you feel better about yourself and the rest of the world. Happy feelings spread like wildfire. Your family can't help but be affected by them.

A mother of four returned to school for a master's degree in special education when her youngest, twins, were 18 months old. She describes how a student role can improve a marital relationship:

> I'm a happier person, much more self-fulfilled. It makes life much more pleasant for me and my husband. He's very proud of the things I've accomplished. And I look better because I feel better. I've even lost weight. My husband knows I'm happier and that's made him happier.

Some returning students will tell you that adding a student role actually *salvaged* their marriages. When Gloria at age 50 went back to school in order to get her master's degree in counseling, she remembers:

> I really kind of wonder whether we'd still be married if I had gone on as a housewife who was becoming more and more frustrated. I wasn't doing what I wanted to be doing, and I was keeping a lot of my feelings inside. He certainly felt the resentment.

"There's so much more to talk about."

Many women find that their husbands are eager to hear all about what's been happening at school. Your husband may not be in a position where he can pursue his formal education at this point in his life, and he may get a lot of vicarious pleasure out of hearing about your classes. "I can't wait to get home and share some of the new things I've learned," says one woman. "It's really exciting for both of us." Some couples actually wind up doing the course work together.

If you have spent a major portion of your time as a homemaker these past years, your husband is probably quite used to hearing about the activities that involve you. If you have been busy raising children, he may be interested in hearing about your day, but the content will be fairly predictable to him. When you return to school, you are leaving his realm of the familiar. Although some men find this threatening, most find the new input very stimulating.

Of interest are not only the courses you are taking, but a whole atmosphere from which he is probably very far removed. A mother of 15 said that when she returned to school "another world opened up" for her husband and her. "We have so much to talk about," she said. "He enjoys hearing about the classroom scene. We talk a lot about the things I do at school." Connie, now a junior, resumed her studies after a 13-year break, most of which she spent being a housewife. She comments:

> It's very satisfying. He's much more interested in me now for what I'm doing. I'm not just his wife. We don't just chitchat about his children and his house and his community. We talk about what *I've* been doing.

You may feel that spending less time together will be a problem for you and your husband. But you may also find that there is more to share when you are together.

"We communicate better."

Many women who stopped their education in order to put their husbands through school wind up feeling intellectually inferior. Lack of confidence in their intellectual abilities can make it hard for them to voice their opinions on issues. When women say there's a lot more to talk about or their husbands say they have become more interesting, what they may actually mean is that the women feel more comfortable verbalizing thoughts they have had all along.

The time pressure can actually work *for* rather than against better communication. There is just no room for nebulous messages in the harried life of a couple who are often juggling time together—time with the children, work, and school. It becomes essential to discuss conflicts and practical matters in a way that will resolve them most efficiently. For couples who are used to having more time together, "efficient" communication may be a problem for a while. Be sure to read the section in Chapter 6 about double messages!

Fortunately, many returnees do find that being a student helps them to communicate better with their spouses—either because they develop self-confidence or because there is no time to communicate any other way.

"The major changes in me have affected our relationship."

Women who return to school find that their self-image often changes dramatically and unexpectedly. One of the changes that is reported by just about everybody is an increase in self-confidence. Other changes include feeling more professional, independent, and assertive, and relating better to people. All of these changes affect your relationships with people close to you.

A 33-year-old Ohio woman who went back to school to receive a bachelor's degree in social work explains the kinds of changes that took place for her:

> My entire life changed. I regained self-confidence. I've instituted a lot of personal changes like giving up an eighteen-year smoking habit since returning to school. I learned to drive, bought a car, and quit biting my nails. Before I went back to school, I'd get up and grumble my way through the day. I didn't acknowledge that I had any choices about my future. It could only help us as a couple that I'm more of a person than I used to be. At least it's worked out that way for us.

Frequently women feel upset about being so dependent on their spouses, but they feel there is no alternative because they haven't got the qualifications or the "gumption" to be more independent. A Connecticut woman who is a senior majoring in psychology commented:

> I've gained a lot of self-confidence in the sense that I feel better about myself. I also feel more confident about my intellect. School was easy! And I made a lot of friends which I never expected. I tore myself away from my husband and became a person in my own right. Our relationship has really improved. I bring more to the marriage now; there's more to share.

"My husband's delighted he's not going to be the only bread-winner in the family."

It wasn't so long ago that if a woman held a full-time job outside the home, many people assumed it meant her husband just didn't have what it takes to hold the family together. The attitude was: behind every working woman was a flop of a man!

Times have certainly changed, as has the attitude. Although there are still some men who feel secure about their own image only if they are sole provider and "the little lady" greets them at the end of the day with pipe and newspaper, the number is dwindling fast.

A 35-year-old Massachusetts graduate student in social work commented:

> When we finally realized that we were living stereotyped roles and how uncomfortable for both of us that was—me home with the kids, him at work—we became mutually supportive about allowing the other person to develop. He is just incredibly supportive.

Having another employed person in the family can open up a variety of options. Your husband might like to explore a career change but knows it's impossible even to bring it up if he is sole provider for the family. Or the added income can mean a drastic change in your life-style—necessities or luxuries that you were unable to consider before, an earlier retirement for him. Another important option is that if you are working you may feel more fulfilled, which could mean an improved marital relationship.

THE DRAWBACKS

> My husband's overall general attitude was: "You want to do it, do it. But don't bug me. You can do anything you want to do as long as everything else you have to do gets done." That was at the beginning, but it's changing. Recently he's been helping more, not fifty-fifty, but not as much "honey, would you please." That used to bug the heck out of me. I always had to ask him as a favor to me to help me out when I felt we were both doing the same things: we both worked forty hours a week, we both went to school, we both had a child. But just yesterday we were talking and he said that he felt we were friends. It was the best compliment he's given me in years. That's how things are going lately.
>
> —A 32-YEAR-OLD FRESHMAN

Even returning students who feel that their marital relationships have greatly benefited will tell you that major adjustments had to be made on both their parts. Your husband may resist your new role in any number of ways, the worst ones of which are subtle. Read Chapter 6 for some clues to the pitfalls and how to climb out of them.

Chapter 5

My Mother the Student— What Children Think

She's never here. She starts going all fast, and she gets mad. She does everything at once. We don't do as many things together. I'd like her to stay home and do errands. Then I'd get to see her more often. Daddy makes bad peanut butter and jelly sandwiches.

—THE 8-YEAR-OLD DAUGHTER OF
A COMMUNITY COLLEGE SOPHOMORE

Yes, it affects our relationship. I look upon her not only as a mother, but as a human being struggling to learn things about her world in the same way I struggle to learn things about mine. Through her education, I have been further educated. I like the feeling of having a mother who believes she doesn't already know everything and has room to learn more. I'm glad she hasn't reached a "stalemate" in her learning as many housewives have. She doesn't read cheap novels, wear curlers or fluffy house shoes, and isn't perpetually watching TV game shows. She's out in the world learning.

—THE 17-YEAR-OLD SON OF A
UNIVERSITY JUNIOR

If you are concerned about your children's reaction to having a student for a mother, you are in good company. Nearly all women who have recently gone back to school, or who are thinking about

41

doing it, find that one of their biggest worries is what effect so major a commitment will have on their children. Unless you have been working outside your home, going back to school probably does mean spending less time with your children.

Over half of American women with children under the age of six are in the labor force. In fact, the "American dream" family—a working father, a dependent mother, and two children—represents only 7 percent of the American population! So if you still carry around an image of the all-American mother who stays home all day to watch over her brood and polish floors, label it obsolete and erase it.

What kinds of reactions can you expect your children to have if you do pursue your education? There are some you can almost count on:

· They'll feel proud of you and happy that you are doing something that is important to you.

· They won't like spending less time with you.

· They'll complain about having to do more work around the house.

· The older they are, the better they will feel about having a student mother.

"YOUR MOTHER IS A *WHAT*?" HOW YOUNGER CHILDREN REACT INITIALLY

Your preschool children will most likely reflect your attitude about school. If you feel that school is something worthwhile to do, they will too. On the other hand, if you feel you must apologize to your children for pursuing your own interests, they will identify with your guilt feelings and the experience will be a lot less enjoyable and productive for you and them.

When you explain to your preschoolers why you are changing the routine at home, be sure to tell them that you are returning to school because it is something that you very much *want* to do. By the age of two, children are already aware that grownups have special work that they do outside of the home. Emphasize that studying and going to classes is going to be your work, and that it is a job just like being a teacher or a carpenter or an airplane pilot.

The kind of child care that you find for your preschooler is the most important factor involved in how he or she will feel about your time away. It will take a considerable amount of energy on your part, but you should be able to find a child-care situation which both you and your child feel very good about. If your child is offered a stimulating and loving alternative, he or she will almost certainly respond well to it. (See Chapter 15 for advice on how to find good child-care situations.)

Initially, elementary-school-age children may be very confused by the announcement that you are going back to school. Isn't school something you were supposed to have done *before* you had children? they wonder. Grownups are not supposed to be in school, so why is it that you have *chosen* to do this? Their friends will most likely share the same misconceptions about who is supposed to be in school and who isn't. Consequently, you may wind up with a child like Connie's daughter who says defiantly: "I don't tell anyone about my Mom."

One seven-year-old admitted trying to keep people from finding out what her mother was doing, because "when they find out, they make fun of me, saying, 'Oh, your mommy is a baby because she's still in school.' " But this same girl defended her mother with a trouper's allegiance: "She is *not* a baby. Almost half the parents in America go to school."

Although it may be obvious to you, don't assume that your younger children know that grownups being in school is nothing to be ashamed of. These children are old enough to understand your reasons for resuming your education. Be sure to explain to them why you are going back to school, and let them share your enthusiasm about your new job. Elementary-school-age children are usually less flexible about changes in their routine than their preschool brothers and sisters, so make sure that they understand that the changes are taking place because of something you believe in.

"MY MOM'S PRE-LAW" HOW TEENAGERS REACT INITIALLY

Teenagers also complain that they see less of their mothers, but they do spend time thinking about why their mothers have chosen to make such major changes in their life-styles. Teenage children of student mothers usually feel proud of them.

By the time children enter their teenage years, they think a lot about what they want to do when they are adults—what kind of job, what sort of spouse (if any), whether or not to have children, how to spend free time, etc. Parents come under close scrutiny during this process.

Teenagers often feel glad that their mothers are involved with another major commitment in addition to mothering. A 19-year-old daughter of a 43-year-old sophomore likes having a mother who is "more than just a mother." She says:

> I find myself comparing her to other mothers her age. She chose to be a mother, and that's the important thing, but I'm glad that's not the only thing she's concerned with. So many women her age, they're always so concerned with their families. That's nice, but they're boring. I admire my mother for going back to school.

You and your spouse are unquestionably the most available role models your children have for adult behavior. Making a major commitment, being flexible enough to change your life-style, and improving your own self-esteem are all traits that can have a powerful influence on your children as they look around for adult models.

It's especially important to discuss returning to school with your teenagers, making sure that they know the reasons why you're doing it. If you share your goals with them, they will understand and respect your choice, and be happy for you. Unlike elementary-school children, who may try to hide your student role from their friends, you can expect your teenagers to boast about you. A particularly inspiring example is a Long Island woman, a mother of 15 children, who went back to school when they ranged in age from 11 to 27. The sixth of the 15, a son, said of her, "I wish I had one-third of her energy. She's got energy and spunk and drive. She gets it all done because she wants to."

BE PREPARED FOR MIXED FEELINGS

A 15-year-old, who expressed happiness that his mother didn't just "sit around" like other mothers, hadn't been so happy at the age of 11, when he sometimes came home to an empty house. No matter how you emphasize what is good about being in school, you can expect that there will be some painful experiences with your children. You can also expect that your children's feelings about your being a student will improve as they get older. When the world stops revolving around them—a perfectly normal stage of development, no matter how long and trying it is—they will find it easier to cope with the realization that you have a life of your own. It's important to encourage your children to become self-sufficient. A mother who gives her children her constant attention is not letting them establish the skills they will need when they are on their own. Going back to school lends itself to the kind of home life that promotes a positive kind of self-sufficiency.

It will take your children a while to adjust to all the changes. Children need and feel reassured by routine, and you will change that routine drastically when you add a student role to your life. Your children may understand that being in school can lead you to an interesting job, more money, a happier you; but if you have been mostly at home for their whole lives, they are bound to have some doubts about your new involvement.

You should expect that your children will like some things about your student role and dislike others. Comments such as "She seems really happy—I think she's getting more out of life," or "She can be of benefit to society, not just us," are quite common. On the other hand, and from the same mouths, "When I need help, she's not around," or "I hate doing my duties every day, and I get mad because she gets home late," are just as common.

Be understanding about the adjustments your children have to go through. Ask them if they notice differences in you or the way things are at home, and listen carefully to what they have to say. Teenagers and their younger brothers and sisters as well discover that there can be a lot of benefits to them from having a mother in school.

Many older children report that one fringe benefit of having a mother in school is that it gets her "out of my hair." Your children may find it easier to get along with you as you make friends with younger classmates. You may both discover a closing of the generation gap as you share your school-related experiences with them. The mother of 15 who was mentioned above—all 10 of whose college-age children have continued their education—reported that when she first became a student, her oldest daughter helped her with term papers. The 13-year-old daughter of another student said jubilantly, "If I'm having trouble with my homework, my Mom knows it all. I'm studying earth science right now, and it just seems like every time I'm doing something, she's doing the same thing and can help me out."

But there is no avoiding it: even if your children beam with pride over having a student mother, they are likely to resent you for spending less time with them. They may not have realized how much they depended on you—to transport them, to rush to school with a forgotten book or lunch box—until you are no longer there to do it. Fortunately, there are practical solutions to problems of this sort: placing lunch boxes and school books in the same spot every day, arranging a backup for transportation when you're not available. If your child comes home for lunch or has special half-days off, making arrangements may be less easy—but not impossible. If your classes are mainly in the daytime, scour your neighborhood for another student whose classes are at night. You can help each other out when help is needed. Or you may have a friend or relative who will have your child over for lunch on a regular basis.

Children often complain because their mother is not home to greet them after school. If this becomes a problem for you, a little resourcefulness ought to produce a solution—a friend or relative to welcome them, at home or elsewhere, or a special activity such as Scouts or a swimming lesson to go to when the school day ends.

"YOU CALL *THIS* DINNER?"

If you have classes that keep you away from home at dinnertime, there are almost certain to be complaints. Probably what the complainers are missing is not so much the food of yesterday as the undivided attention of the mother who once served it. Now this same mother is home only long enough to whip up a five-minute special, or is off for class halfway through the meal. Or all that remains of her are some hurried instructions about what to put on the table. Being asked to cook for themselves does not usually go over well with children who are used to a full-time mother.

It is hard to make light of complaints that focus on meals. But there are things you can do to make it all go more smoothly:

• When you *do* have time, prepare the kind of meal you know your children like. Even if this happens just once a week, it will really be appreciated.

• You can ease the load on everyone by spending a few hours a week making casseroles that can be frozen. It doesn't require much talent or energy to pop one of these into the oven, and it counts as a home-cooked meal whether or not you are there to enjoy it. A cookbook that specializes in meals of this sort is *The Elegant but Easy Cookbook* by Lois Levine and Marion Fox Burros.

• If you are married, buy your husband a cookbook that he will find simply irresistible!

• If you can't be at home for dinner and your children are responsible for preparing their own meals, make a point of having someone there occasionally whose company they enjoy.

• If you are anxious about something at school, dinnertime is *not* the time to complain about it. Your children will not be sympathetic at this particular moment, since they may already feel put upon. Talk about good things that have happened, about what you have learned—not about what you're annoyed or worried about.

"WHY CAN'T WE GET A MAID?"

Another complaint by the children of mothers in school is about having to do more housework. Like cooking, this can become an emotional issue. If your children have become accustomed to a mother who made it her responsibility to keep the house clean and in order, it is natural for them to balk at suddenly being assigned new tasks.

You can deal with this potential conflict by calling a family meeting at which you collectively make a list of everything that needs to be done. You should also decide together on some activities to be done as a group, as a reward when the system is running well.

A painless way of getting the housecleaning done is to do the job together once a week. If everyone pitches in and does it all at once, you'll find that the housework gets done a lot faster. The 10-year-old daughter of a student mother in Maryland reported, "We get to go to the movies and do things like ice skating together because we all work together on the house and we wind up with extra time."

BE PREPARED FOR SOME TENSE MOMENTS

Your children may notice that your fuse is a lot shorter as pressures begin to pile up. It may not be apparent to either you or your children why you are feeling tense or angry. But it is important to know whether what you are getting angry about is what is actually bothering you. If you have a huge assignment to do, a child's messy room can set you off a lot quicker than if your homework is all done. You will need to explain to your children that assignments are closing in on you, but that it isn't forever.

Get your children to signal if they see you building up the kind of tension that can result in unwarranted anger. Nonthreatening

signals can be worked out at a time when everyone is feeling relaxed. You can offer a few choice examples of the kind of outburst
you mean: "How come I'm the only one who ever does any work
around here? This place is a mess! If you don't start cleaning up immediately, you can forget about going to the beach. I've just about
had it!"

It's at this point that your children are entitled to ask whether
you're being fair—and the question becomes your cue to stop for a
minute and think about what is upsetting you. Is it really true that
your children are contributing nothing to the housekeeping? Did
you take time to praise whoever cleaned up the kitchen that time,
without being asked? Where is the pressure on you really coming
from?

Your anger *may* be appropriate. But if you realize on second
thought that it isn't, you should take the time to explain what's
really bothering you. Everyone will be happier with a procedure
that forestalls unnecessary arguments and hurt feelings.

If the signals of tension become more and more frequent, no
matter how determined you may be to do well in school, it's important to allow yourself some time off. Even half an hour spent
taking a walk, with or without your children, can help make things
go more smoothly for everyone.

IN CASE YOUR CHILDREN ASK . . .

You might encourage your sons and daughters to read this
chapter as a preview of coming attractions and distractions. In addition, they are bound to know other children their age whose
mothers are in school. A get-together involving mother and children can help to set the stage for what lies ahead and can provide
you and your children with allies to support you in your new
life-style.

If your children would like some advice from other children
whose mothers have returned to school, that is what follows.

Learn to cook. You're going to have to find something to occupy
your time so that your mother can have the time she needs to study.
You need to accept your mother and know that she's doing something for herself and will not always have time for you. You'll have
more free time, and that's a good thing because it allows you to develop your own interests.

—THE 17-YEAR-OLD SON OF A
UNIVERSITY JUNIOR

Make sure she doesn't depend on you to do all the housework. For a while there, my Mom had us doing all the cleaning and straightening at our house, and we didn't even have time to do our own homework. Let your mother know when she's asking you to do too much.

—THE 14-YEAR-OLD DAUGHTER OF A
COMMUNITY COLLEGE FRESHMAN

Let your Mom study. Be aware that your mother is going to need a lot of time to be by herself and that she has to have room and time to be alone. She will need *complete quiet!* She should find a place where there's no traffic because otherwise she won't be able to concentrate. Our Mom spent a lot of time in the kitchen with everyone going in and out, in and out, and she just got so frustrated. Now she studies in her room with the door closed, and we really try not to bother her.

—THE 15-YEAR-OLD DAUGHTER OF A
UNIVERSITY SOPHOMORE

You'll have to help out more. Your mother being back in school means that you'll have to do a lot more around the house. Being helpful is a good way for you to support what your Mom is doing. You should be as encouraging as you can, because it's hard for mothers to be students, and they need an understanding family. Education is a wonderful thing and it will open up all sorts of doors for your Mom and maybe even for you.

—THE 21-YEAR-OLD DAUGHTER OF A
GRADUATE STUDENT

You can both learn together. Take advantage of the knowledge that your Mom gains at school. You'll be surprised that she is learning so much, and you'll wind up learning many things from her. Be patient. She will no longer have time just for your problems. Get involved with what she is learning.

—THE 17-YEAR-OLD SON OF A
UNIVERSITY JUNIOR

Your mother will need support at home. For mothers who have doubts about their abilities to "reenter" student life, stock family criticisms about what is being served for various meals and the way the house is being kept can be critical to success or failure. Your critical attitude at home can affect how she does academically and professionally. Try not to make your mother feel guilty about spending time on "her own thing" instead of on housework and meals.

—THE 33-YEAR-OLD DAUGHTER OF A
FORMER RETURNING STUDENT

"I'LL HOLD YOUR HAND, MOM, BUT WHO WILL HOLD MINE?"

Teenagers spend a lot of their energy sorting out who they are. It can be hard, when you have an identity crisis of your own, to cope with a mother who is going through the same kind of transition. A woman who was a college freshman when her mother went back to school in 1962 remembers:

> I disliked the amount of family support it took to carry Mom through school. Since I carried myself through by working on campus and holding a scholarship, I had a hard time understanding her constant need to be encouraged and supported. I had to take a summer off from my campus job after graduating from college to come home and "hold the family together" (as my father put it), so that Mom could complete her course work. It was hard to keep her spirits up when I was wrestling with career and life goals of my own.

It is to be expected that you will sometimes need emotional support as a student. Mothers, who are used to being in a supportive role themselves, sometimes have trouble finding the right person. But there are sure to be people around who will give you the help you need—friends, relatives, even members of the university staff. It's a matter of learning to ask the right person at the right time.

Returning students tend to be extremely grade conscious, and to set very high standards for themselves. As a result, their children can sometimes end up feeling threatened by being placed in what looks like direct competition with their own mother. One junior high school student mused, "I sometimes wonder where I got my brains, I really do. I don't do half as well as she does."

A college student who is expecting good old Mom to be standing by the door waiting to hear the latest about what he or she has been doing will be disappointed by discovering a Mom who's engrossed in assignments of her own. One such student reflected:

> At first I felt kind of cheated. It takes all the glory out of the fact that I'm in college too. I thought this was supposed to be *my* time. When you come home, she's supposed to say, "How did you do on finals?" But when I come home, she says, "Guess what I got on my

finals?" She's proud of what she does, and we're really proud of her. It's just that she likes to brag about it.

So if your children begin to resent your enthusiasm, it may be a sign that it's time to take stock of whether you're showing enough interest in their accomplishments. If you know that your children really enjoy having you review for exams with them, try to find the time to continue this kind of sharing. Your children will almost certainly be supportive of your school-related activities if you are genuinely supportive of theirs.

"CAN WE TRADE NOTES ON *MOURNING BECOMES ELECTRA?*"

Actually, most children of returning students report that their mothers show more interest in their school-related activities than they did before. Both mother and child enjoy it when what they are studying turns out to be the same subject material.

Even if what you are studying is totally different, the fact that you are both studying creates a strong bond which children of all ages enjoy. Younger children often like to read curled up next to their mother while she is studying. And they often find it amusing that their mother talks about homework and teachers just like they do.

When the support flows two ways, college-age children are awfully glad to have a mother who is having experiences similar to their own. One daughter says:

> She can relate to long registration lines and other hassles like that. It's nice to know that I'm not the only one who has to go through all this. I can learn from her mistakes. I think my Mom being in school has really enhanced our relationship.

Should you bring your work home with you? The answer is definitely *yes.* By sharing the experience of studying, you have the potential for adding a very enjoyable new dimension to your relationship with your children.

Here are some points to be kept in mind as you go through the reentry process:

1. *Almost all change is met with resistance.* Children are creatures of habit just like everyone else, and any kind of change, whether positive or negative, is apt to be upsetting.

2. *Let your children know why you are back in school.* Take the time to talk about why being a student is so important to you. Your children will catch on quickly and respect you for wanting to change things.

3. *Less time spent together is not synonymous with a bad relationship.* Children soak up guilt feelings the way blotters soak up ink. If you feel guilty about being home less, your children are bound to get the message. Remember that although you may wind up being with your children less, the time you do spend together will most likely be quality time.

4. *Children benefit from taking on more responsibility.* It simply is not good for children to have someone "doing" for them all the time. Your children will benefit from feeling that they are members of a team that is working toward common goals. Be sure to let them know that you are genuinely pleased when they perform their assigned tasks.

5. *It's not all that important to have an immaculate house.* Returning students do report that their houses are less tidy, but that it doesn't bother them or their husbands nearly as much as they thought it would. You can save a lot of wear and tear on your nerves by supervising your children's rooms less than you did before. You might want to strike a bargain: I'll stay away from your room if you will take on more responsibility for helping me keep the living room and kitchen clean.

6. *Share your enthusiasm about being in school.* If you enjoy school, your children probably will too. But beware of the fine line between enthusiasm and bragging—it can make the difference between whether your teenagers are proud of you or resentful. If you see them turning sour each time that you report a major triumph, think about how you are presenting yourself.

7. *Discuss school-related experiences with your children.* Children love to feel that their mothers are interested in what happens to them at school. Student mothers can compare notes with their children on interesting things that they have both learned. Children of students really enjoy this dimension of their relationship.

8. *Arrange it so that your children always know how to find you.* Develop an efficient system for locating you in case of emergency. A good idea is to draw up a weekly schedule of your classes and related activities and post it in a convenient location, such as the refrigerator door or near the telephone. Your children's schools should also have copies. It will mean a lot to your children to know

that you can be found. Have a backup system of friends and relatives organized just in case.

9. *Your children need a special, inviolate time with you each day.* You will be very preoccupied during your student years, and it is important to spend some time each day just "regrouping." A good idea is to spend 20 minutes at bedtime reading and talking with your children. When your sons and daughters can count on having your undivided attention at that time, they will be more flexible about the times when you are unavailable.

10. *The university has something to offer everybody in your family.* Be on the lookout for special exhibits, craft fairs, movies, sporting events, concerts, plays, interesting speakers, etc. The most inexpensive cartoon festival in town will probably be at the university. Campus newspapers and various bulletin boards can keep you posted. You don't need an excuse to bring your children to campus; a trip just to see where it is that you actually put your nose to the grindstone is guaranteed to intrigue them.

Chapter 6

What Husbands Think

At times she is very uncertain about her abilities and potential. I guess this is to be expected, but it's not as easy emotionally for any of us as when she was secure inside the world of her home. She seems to be riding an emotional roller coaster where the highs are higher and the lows are lower.

—THE HUSBAND OF A 35-YEAR-OLD
FRESHMAN

The all-consuming business of keeping the house neat as a pin, always having a meal ready on time—good grief, why these things were ever important, I'll never know. They have now been replaced by things of far greater importance. She's begun to think about herself, her worth, the contribution she might be able to make in so many different ways.

—THE HUSBAND OF A 59-YEAR-OLD
SENIOR

If you are married (or otherwise committed) and considering a return to school, you are bound to be concerned about how the man in your life will react. What kinds of effects do husbands usually see? What sorts of things worry men when their wives take on school? Can you expect your husband to be encouraging? It's only natural that these unknowns may make you feel anxious.

Unfortunately, you can't rely entirely on what other returning students say about their husbands' feelings. Studies about the ways couples communicate show that husbands and wives often perceive the same event in totally different ways. Two economists from the University of Michigan, Stafford and Duncan, surveyed 1,500 people and found that the typical married man and woman average only about 15 minutes of conversation as a primary activity each day. It's no wonder that couples misunderstand each other—even without the added involvement of school!

You also can't assume that what your spouse says he feels about a return to school is actually the way he feels. Many returning students report that their husbands say they think taking classes is great, but that in fact they are expecting no changes in the routine at home.

So it's important for both you and your husband to be as honest as possible with each other and yourselves. Learning about how other husbands say they feel is a positive step toward peace of mind. Many of the topics in this chapter can serve as springboards for discussion between you and your husband *before* you take on a student role.

THEY SAY THEY AREN'T WORRIED

Husbands seldom report being concerned when their wives first decide to go back to school. Although some men express fear about unknown changes, the most common worry that is expressed has to do with how it's going to be paid for.

It is important to find out what your spouse is feeling all along the reentry route. When he says he's not concerned, it could mean:

- He is worried sick but not talking about it because he knows how worried you are.
- He's convinced of the worst: you plan to leave him as soon as you are financially independent. He's afraid to bring it up.
- He thinks everything will be exactly the same as it is now.
- He may not believe you actually plan to go through with it.
- He may have thought it all out and really not be worried.

For starters, be sure to ask your spouse specifically how he feels about your new commitment. If he seems unworried, try to talk about what he thinks it's going to be like to have a spouse who is a student. Does it sound like what you think it will be like?

THEY FIND MUCH TO BE ENTHUSIASTIC ABOUT

Most women are delighted by the kinds of changes they see in themselves when they take on a student role. But do their husbands share in their enthusiasm? Happily, they do! Spouses generally see the same kinds of positive effects as their wives, and they identify a lot more pluses than minuses resulting from the return to school. Most men don't like the way school infringes on family time and time spent as a couple, but they are still pleased that their wives are back in school.

Some of the changes that men feel good about follow.

"She's becoming a more independent person."

Men often notice that their wives are more independent as a result of returning to school, and they report it as one of the fringe benefits. Interestingly, wives often fear that their becoming more independent is something that would bother rather than please their husbands.

Husbands say they feel good about the change for several reasons. For one thing, they feel excited by the prospect of having a companion who is genuinely concerned with attaining her own goals and becoming her own person. As a Massachusetts man whose wife is getting a master's degree in social work commented:

> We found that after so many years of marriage, we were beginning to mold together into a kind of blob. I'm fascinated by the way she's changing now. Life isn't centered around me and around this house and around where I put my boots anymore.

Another husband, whose wife is a medical student, expressed it this way:

> It's a wondrous thing, amazing to know that she will be able to do with the rest of her life what she wants to, or at least to know that she has the credentials and training for it.

A return to school is also a step toward independence in the sense that a woman could be in a more secure position should something happen to her husband. Spouses are relieved that their wives would probably have less trouble finding a meaningful job after getting a college degree.

Although many men complain because they see less of their wives, others feel that some time apart can help their relationship. For example, being apart more may mean an increase in intensity during the time spent together. As one spouse commented: "Time is precious, so we talk more when we're together." "Being apart and doing things you want to do," said a man from Texas, "tends to bring you back into a relationship." So for some men, having an independent wife means feeling less cloistered and having more time to themselves.

It is important to understand what both of you mean by *independence*. Your husband, with the best of intentions, might say he looks forward to having an "independent" wife, but the meaning he gives to the word "independence" may be completely different from yours. If whatever you mean by "independence" is important to you, be sure to explore what you both mean.

"She's home less and stimulated more."

Returning students are often plagued by guilt feelings—guilt about spending less time with their children and husband, guilt about having a messy house, guilt about taking on a major commitment. Yet husbands frequently report that they feel a relief from their *own* feelings of guilt when their wives find something that occupies them outside of their home. As one husband put it:

> She has a world of her own outside the house, and that takes a lot of pressure out of it, because when I come home and kick off my shoes, it doesn't destroy the whole thing. I don't feel quite so guilty indulging myself in my own work and talking about it when she has something she can indulge herself in, too.

If your present situation is making you restless, your husband knows about it—whether you have discussed it or not. Knowing you are less than happy with your current life-style can be as frustrating for him as it is for you. So it is perfectly natural for him to feel relieved that you are adding a new dimension to your life. "This is the first step in the transition back into the world," says one man in Maryland whose 35-year-old wife had expressed feelings of deep dissatisfaction with her life at home.

"She just feels better about herself."

Husbands and wives both report that a return to school can make you feel as if you're on top of the world. One husband explains the kind of upward spiral effect that is often found when you are feeling better about yourself:

> My wife is happier within herself, which gives her more confidence and more courage to try to reach out because she feels better about herself. The more success she has, the more willing she is to try.

Studying hard leads to success, which leads to self-confidence, which leads to more success, which leads to an improved self-image. Feeling better is one thing that almost everyone involved mentioned.

Aside from a dramatic increase in self-confidence, spouses notice their wives have a lot more energy and enthusiasm—more "vim, vigor, and spice" as one man from Maine says. "She feels more like getting up in the morning and more like talking to people," he continued.

Husbands mention that they are amazed by how much their wives are able to pack into each day. As your priorities become clearer, you will discover energy you never knew you had before. Most reentry students become excellent managers of their time, according to their husbands.

"She knows more—it makes her more interesting."

As one spouse of a California reentry student remembers: "She's learning all of those things that have been a mystery to her. It's been exciting to watch her understand things she's wanted to know for such a long time."

Some husbands remark that their wives used to feel defensive about their lack of formal education and were reluctant to get involved in discussions socially. This changes, most husbands observe, as the women develop confidence in their intellectual abilities. "She's much more comfortable with a spectrum of ideas on any subject, and much less timid about voicing her opinions," comments the spouse of a 48-year-old junior who juggles being a student with being the mother of 10.

As reentry students who are heading for a career gather knowledge and get closer to graduation, their husbands say that they enjoy watching them define a professional image for themselves. One man discusses the kind of satisfaction he feels from having the woman he is involved with back in school: "I am stimulated by her pursuit of her career. It makes me feel good about her and good about me and good about us."

Many men report that there's a lot more to talk about since their wives started attending classes. Comments such as the following are typical:

> I used to come home at dinnertime and we'd talk about the daily domestic problems. Now she's bringing home new ideas from the classroom and her job experience, and it's really interesting. I think she's a lot more interested in what I'm doing, too.

"She's better with the kids."

Although women worry a lot that their husbands will not approve of "what they are doing to the kids," most men report an improved mother/child relationship.

Time apart from the children can help mothers and children to get along better, husbands observe. One husband reflects a general attitude about this: "When you have less time to spend, you try to make the quality of the time better. She actually pays more attention to them now than she used to."

Time away can also help to alleviate tension. Mothers often complain that mealtimes can be especially exasperating with their teenagers. Breaking the pattern of eating together every night can be a relief for everyone involved. When Gloria went back to school at age 50 to get a master's in counseling, her husband recalls:

> She was away three nights a week at suppertime, so the boys and I were getting better acquainted and getting along really well. All this happened to be at a time when she wasn't getting along well with them. When we would have meals, there would be a constant, what the boys would call "nagging." The boys really resented it. So she was glad to get out. And it was a great thing for me to have more contact with the boys.

Mothers and fathers agree that having a student for a parent serves as a terrific role model for their children. Fathers notice their children becoming much more involved with studying. Having a mother who studies too makes the whole job of studying seem more relevant. "It shows them that studying isn't just an artificial thing that only kids do," concludes one father.

And fathers are quick to attribute their children's interest in going on to college to the satisfactions that they see in their mother's student role. In a family with 15 children, all 10 of the college-age ones have gone on to college. It is not uncommon to find people in their late 20s and 30s reentering school after their mothers have resumed their studies. "A mother working hard to achieve a goal can serve as an incredible source of motivation and inspiration," claims one father.

WATCH OUT FOR DOUBLE MESSAGES!

Although husbands for the most part speak really enthusiastically about their wives being back in school, their wives often say that the support their husbands give verbally can be a far cry from what they actually do to help. And actions speak a lot louder than words to the overloaded returning student.

On one level, the following husband is quite supportive of his 36-year-old wife's return to school:

> It's taking her mind off things that have bothered her in the past. I'm glad she's back in school. We all recognize that there are some things that will have to suffer a little bit, but she's being given the chance to go out and think about something besides what she feels she's required to think about because of being a wife and mother. It's a chance for her to become more self-reliant and happier and a more rounded person in every way.

Although this spouse has many of the words right, his wife, a freshman who has been out of school for 18 years, does not characterize her husband as supportive:

> He could do a heck of a lot more. He comes in, grabs a beer and the paper, and sits down. Then I come dragging in thirty minutes later after being in a lab for four hours, and I don't get any farther than the kitchen. He could have started dinner. And when I'm very excited about something that's happened, he doesn't have the time to

listen to me. He's too busy working the crossword puzzle. I resent this.

If you find yourself in a situation where your spouse thinks it's great that you're in school but complains because you aren't turning out four-course meals every night and his socks aren't folded the way they used to be, try to talk about it right away. There's nothing like the double message for building up resentment. And feeling resentful is a terrific way to waste time and energy.

To begin with, find out if your husband is aware that there is a difference between what he says and what he does. Change, whether good or bad, is hard to adjust to. Your husband may not be contributing as much as is needed because it's not part of his familiar routine. Or, since you are the originator of the changes, he may be waiting for you to provide him with some very specific clues as to what he can do. You mustn't assume that he will know what will be most helpful. Silent messages definitely don't work as a reply when someone is giving you a double message!

When all is said and done, the husband quoted above can justifiably argue that he's worked an eight-hour day and deserves to relax before getting involved with household activities. But it doesn't have to be an "either/or" situation; a schedule can be worked out for this family where the couple and their 14-year-old daughter take turns starting dinner.

Accusations don't sit well with anyone. "You don't ever listen to me" is not a constructive approach. "I would really like to share what's been going on in my day. When's a good time to talk?" is better and more productive. You may discover that your husband can't stand to say more than three words to anyone between 5:00 and 6:00 P.M., but that after dinner he loves to spend a half-hour doing nothing else but talking. If immediately after dinner is when you crack open your books, you'll have to work out some sort of compromise.

SOME STUMBLING BLOCKS AND HOW TO GET PAST THEM

It would be surprising if either you or your husband could take on something as major as school without a few tremors along the way. There is no way to know how many women have dropped the idea of school because their husband resisted.

A study done by Gail Berkove does indicate, however, that women whose husbands don't pitch in around the house drop out of school more than women whose husbands share in the household responsibilities. Amazingly, in a study of doctoral candidates by S. B. Mitchell, only 7.3 percent said their husbands had actually encouraged them in their educational plans. The overwhelming majority of spouses had been either neutral or nonsupportive. Spouses have made comments such as: "If I'd thought it was going to affect her negatively, I wouldn't have allowed her to go to school." *Allowed?!* If your husband reacts this way, the reentry route will most likely be a painful one.

What kinds of things don't sit well with husbands of women who return to school?

"We never see each other."

The most common complaint by far that men bring up when their wives return to school is that they see a lot less of them. There is usually a dramatic change of routine at home, and peaceful time together is one thing that can easily be obliterated from a busy schedule. Weekends, which before may have been exclusively family time, are often used by reentry students as a chance to catch up on their homework.

Although many women decide that their family will come first, no matter what, others have found that what comes first is what is most pressing at the moment. The pressure of homework yet to be done can easily conflict with the needs and desires of other family members. As one California man involved with a master's degree student remarked:

> I'm aware of the fact that when I think I'd like to go away for the weekend, the first consideration is her homework, and it's probably the library for her this weekend. I've made a real point of leaving my work behind me at the end of the workweek, but she can't do that.

It's important for you as a couple to keep in mind that your student role will not last forever. A Rhode Island man whose 51-year-old wife is back in school commented: "Figure a span of a lifetime and figure four to six years out of that: It's a small price to pay for all the pluses she will have and you will have as a family unit." If you have decided to pursue a career after graduation, you will obviously be spending a great deal of time away then as well, but your schedule will be much more in tune with your husband's if you are both working traditional hours.

You have a goal in mind if you have returned to school—whether it's to learn more or to gather the necessary credentials to pursue a job or career. As you and your husband become involved with the time conflicts that surround your being a student, you should both keep your goal in mind. How would your husband feel if he did not have some kind of goal or continuing activity?

A good way to look at your student role is to think of it as your job, your work for the next however many years it will take. A certain amount of your husband's life is tied up with his work, and a certain amount of yours is tied up with your work as well. In a few years, your work schedule should improve!

In the meantime, be sure to set aside time for your relationship. This is something that you may have to make a deliberate, conscious effort to do as your obligations at school increase. Organize your study schedule, and when you have worked for the allotted amount of time, leave your work behind you. Having some fun will help give you the energy that you will need to resume your studies when you have to.

You should arrange a special, inviolate time each day that you and your husband share. Both of you will be able to depend on this time together as being exclusively yours when the pressures of schoolwork start to mount.

"She's a lot more temperamental than she used to be."

Many men mention that although their wives seem happier because they have taken on a student role, they are also more prone to mood swings than they were before they returned to school.

For instance, some men notice that their wives are much more anxious than they used to be. In many cases, women feel obligated to accomplish all that they did before in addition to their school-related activities. The pressure of having to stick to a rigid schedule makes returning students tense, according to their spouses. As Connie's husband commented when she became a nursing student:

If there's one negative effect it would be her inability to relax about not getting everything done or everything done in the way she wants it. Obviously, if you substitute school time for other time, something has to give.

Another kind of anxiety comes up for returning students as they get closer to graduation, if their goal is to find a job. On the one hand, observe many husbands, women feel much more self-confident because they have done so well in school. On the other hand, they are deeply concerned about whether they will be able to use what they have learned in a fulfilling job. The process of the actual job hunt is very worrisome, according to the spouses.

Husbands find that the pressures of school can make even the most easygoing of women more short-tempered at times. Having to get up early in the morning to catch a bus to school means not getting as much sleep as is needed and not having enough time for oneself and with one's family. There is a seemingly endless amount that has to be accomplished.

It is interesting that when you ask most returning students if they see any negative effects on them from a return to school, they usually say, after considerable thought: "I can't really think of any, but my family probably can!" And when you ask husbands the same question, they often mention temperamental changes, such as being more irritable, tense, short-tempered, or anxious.

Could it be that returning students do not see themselves as more nervous, short-tempered, etc.? This is very likely the case! When a husband sees his student wife as tense, *she* is usually seeing herself as having an incredible amount of work to do in a very limited amount of time. For instance, one returnee, when asked about negative effects, said: "They say I'm less patient, but I wouldn't call that negative. I would say I'm much more aware and concerned about my time."

You will probably become quite preoccupied with all that you have to do, and it is certainly possible to be climbing the walls without being aware of it. Remember to stop every once in a while to think about how you are projecting yourself to others. Your husband may see you as tense, nervous, or impatient—all signals from you for him to stay away. You, thinking about how much you have to accomplish, may wonder why he is steering clear of you, *especially* when you could use some support.

Things will run smoother if you let each other know about your differing perceptions: If your husband feels your tension start to rise, he should tell you about it in a nonthreatening way. If you are under a lot of pressure, explain to your husband what you are up against.

"There's no need for her to study that much."

Women who return to school are, as a group, determined to do really well academically. Many husbands feel that their wives are overdoing it, that they study more than anyone else enrolled in the courses.

Staying up later and getting up earlier in order to study is not at all uncommon for reentry students. One spouse remembers: "She'd sometimes stay up all night studying, always afraid she didn't know enough." Nor is it uncommon for a reentry student to do more homework than is required of her. "She did ten times as many drawings (by her own admission) than anyone else in each of the two courses," said the spouse of a 40-year-old reentry student who just received a master's in fine arts. Husbands really resent their wives devoting more time than is "necessary," and this can cause tension in your relationship.

Even if you are bound and determined to do as well as you possibly can, you need to set limits on your study schedule—for your own sake as well as everyone else's. It's important to have sharply defined intervals when you study, and to be able to leave your studying behind, even if your assignment is not 100 percent perfect. Your family will probably accept it if you say you must study until 10:00 P.M. They will be resentful, however, if you then continue until 1:00 A.M. If your husband does start to complain that you are overdoing it, take serious stock of how much time you are spending on school-related activities and think about whether or not you want to be spending that much time on them.

Sometimes the length of time a woman plans to take in order to get her degree may be a source of conflict for a couple. Your husband may not understand why you want to get a degree as quickly as you can. What difference does it make if it takes you two or three years? If you are eager to get started on a career, the extra year in school can seem endless and frustrating. Be sure to explain your reasons for wanting to finish as quickly as possible. Never assume that someone else understands your rationale for anything!

"This isn't exactly the way I envisioned our life together!"

A return to school is certainly not just a matter of four years spent in an academic setting if the end result is to pursue or change a career. A return to school often causes a dramatic change in your future life-style. Sometimes, for example, a woman who is just setting off on a career path will find that her spouse is just beginning to think about a time when he won't have to work anymore. Gloria's husband was 62 years old when she returned to school at age 50 in order to get a master's degree in counseling. He said:

> Thinking about her starting a career when I was ready to retire gave me some reservations. Fifty weeks out of the year, I was working from eight to five. It's very demanding and interferes with your private life. So you dream about a time when you can just pick up and do things without a whole lot of planning beforehand. With her fully employed, it could interfere with a few of those dreams.

This couple appears to have the necessary tools to deal with a potential conflict about the type of life-style they will have together. There are several possibilities that could satisfy both of them. For example, Gloria could try to find a nine-month counseling job at a university. Three months off in the summer plus other vacations is certainly plenty of opportunity for traveling.

When you and your husband first talk about a return to school, you should be sure to discuss what each of you would like to be doing five and ten years from then. Will your return to school conflict with these plans? Will it aid in these plans?

When being back in school produces basic ideological changes in you, this can certainly affect your life-style and therefore your relationship. One couple who have been living together for several years are experiencing this kind of conflict. He is an independent businessman who is aspiring "to join the upper middle class," to have the same kind of life-style as the parents of his companion. She, on the other hand, because of her involvement and commitment to social work, has developed strong feelings about social change. She now believes that there should be ceilings set on how much money any one person can make. You can imagine the potential for conflict here!

Speaking of life-style changes, a woman's return to school can prompt her husband to do some reevaluating about his direction as well. If your goal is to work after graduation, this gives your husband the option of working less, switching fields entirely, or taking on a domestic role. Encourage your husband to use your change in life-style as an impetus for exploring new options himself.

"The kids don't see nearly as much of her."

Although most husbands feel that a return to school can improve the mother/child relationship, they do mention that there are problems involved with trying to combine the mother and student roles.

The main problem is the decrease in time spent together. One husband describes their routine:

> In the morning when we get up and go to work we're together as a family, but we're just getting everyone prepared to leave the house. In the evening we have dinner together and then put the kids to bed, and that's really the only time we have with the children during the week.

Although this schedule sounds pretty dismal, you should remember that it's not unique to families with student mothers. Any mother who works traditional hours outside the home has to confront the same kind of time limitation with her family. Most returning student mothers and their husbands would agree that the quality of time spent together is more than enough to make up for the quantity.

Nevertheless, as student mothers become preoccupied with their studies, their husbands observe that they are sometimes more short-tempered and impatient than they were when they did not feel so pressured by time. If you find yourself losing your temper more frequently than before, learn to recognize the pattern that leads up to the explosion, and see if you can devise a system to short-circuit the anger if it is unjustifiable. Your husband and children can signal you in a nonthreatening way when they feel that you are about to go off the wall. (See Chapter 5 for some advice on how to do exactly that.) Or, if you find yourself frequently blowing up at a particular time—say, when you walk in the door—spend an extra ten minutes at school talking with a friend. See if that makes a difference in your mood when you get home.

Having a student mother usually encourages children to become more independent, and most fathers identify this as being a positive effect from a return to school. Some fathers feel, however, that too many responsibilities are placed on the children because their mother is unavailable.

It is certainly important for your children to learn self-reliance and responsibility. These are not genetic traits that suddenly appear when children attain their majority! They are learned and therefore must be taught. Being responsible for sharing in household tasks is one step in the right direction.

Also, it is important for children to learn that other people aside from them have needs. As one proud father put it: "Our kids are not under the illusion that adults are only there to serve them."

Your children will most likely reflect your attitude about school. If you feel guilty about spending so much time away from them, they will pick up on your feelings and complain about your student role. If you are enthusiastic about being in school, your children probably will be, too. Feelings, both good and bad, are contagious.

A FEW WORDS ABOUT TEAMWORK

Ideally, a couple approaches a woman's return to school as a team. The reentry process will be much easier if the family works together to get everything done that needs to be done.

One characteristic of a good team is noncompetitiveness among its members. If you feel your husband resisting your return to school, try to find out how he feels about women pursuing careers. Is he threatened by this? It shouldn't surprise you if he is. Many men have been raised with the idea that it's the man who is supposed to be the sole provider for his family, and that the woman's place is you-know-where. It wasn't so long ago that it was considered a failing on the man's part if his wife went to work. If you suspect that your husband may be feeling this way, don't be surprised; it can take a while to unlearn an attitude that has been firmly implanted.

If your husband feels that his main job is to be the breadwinner, and your main job is to stay at home and take care of the children, he will be totally bewildered if you announce that you are returning to school and that he is now to take on half of all the household responsibilities. And it will not be long before the bewilderment turns into resentment.

If your return to school is to go smoothly, it really must be a joint decision and consequently a joint effort. Perhaps you are one of the countless women who quit school in order to support her husband while he finished *his* education. When women who have done this decide to resume their studies, they often feel that their husbands "owe" them an equally shared responsibility for the household. *No one* likes to be presented with a debit sheet, or to be told: "You owe it to me!" Don't ask your husband to share in the household responsibilities because he *owes* it to you—instead, approach the whole venture as a team project and without any debts. Things will go a lot more smoothly.

You will know that you are making it as a team when you and your husband consider what he does around the house *not* as "helping" you but as sharing in the responsibility.

The following suggestions may help as you approach the reentry process:

1. *Take the time to discuss changes as they occur.* Don't assume for a minute that what you are feeling is being transmitted accurately to your spouse. You will be just too busy for subtle forms of communication. So when your husband sees you start to become tense, and that makes him uncomfortable, he should already have been urged to somehow let you know about it. You will both feel more comfortable once you have discussed your differing perceptions. Maybe your partner will have some ideas about how to alleviate what he sees as tension. Or maybe, once you are aware that what you are feeling is coming out in a way that makes him uncomfortable, you can channel the energy differently.

2. *Get together with other couples who have been through the reentry process.* It will help both you and your husband to hear firsthand about the kinds of changes other couples have experienced. If you don't know any reentry students, ask your friends whether they know any, or ask your children about their friends' parents. Another good resource is the university itself: inquire at the reentry and continuing education offices, or of the secretary in the department that interests you. Most people are delighted to talk about how they are managing their various roles. Encourage your husband to read this chapter, too.

3. *Ask for help in a nonthreatening way.* At a time when you are involved with a great many changes in your own life, remember that your spouse is also experiencing these changes—but from a different perspective. Talk about these differences. One change is almost guaranteed—he will need to share in the responsibilities of running the household. Discuss the change in a nonaccusing way. "It would really be such a help if you . . ." is a lot more productive than "Why don't you ever . . ."

4. *Thoroughly discuss your reasons for returning to school.* Don't expect that your spouse will automatically grasp your reasons for making this major commitment. Discuss your long-term goals as well, and let them serve as a source of motivation to you both.

5. *Involve your husband with the university.* There is always something happening on campus that could be of interest to your husband—movies, concerts, plays, sporting events, exhibits, and so on. Don't forget about your student discount when you buy tickets—it can make a big difference.

6. *Reserve some time each day for just the two of you.* Even if it's no more than 10 minutes after dinner, don't scrimp on it. This kind of "regrouping" when nothing else is happening is very important.

7. *You'll need rewards all along the way. Involve your husband.* Set short-term goals for yourself, such as finishing a paper or reading six chapters of a textbook. When you get there, take time to "celebrate" with your husband. Go see a movie after you finish writing the paper. Go out to dinner, just the two of you, after you read the six chapters. Don't forget about having some fun together.

8. *Minimize the upkeep of your house as much as possible.* You can shift an enormous load from your mind by sending your clothes to the laundromat once a week and by having someone clean your house every 10 days or so. Try the university student employment center for affordable help with house cleaning.

9. *Encourage your spouse to take some courses, too.* Now might be a good time for your husband to be doing some reevaluating of his own direction. If you have chosen to go to work after graduation, perhaps your husband could also arrange for some big blocks of time to explore his interests.

10. *Maintain a sense of humor.* Many of the problems that come up can be solved by good-natured and well-intentioned participation on both sides. Once it's over, couples love to rehash what it was like to be going through the reentry process. Maybe you will, too!

Chapter 7

The Single-Parent Family

Aside from worrying about looking like the class matron, are you also concerned that you are going to be the only "married-looking" woman in the class who doesn't have a husband to run home to? Forget it! The number of divorced women back in school is increasing at an astounding rate. Many centers for continuing education for women report that over half of their students are divorced. The married woman who is dilettanting her way through school is not frequently seen on campus these days. The woman in class who is keeping one eye on the clock and the other eye on the door (hoping that her friend didn't forget to pick Junior up at day care) is *very* common, however.

The amount of juggling you will have to do is about the same as your married colleagues', but the emphasis is different. If your children live with you, you will be solely responsible for making sure they are happy and busy while you are away. Even if your "ex," plus parents, plus friends are helpful, it is *you* who will probably be doing the arranging and the worrying about whether or not child A has made it from point three to point four. On the other hand, you will not have to worry about whether your *spouse* is busy and happy! Many single-parent students say that they feel it must

71

be infinitely more confusing to have the role of wife added to all the others.

If you are recently divorced or separated, you have probably invested a great deal of your energy and brain power in trying to find some kind of resolution of problems connected with your marriage. A wonderfully supportive book on the subject is *MOMMA: The Sourcebook for Single Mothers,* edited by Karol Hope and Nancy Young. A section entitled "Moving On" includes an article by six single mothers at the University of California, Santa Barbara. It was their conclusion that being students brought them closer to their children: "Our kids really understand and participate in the meaning of our lives."

Going back to school means an opportunity to direct all the energy and brain power that went into trying to hold your marriage together toward molding your own future. A study by Saul Feldman showed that in graduate school, divorced women (70 percent of his sample were mothers) do best of all. The reason is obvious: if they're in school, it's not for frivolous reasons. They are there to get the necessary credentials for a job or career. No group of returning students feels the pinch of poverty more than single mothers. As one California woman put it, "I have four years of poverty staring me in the face. But what's my alternative? I'm sick of getting jobs that exploit me."

For a single parent going back to school, finding good child care is crucial. Chapter 15 gives the details about how to proceed and what to expect. You'll know when you've found the right place by the fact that you're not worrying after you leave your child there, and that the child is happy and alert when you go to pick him or her up. Ten years ago you might have had months of research ahead of you in order to find the right situation for your child. Luckily, this is also changing. Be sure to see if your campus has a center.

The experience of going back to school will be much better if you have somewhere to turn for emotional support. Since there won't be a built-in adult support system at home, you will want to establish one through school. If there is a reentry or women's center, you will find it simple to seek out other single parents. If you have a child in a campus day-care or preschool program, you'll discover that many of the children have single parents. Some campuses even offer classes on how to juggle the roles of student and single parent. You are likely to find other single parents in whatever corner you claim for yourself at the library, cafeteria, etc. Just keep an eye out, and you'll be sure to recognize some allies.

Single-parent students can be ingenious about helping each other with the juggling act. "If you pick Willow up at five on Mondays, I'll meet you at my house and feed Matthew and her dinner while you go to class. Then on Tuesdays, you can get her at lunchtime and we'll meet in the park when my class is over." Talk about good training for an administrative position! Your children will probably find the group effort exciting—so long as a dependable routine is maintained and they still have some time alone with you. Many single-parent students have discovered that close friendships with kindred spirits become a precious bonus of going back to school.

THE MEN IN YOUR LIFE

A social life is pretty hard to manage when you are trying to juggle school and your children *and* your own peace of mind. Surprisingly, most single mothers who go back to school say they don't miss having men (as mates) in their lives. When you are determined to do whatever it takes to arrive at a satisfying career, "dates" may turn out to be quite low on your list of priorities. But your priorities are your own, after all.

If you do become involved with a man, he will probably have to do a bit of adjusting. Most men aren't used to being associated with anyone whose life is as tightly scheduled as yours. One man who did commit himself to a relationship with a single mother in school had these observations about what to expect:

• *Little frivolity.* You will find that the returnee has little time to spend on nonessential activities.
• *No spontaneity.* You will not find this woman "hanging out," waiting for something to come her way. In fact, you will find little opportunity to meet this person at all unless you are involved with the campus.
• When she says she *has to do homework*—she WILL!
• Casual *relationships will probably be specific*—every third Thursday between 7:00 and 9:00 P.M. (unless she has a midterm)!
• This woman *is very serious about her priorities.* First come her children, second comes school, third is herself, and fourth is miscellaneous. You fit in somewhere between three and infinity.

• Mostly a returnee *needs emotional support.* Physical assistance may be welcomed, but emotional support is essential if the relationship is to work.

• This person *is very definite about things.* She knows what she wants, often because she has had to overcome bitter self-doubts and apprehensions. She will want no interference with her hard-won progress.

Chapter 8

Role Juggling

There aren't enough hours in the day. Being in school is a full-time job and so are the three children. Plus I do all my husband's bookkeeping at the store, and I'm a member of the school board. It's a lot of hats. Sometimes I get very confused about which one I'm supposed to be wearing when.

—A 43-YEAR-OLD SOPHOMORE

Scheduling your classes around the needs of your family, constantly switching gears from one role to another, trying to get it *all* done—and done *well*—probably seems like an impossibility.

Role conflict is a natural consequence of not having enough time to do everything that needs to get done, and it's something that just about every reentry student experiences.

Do not despair! Although there is basically no resolution to the problem of role conflict, most returnees come to terms with it and develop very constructive coping mechanisms. How you *feel* about juggling so many roles is much more critical than the actual number of roles involved.

Do you imagine that the woman who is constantly trying to juggle roles is impossible to be around? Are you afraid that you will turn into a monster? There are probably some dramatic exceptions, but in general, and much to her *own* surprise, the reentry student leads a tremendously busy but happy life.

Would you believe that 92 percent of the women interviewed for this book said they gained self-confidence as a direct result of being back in school? An improved self-image is almost a guaranteed outcome of returning to school. Three-quarters of these same women said they had become more assertive, and two-thirds of them indicated that they managed their time better. When asked if they noticed any negative changes in themselves, almost half of them couldn't think of even *one!* Yet these women are all involved with juggling many different responsibilities, and listed role conflict as one of their major difficulties.

When you first resume your studies, you will probably feel that you are being pulled in a thousand different directions. If your main job has been as homemaker, your family is probably accustomed to your being able to arrange your schedule around theirs most of the time. Suddenly, it may seem as though every time your child suggests anything you might do together, you have to go through an anguished process of decision making.

Do you cut class to take your daughter to the orthodontist? Do you give up a weekly meeting that is important to you, or decide that you'll make up for it by staying up until 2:30 A.M. once a week? Do you say no to your husband about a weekend trip, or resign yourself to getting less than an A on the test Monday morning?

Time management and assertiveness are survival skills that reentry women say they develop very quickly. You will probably become an excellent decision maker as well—if only out of self-defense and because you have a lot of practice. These skills will also be a real plus to you if you plan to become involved in the job-hunting process.

The problem is not only one of juggling your various roles, however. The transition from role to role, the shifting of gears, can be extremely difficult if it is made too abruptly. You may welcome the opportunity of taking your mind off a lecture that you had to leave in order to meet the school bus. There will be other times, though, when you might really want to think through what you have just learned in class. Instead, 20 minutes after the period has ended you are in the middle of hearing about your child's day at school.

The sudden immersion into a different role can make you feel as if you were four or five different people all wrapped up in one rather frazzled and fragmented bundle. One study, made by Eileen

Gray, showed role conflict to be the number-one problem for women going back to college.

Student mothers do not have a monopoly on role conflict. Single women, married women without children, or whose children are grown, also find themselves torn. Single women often have to choose between studying and being with a close friend. It can come as quite a shock that even the transition from hard concentration to a warm, relaxed atmosphere can be difficult when it is too abrupt.

If you are married, your husband's attitude about your being a student will have a huge effect on how you come to terms with role juggling. If he is supportive of your returning to school, things should work out well because you can talk them over. But some women have said that their husbands, although they "allow" the re-entry, do not want to participate in any of the school experience. The general attitude is: "If you can do it without disturbing anything else, fine—otherwise, quit." If anyone close to you is reacting in this way, things are likely to be very difficult unless you can find support elsewhere.

There is no way to *resolve* the problem of role conflict. Your aim, really, is to adopt an attitude about it that feels comfortable to you. Some of the following suggestions might help you with the process.

1. *Keep assessing and weighing your priorities.* It is absolutely necessary to take the time to decide which commitments are most important to you, which ones you are unwilling to sacrifice. You will probably find this clarification process very satisfying. Nevertheless, within the general framework that you come up with, it is crucial to cultivate flexibility.

You will find that your priorities change from hour to hour, along with your own needs and the needs of those around you. Allow yourself to become an expert at gauging the stress levels of those close to you. If you see that your child is really needing your attention, and you'd planned to study, don't consider it a "failure" that you've changed your plans.

You will encounter far more difficulty if you approach the problem of role conflict with blinders on: "I will not leave this desk until this assignment is done, no matter what happens." Avoid this kind of "either/or" rigidity. Thirty minutes spent with a child who needs your attention can give you the peace of mind to study more effectively the rest of the evening.

2. *Discuss the new demands on your time with those close to*

you. In general, people don't respond well to sudden changes in routine. You should try to keep those close to you updated on your changing needs as far in advance as you possibly can. If you know that you will have to spend more time studying during midterms, tell them how you think this will affect them. Explain to your children, for example, that you will be spending two extra evenings at the library and that you won't be cooking at all that week. At some point that week, try to remember to order in something they really like.

After you have organized your overall study schedule (see Chapter 16 on budgeting your time), explain what it means to those close to you. Post your schedule in a spot which can be easily consulted by anyone concerned.

3. *Find a support group; look for role models.* It can really help to talk with women who have successfully come to grips with their own juggling acts. Seek them out and ask them for tips. You will probably discover that feeling somewhat fragmented at the end of the day is generally accepted as an occupational hazard.

Joining a support group through the reentry or women's center can also help. Spend a session discussing the kinds of role conflicts you have been experiencing, and then brainstorm through to some ways of dealing with them.

4. *Allow yourself adequate time for transition from role to role.* Sudden switches from one role to another can literally send you reeling. Don't expect to be able to plunge from Plato into Play-Doh without some transition time!

Arrange a break, no matter how small. Quit studying 10 minutes early, for example, and spend the extra time doing something mundane but enjoyable (read a magazine, take a walk, think about a vacation). This will help get you out of your studying frame of mind so you can be receptive to whatever is next on the agenda.

Feelings of guilt sometimes prevent student mothers from taking even the smallest break between study and children. But the transition time can mean the difference between being a mother who is distracted and one who is all there. Don't scrimp on transition time!

5. *Bone up on your time-management techniques.* As mentioned earlier, two-thirds of the women interviewed for this book reported that they managed their time better as a direct result of returning to school. Be sure to read the section in Chapter 16, on

budgeting time. Talk with other reentry women about how they manage to create a study schedule and stick to it.

FEELING GUILTY

When you are working really hard at role juggling, you're likely to wind up feeling terribly guilty because you're not perfect at everything. Mothers are especially vulnerable to these feelings, but they're not alone. A study by Anne Kolar and Barbara Hills showed that 65 percent of mothers—and 28 percent of non-mothers—felt guilty about some part of their role as students. In another study, covering 361 women who had gone back to school, Shirley Emerson discovered that all admitted to feeling guilt at some point during their student days.

Returning-student mothers have done amazing things to try to alleviate the feeling that they really should be home next to the hearth after all. One California mother would leave class and take a quick, furtive look through the window of the campus child-care center to alleviate those feelings. Convinced that she was the only one who ever gave way to these palpitations of anguish about leaving her child, she was astounded one day to find another mother peering through the same window. (Both children were fine, by the way.)

"I was home all the time with my first," says an Oklahoma mother of two. "The second wasn't even a year old when I started school. I worry that I've neglected him. If the first should do better than the second in school, I'll be convinced it's because I paid less attention to him."

You may tell yourself that it's important for a child to learn self-reliance, but you'll still feel guilty. You may be convinced that it's important that your child have certain chores to do—and at the same time you feel guilty about assigning tasks that you might have done yourself. Ambivalence galore!

All the same, those guilt feelings aren't doing you or anyone else any good. When you act out of guilt, you can put a tremendous amount of pressure on those around you. If, for instance, you feel that you should be studying, but also that you're neglecting your children, you may wind up preparing a lavish meal to placate those guilt feelings. But if you are frantic and preoccupied during the meal because of the study time you've lost, your children won't be receiving what they really need—time that's focused directly on themselves. Instead of the elaborate meal that takes precious time, you might arrange to have them eat at a friend's house. By the time they finish, you'll be needing a break; so spend 45 minutes or so taking them for a walk.

Explore why it is that you feel guilty about being at home less of the time. Would you feel just as guilty if you were a man? What if you were at work all day instead of going to classes? If it appears that what makes you feel guilty is spending less time with your children, remind yourself that what's important is the quality of the time, not the quantity. It's likely that the guilt you feel has to do not so much with your own personal situation as with your reaction to what's been traditionally expected of women.

GUILT AND SUPERWOMAN

"I went into some gear I never knew I had," said a 33-year-old mother of two. "I baked tons of cookies and read fortunes at the P.T.A. carnival. I became the main source of transportation for all the kids in our town. I wanted to make sure I didn't inconvenience *anyone* by my return to school. Actually, I didn't really return to school—I snuck back, hoping that no one would notice."

Many women think the best way to alleviate guilt feelings is to be perfect at everything. They make incredible demands on themselves: the house has to be in perfect running order, everyone in it has to be perfectly happy all the time, and this supermom has to be a perfect student besides. Those demands are impossible to meet, all at once, for very long.

The superwoman solution—the valiant attempt to make your own school experience a positive one for everyone around you all the time—can turn out to be the very reason why things do not run smoothly. For one thing, you will quickly become exhausted. Being overtired will eat away at your cheerfulness and optimism. Your family will respond to the change in your mood by making more demands on you, and inevitably your fuse will blow. The full-time mother of three who also does all the bookkeeping for her husband's store and is a member of the school board sleeps three and a half hours a night! "I was used to getting by on five or six hours' sleep," she said, "but this new schedule is beginning to show on me."

Women who have been through the superwoman phase advise you to try to avoid this path from the beginning. Erase the "super" from in front of mother, wife, student, and companion, and things are likely to go a lot more smoothly, if only because your mood will improve. There's no law that says you have to be perfect!

By deciding that it's okay not to be perfect at everything all the time, you give yourself the chance to be perfect at some things some of the time. Being a student does not mean that you cannot be a perfect mother, wife, or companion. It just means that you can't fill all of these roles perfectly all of the time. Reentry women can throw terrific parties and plan splendid camping trips just like everyone else—but just not as often. Watch out for superwoman—people find her really hard to get along with because she's suffering from overexhaustion.

SUPPORT FROM FRIENDS, AND WHEN FRIENDS FEEL THREATENED

If you have not already been sharing feelings with your friends about wanting to make changes in your life, you will probably discover that many of them are also involved with deciding what to do "next." The fact that you have already chosen a *route* will be of great interest to anyone who is spending energy studying the map.

Going back to school can be contagious. Did you catch it from a close friend? Many returnees say they did. Those friends will be especially supportive.

As one student put it, "They have experienced it and feel so much better for having done it that they want you to share the same feelings." A 45-year-old student in Washington, D.C., reported, "As soon as I said I was going back to school, several of my friends began to talk about doing it too. I think I provided them with the motivation to deal with things they had thought about only on a very subliminal level." She went on to say that now the friends of friends are calling her for advice and support during the decision-making process.

Approximately two-thirds of the women interviewed for this book said that their friends were encouraging. Quite a few women will tell you, in fact, that their friends offered more support than anyone else for their plans to go back to school. But the women interviewed for this book also warned that some friends may feel threatened by your decision. Some may see it as a value judgment not only about your own life-style but about theirs as well. And once you're actually in school, these same women may feel even more threatened.

It can be confusing to find that people who offered you support in the past are now saying things that undermine your enthusiasm. How can you possibly do this to your children? Is there something drastically wrong with your marriage that's made you resort to this? What in the world would make you want to get up for a class at eight in the morning? Questions of this sort are clues that your friends are feeling threatened.

If your friends feel that they are being judged, it is natural that they will feel threatened. The decision you've made is a very personal one, and you should make it clear to them that it is not to be construed as a value judgment on anyone's life-style. If you notice that your friends are concerned, you should try right away to alleviate that pressure. One of the reasons why women get so much out of school the second time around is precisely that they have *chosen* to go back. This time, it's not a matter of family or social pressure as it may have been the first time.

As you adjust to your role as a student, you will find that you have to cut down on your social life. Women who have gone back to school report that they have much less time to spend with friends in person, on the telephone, or by writing letters. But you will also discover that when you are busy in a productive way, putting in time with other people becomes less important. Connie, studying to become a registered nurse, commented, "My social life has come to a screeching halt. My life right now is school and family. I don't miss the social life. I'd much rather be doing this right now."

But although there will be less time to spend with your friends, you're likely to find that what time you *do* have will seem more worthwhile. "I used to have morning coffee with friends," says a junior-college freshman in Maryland, "but that was just to fill in time anyway. When we get together now, it's much more satisfying because I'm not constantly complaining about my lot in life anymore."

You may also discover that you have less in common with your friends than you once did. As one 35-year-old freshman put it, "I've realized that taking care of the house and cooking a pot roast for six hours just isn't that important. It's very difficult to relate to my friends sometimes because that's their whole world."

Don't become discouraged if you find yourself feeling lonely at first. You tend to be friends with people who are in situations similar to your own. It may take you a while to sort out which "situation" you identify with most strongly. Many women attend classes and leave campus without having said a word to anyone. Others enjoy spending as much time as they can at school.

One surprise for women who return to school is the discovery that they become experts at getting the important things done. If it is important for you to maintain old friendships, you will manage to do it somehow. If you have grown away from your old friends and are ready to make new ones, you will find them in your new surroundings.

Most returning students will tell you that although a few friends may feel threatened, many others will be supportive and encouraging. Just as with members of your family, however, relations with friends need time and work to maintain. You might arrange a special time once a week for seeing one or more friends—perhaps lunch at school every Friday. And as is mentioned in Chapter 16, you can use a telephone conversation with a friend as a kind of reward for finishing a study assignment.

If there is a reentry or women's center on campus, be sure to go there on your class breaks because it will be a great opportunity to meet other women who are in comparable situations. You might want to enroll in a self-development course which will probably use small group discussions as a teaching/learning technique. The process of returning to school can seem frightening if you feel that you're surrounded by people who are not receptive to change. But the process can be exciting if you feel you're getting support from other people. Look around, and sooner or later you'll find them.

Chapter 9

Your On-Campus Relationships

CLASS MATRONS AND MOTHER FIGURES

Do any of the following nightmares sound familiar to you?

- Students are settled into their seats waiting for class to begin. When you arrive, everyone assumes *you* are the professor.
- The first day of class, you break into small groups for a discussion. When you exchange first names, a bright-eyed 19-year-old says, "I couldn't possibly call you *that!*"
- You are called on to explain one of the concepts from last night's homework assignment. When you finish, the professor says, "Now, if Mrs. ——— can understand it, *anyone* can."

If you are worried about being the odd person out because of your age, you are certainly not alone. Many returning students express such misgivings.

First of all, you need to remember that more than one out of every three college students in the United States these days is over 25 years old. Unless you are planning to enter a very esoteric field, you are quite unlikely to find yourself in a class without some other students your own age.

Furthermore, if your mental picture of a college professor includes jacket, tie, and formal title, be prepared for a jolt. The dress code on campus is far more casual than ever before, and many professors prefer to be called by their first names. You will also notice more women professors than you would have 10 years ago. In sum, the faculty is much more approachable than it used to be.

The advance fears of many reentry students about the reaction of the other students and professors almost always are quickly forgotten once classes start. The women interviewed for this book were asked to rank 17 difficulties, one of them age embarrassment, that they might have encountered. Only 4 percent gave age embarrassment as one of their top three difficulties.

FACING YOUR PROFESSORS

You will find that faculty members generally respond enthusiastically to older students simply because they have earned the reputation of being extremely hard-working. They may have confidence in your abilities even before *you* do.

They also know that older students can liven up classes. You will discover that age is to your advantage in many classrooms because you will have more to say. This may not be true in a statistics class, but what about modern American history, or any number of psychology and sociology courses which rely in part on experiential knowledge? When your American literature professor is trying to explain the emotional climate that influenced writers following World War II, you may find your own memory to be a valuable resource. Life experience can provide you with an invaluable tool—perspective.

One 33-year-old woman who graduated with a bachelor's degree in social work commented:

> I felt I was treated differently by my professors because I was an older student. This is probably because I felt like a peer to the professors since I was an adult. I know I felt more at ease with them than the younger students did. My relationships with my professors were much more personal than they were ten years ago. We've really gotten to know each other, mainly because I would participate a lot in class and it would just continue after the class ended.

Lorraine, who has nine children and went back to school when she was in her late 30s, declared, "The professors really appreciated the older students and bent over backwards for us. They were just wonderful."

Not all professors will treat you fairly, of course. As an older student, you may find that some of them will exert more pressure on you than on younger students. Because it is known that you are determined to do well, you may be called upon to do more than your share in class. Some professors figure it means less work for them when they notice a few older students in their classroom. Older students usually get very involved with class discussions. Watch that you don't get saddled with the responsibility of leading the pack while your professor takes a series of mental coffee breaks during class.

Another type to watch out for is the professor who feels threatened by your presence. Although a good professor encourages and feels stimulated by a lot of questions, there are also teachers who would rather not be questioned at all—they talk while you listen. If you interrupt this routine with thought-provoking questions, you may quickly find yourself being made to feel unwelcome. Most returnees deal with the situation by resigning themselves to the fact that the professor just doesn't want to be dislodged from the rut he or she is in. Younger students must face the same realization, but their cries of anguish about it don't seem to be as loud.

Occasionally you may run into a professor who has not had much experience with older students, and who is guilty of the stereotyped behavior you have been dreading. But you can almost count on a rather drastic change in attitude after you've turned in a few assignments. A woman from Rhode Island, back in school at age 42, described the kind of turnaround that can take place:

A few professors treated us in a condescending fashion at first. There were lots of jokes about why we were giving up cocktail parties and golf and cake baking in order to come to class. It was only a matter of a few weeks before they realized we were serious students. They actually wound up admiring us.

The chances of your running into a professor who hasn't been exposed to reentry students grows slimmer as each quarter goes by. The stereotyped image of the older student—a dilettante club-woman who has nothing else to do—has left college campuses long ago. Almost all the professors you encounter, *if* they prejudge you at all, will figure you are another one of those committed, hard-working, goal-oriented students. Faculty members appreciate and welcome students who are sincerely interested in being in school!

FACING YOUR CLASSMATES

Four or five years ago, if it ever came up, I made absolutely sure no one could figure out my age. Then I realized this was a ridiculous position to take, so I decided to surprise everybody. I announced that I was sixty-two, and everyone told me I looked twenty years younger—which made me feel great. Now I realize *that* approach was ridiculous, too. Making an issue of your age is no more relevant than making an issue of any of your other qualities. Now, I'm proud to have reached this place in my life, to have the wisdom and experience, and yet to be as youthful thinking and feeling as I am. I've gotten so much positive input from the friends that I have made.

This statement by a 64-year-old graduate student in counseling suggests that many returnees, after just a few weeks of attending classes, discover that the emphasis on age is much more in your own head than in anyone else's.

Nevertheless, women of all ages, when they return to school, worry that they will stand out in the crowd. The fears of a 26-year-old woman that everyone would be staring at her because she is older are just as real as if she had been 70.

If you have teenage children at home, you may feel at first that other students regard you as a mother figure. When Lorraine, the mother of nine, went back to school, she wasn't sure about how she would fit in. "There I was," she remembers, "old enough to be everybody's mother, including most of the teachers. Would we be able to relate to each other? I wondered. The worries were completely unfounded. As soon as I opened up, everything was fine. No one at the university ever made me feel as if I didn't belong there."

If being a maternal figure feels comfortable to you, then why not be one? You may find younger students coming to you for advice and support. Having students say they wish you were *their* mother is not at all uncommon! If you decide that you want to relate on a different level, however, the option is certainly there. It's up to you.

As a general rule, people will pick up on how you feel about your own age. If you feel odd because you are older, they'll react not to your *age*, but to your feelings about it. Age will most likely become an issue only if you feel it is one. Haven't you found that in general people accept you the way you present yourself?

It may take you a month or two to find the image that you want to present of yourself as a student. Many women have said that they dressed in jeans at first, in order to blend in with their younger classmates. One 43-year-old returnee from Maine says, "Now I dress the way *I* want to dress, which is usually a blazer and skirt." Finding clothes, an image, and an attitude that feel comfortable to you can be a very important and interesting learning experience in itself.

If the younger students stereotype you at all, you may find that it will be as an average-raiser and apple-polisher. (How does *that* affect your fears about not being able to get good grades?) A California woman who returned to school at the age of 35 remembers, "They always expected me to be the best student. They always looked up to me because they figured I must know everything since I was older. There was no way to establish a relationship as peers."

The reputation older students have developed for being conscientious can sometimes antagonize their more relaxed younger colleagues. You may find yourself totally dumbfounded by how few of your classmates participate in discussions or turn in their homework on time. But remember that your younger classmates will be equally astounded that your homework is always in on time and that you are constantly raising issues in class.

Although you might find yourself feeling lonely on campus at the beginning of the reentry process, most women report that friends are easily found *if* you take the time to find them. In fact, almost three-quarters of the women interviewed for this book said that they had made meaningful friendships in school. Others said that there simply wasn't a spare minute to talk with anyone.

A lot will depend on what your priorities are. If one of the reasons you have gone back to school is because of feelings of isolation, you will most likely find friends very quickly. One Ohio woman, recently divorced and with only one teenager left at home, enjoys eating lunch with her younger classmates on a regular basis. "All of my friends used to be my own age," she commented. "Now I have close friends of all ages."

If you are entering as a graduate student, you may find that the people in your program become very involved with each other, intellectually and emotionally. If you have the time and inclination, it would be most surprising if you were excluded.

Certainly there are other older students out there looking for friends as well. If there is a reentry or women's center, it will be easy for you to find each other. A returnee from Rhode Island said that the basic reason she and three other women managed to stay in school was their friendship, which started the first week of class. "It feels so good to have friends to share your ideas with," she said. "We would quiz each other, study for tests together, and, most important, we gave each other moral support."

If you still feel self-conscious about your age, be sure to seek out the reentry or women's center. Also, include a course in self-development or women's studies in your schedule for the first quarter. Since other reentry students will be taking advantage of these courses, this will be a good opportunity to meet some of your peers on campus. And since these classes usually involve small group discussions, it is a great way for you to become involved with your younger classmates as well.

Chapter 10

We Were Worried Too— Reflections

PERSONAL POSITIVE CHANGES

• I feel very fulfilled in a way that surprises me. Frankly, I really thought I had blown it when I quit school and that I would never get to the same point as the people around me. Being in graduate school was a real joy—the kinds of work experiences I had were really exciting and broadening. I feel so much more competent because of it. School was a major good step because it led me to something I feel fantastic about—my career. For two years, I took my professional life into my own hands and plotted what would get me where I wanted to go. It gives me a lot of satisfaction looking back.

• I've become far less angry and much more open and receptive to other people. I discovered that I really am smart and that I can keep up with other people whether they are 18, 40, or whatever. I like to study and participate in class. Being back in school has given me a lot of self-confidence. There are a lot of things I enjoy doing, and it turns out that I do them well. Coming back to school was the most positive thing I've done in a long time.

• I've changed completely. I'm much more confident and much more independent. I am, most of all, myself. I've had an opportunity for a second career. I enjoyed every minute of my first career, raising my kids. I'm not a housewife and I'm not a homemaker. I don't thrive on that part of it, but I really enjoyed the children so much that I didn't resent any of that time. But I could not have subsisted without a career right now. I really love teaching.

• Being in school has given me the background that I needed. I've never been ashamed of my gut feelings, but now that I have the basics in history, literature, mathematics, and even physics, I know from where I speak. I'll venture into things without that basic fear that I had before. I'm much more confident in every situation because of going to school.

• I'm a lot more outgoing. I just feel more capable. I handle things better. When I used to be home, I'd wonder how I'd get all the housework done. Now I work and go to school and get my housework done. You always say you can't do it, but you can.

• My outlook on life is much more positive. If I'm tired now, it's because I'm physically tired, not because I'm bored or depressed. It was cheaper for me to go back to school than to pay the doctor's bills. Being in school is a real ego booster for me. My school has very few older students. In fact, I'm the only one who goes full-time. It's been just great for my self-confidence, because I'm doing really well.

• The biggest change is how I feel and my relationships with other people. I tend to relate to other people as myself now instead of as somebody's wife or mother.

• I'm enjoying life right now. When all three kids left, were out of the house and living on the Coast, I went into a depressed state. This year has been just great. Going to school has been stimulating, working has been stimulating, and so have old and new relationships. School was the initial step.

• I'm more assertive. I can tell people what I'm thinking without letting them turn it around and get me all upset. Learning that I don't have to keep the house spanking clean is such a relief!

• Everyone has always told me that I am creative, and I'm much more in touch with that creativity now. I feel that I have a good mind and good ideas, and I wasn't so sure of that before. I have the awareness now that I can set a goal, know what the steps are, and get there. I think in a much more organized way. I don't "panic" as much any more.

• I'm much more independent. I feel really strong about being able to get through school and be a mother at the same time. To come to school here, I had to pick up and just come, leaving everyone I knew. Sarah was just two then. I had to find housing, child care, and start school. It was a good feeling to be able to accomplish it all—and to do it well.

• I'm more accepting of different life-styles. The young people at school are talking about living together and birth control. These things were unacceptable as topics of conversation to me even just a few years ago.

• I feel better about myself, proud of myself. It was a big step for me. I didn't just go for two weeks and quit or hate it or flunk out. I have a lot more confidence in myself, and that changes everything else in my life—my relationships with other people and my feelings about myself.

• I can follow through on things. I can set a goal, go after it, and do it. I wasn't so sure I'd stick to it since I dropped out before. I always knew I was dependable for *other* people. The big thing is that now I know that *I* can depend on myself.

• Having worked all that time, I don't really find it all that different. It has been quite a long time since I've been a student, and I find that I enjoy turning in papers rather than correcting them. I found I could do well as a student and that has helped me to gain self-confidence.

• When you try something and you are able to do it, you can relax with it. I'm proud of going back and undertaking something very difficult and very remote from what I ever had before.

• I feel so much more self-confident. It evolved from feeling that I knew a lot about an area that I had chosen to go into. Going back to school, studying what I wanted to study for that year, and really being devoted to it contributed to making me feel competent and intelligent. I discovered in me a desire to succeed, to make something of myself, to follow through.

PERSONAL NEGATIVE CHANGES

• I get more angry with my daughter than if I didn't have the pressure of school, especially during midterms and finals when I was really trying to study and she would interrupt me. We don't have as much time as I'd like—for me to play with her and read her stories.

• I got really tense, just like every other time I've been in school. I started chewing my nails again, a lifelong habit that I had finally given up.

• My husband and I used to have some of the most awful fights before exams. I'm not sure why, but it happened a lot. He says that it was my nervousness, although I was always certain that it was his uptightness about me locking myself up to study.

• I'm touchier and sometimes crabbier when I know I have this big load of schoolwork to do. And I don't have enough time to do all the things I want to do—relax, see friends. I'm under a lot more pressure, and it shows on me.

• It's much easier to feel guilty about things. There's a kind of tenseness and drive about being in school.

• I don't listen as well to other people because I'm too busy thinking about everything I have to do.

• I'm always running and trying to stay on top of things. I feel a lot more anxious. I sleep less, rest less. I'm just unable to relax. My muscles are really tense.

• I feel anxious. I'm not sure if I should be working or going to school. I feel somewhat misplaced. I don't *have* to go to school, so I wonder if I should be doing something else. Should I be doing something for myself or should I be helping someone else?

• There was a time there when I was pretty hard on my husband, attacking him and being argumentative. I felt I was fighting him for my own rights. I overdid it, and I've pulled back now. I don't feel that I need to attack him on every little thing that comes along any more. I keep remembering that he was brought up to be such a macho, and I can't expect him to do an immediate about-face.

• My biggest problem is that some days I feel very depressed. I wonder why I signed up to go back to school. I think about how I want to go to school to prepare for a job, but I don't feel that I'm smart enough to get good grades. So, if I can't make it in school, I won't be able to get a job. This always happens right before or right after a test. And then the feeling passes, and I feel fantastic again.

• I'm more irritable and somewhat less tolerant of myself and others. It's probably the pressure of school, because I have so much less time for all of my commitments.

• I'm more tired and that makes me more grumpy. Working and going to school is hard. My daughter has started doing homework, and that means I have to give her more time, too.

• I always have things that I have to do now. It's not like going to work and then it's over. There are papers *all* the time. It's hard for me to *feel* available to my son.

• I have less time for friends and I'm much more selective about the people I choose to spend my time with. It's negative in that I get a little lonely now and then. I need to think of ways to nurture myself, to give myself some of the attention I get from other people. I just can't get it and be as busy as I am now. I don't take enough time to be by myself either, to renew myself.

PERSONAL CHANGES THAT OTHERS MIGHT IDENTIFY AS NEGATIVE

• It depends on who's considering what's negative. Because I'm taking less flack from people, they are sometimes shocked by the changes in me.

• I don't know if this is negative, but I've become awfully independent. I think it's positive, but some people might not agree with me.

• I don't consider selfishness with my time to be negative, although maybe my children do.

• I don't think I'm as sweet as I was, as totally agreeable. I'm much more inclined to say no. I'm not as passive. I think it's good.

• Perhaps before school, there were things that might have gone on that I objected to or felt bad about, and I'd not only be reluctant to bring to anyone's attention, I'd simply not see it. Now I feel more assertive and can say that I feel very upset. Nobody gets wiped out, but it creates some pretty negative conversations. It's not negative in the end, but it's negative in that conflicts come up that didn't come up before.

• My being more assertive might make other people more resentful of me. I'm more dogmatic. I have more facts at my disposal, so if I'm going to hornswoggle someone, I can do it with greater ease.

SURPRISING GAINS FROM BEING BACK IN SCHOOL

• I've gained the time to read widely. As a teacher I didn't have time to read except in my own subject matter. I also have more time for sports.

• A lot of men friends.

• A real sense of people's diversities. I knew it in a theoretical way, but being in school and having to do team projects, I realized that if one person is good at statistics and another at drawing and another at writing, you can really work together and come up with a good product, using each person's skills. I've always been a very independent worker, and I've never given much thought to kinds of skills other than my own.

• More confidence in myself as a professional in the field I've chosen. It makes me think I'm on the right track. Even though I haven't had as much work experience in the field as some of the other students, I think my instincts are right. I went into the program realizing that the competition would be stiff, but I'm doing fine.

• I've revived an interest in writing, and I'm surprised by how excited I am about that.

• I was not expecting all the extras. I was just planning to come and take classes. I didn't expect to meet peers, make friends, and to be in an exciting atmosphere. And I thought I was slower than I am. I can be on top of things and catch on quickly.

• If anything surprises me, it's the degree to which all the changes interrelate and support each other—my changes of greater confidence and greater independence—and finding that everyone in the family does better with the changes that occurred in me. It's been very difficult for everyone, especially my husband, but it's been extremely healthy for all of us.

• It's a lot easier to learn when you're older than when you're younger because you somehow have an overview.

• Surprising? Yes! My first orgasm!

• The surprise to me is how much I enjoy women, how much I respect and like them.

• I feel on a par with any other professional. You'd be surprised how, when you go to meetings, you feel as if there's nobody there who knows any more than you do, because you've been where they've been. Before, I thought that since they'd been to college, they knew more. They probably didn't, but I thought they did.

• Assertiveness. I was never very assertive for myself. I was assertive if I had a job to do, but anything that was for me personally, I always considered selfish. Even in my job at the hospital now, I have pushed my way into jobs and responsibilities I never dreamed I'd have the nerve to pursue and obtain.

• I dreaded the required speech course, but the confidence I've gained is partially related to that course. I never thought I'd make it through, be able to stand up in front of an audience and speak, but I did fine. It's helped me in all my classes.

• I've learned to relax more. When I first started school, I remember sitting during the day and reading stuff, schoolwork that I loved, and thinking, "Ha! I don't have to feel guilty about sitting and reading in the daytime now because I'm going to get credit." That felt as if I had permission to goof off from things that I *ought* to do. Since school, I don't have any qualms about sitting down and reading anything I want to. I do a lot more things that I want to do now.

• I enjoy the camaraderie, sharing the insights. I never expected to.

• I had no idea that young people in college would be as open to people of other age groups. I'm really learning a lot about their generation.

• Being exposed to so many different people. It's changed my perspective—what I'm impressed with, what I'm not impressed with now. I value different things in people now—like sincerity, gentleness, sensitivity. I'm much less impressed with credentials.

• I found that everything I learned was valuable. Even something like physical geography, which I probably would never use, was exciting to learn just for learning. I really enjoyed school, and I hadn't counted on that.

• Since I gave up my well-paying job in order to come back to school, I've become a lot less materialistic. Material things just aren't that important anymore. I don't want to get a job just to earn money. I'm considering a year in VISTA after I finish, and then I'll wait until I find something I really want to do.

• A sense of my own identity. I hadn't realized I'd lost it.

• I'm learning more from the other students than I am from the professors.

• It's surprising to me that I can have lasting friendships with people so much younger than myself. I still see the friends I made when I was in school. Some of them are only a year or two older than my oldest child. They give me a completely different perspective on things.

• I can handle the academic work quite well and speak out with confidence. Before, I had great difficulty expressing myself. I've also learned that college teachers aren't as intelligent as I thought they were. And I can relate to and interact with a much wider variety of people than I ever imagined.

• I finally had the courage to take an art class my last quarter in school. The last art class I had was in the seventh grade, when I was told that I had no talent. I absolutely loved the class!

• That I could make something positive out of the experience. I really have learned some neat things. I follow through a lot, and I'm surprised every time.

• About 20 pounds!

• Being able to manage things on a really low budget, gaining a lot of self-confidence, doing really well in school. Each quarter I do better and better. Being able to be a student and a mother at the same time.

THINGS THAT HAD TO BE GIVEN UP

• Leisure time. Weaving, reading for pleasure. There are a lot of things that I've had to give up that I've given up with great pleasure—P.T.A. meetings, Campfire Girls, being on call at all times to drive people here and there. I used to hate that. I miss lunch with friends and being close to some of my women friends, but I've met a lot of other people, too. One of the nice things about school is that it's finite. You can tell yourself: "I'm not going to see this person very much now, but wait until I get through."

• I like to see a mother at home making bread and cookies. I like to see a mother always home when her children get there. Some days I'd get there late, and I'd feel bad about that. I bake a whole lot less than I used to, and we all miss it.

• No time for talking. Television viewing? Forget it! No movies. Nothing that takes time. I had to devote myself to home, school, and books, and that was my entire life, for the first two years anyway.

• A great deal of my social life. I couldn't handle school and seeing friends as often. You make a certain choice there. There were a lot of little things, too—not mailing as many Christmas cards, not visiting people who weren't feeling well.

• A sense of security that was based on my being in a comfortable rut—always doing the same thing, always knowing where I'd be. I never know what I'll be doing next now.

• The financial comforts. I'm living with roommates, both very nice, but I would much rather be living alone. I had to move from San Francisco, which I love, to Los Angeles, which I hate. All my close friends are in San Francisco. I had a good job there and was making a very good salary. I was suddenly reduced to living on $300 a month. It was quite a jolt. I had to sell my car and borrow my brother's '64 Chevy.

• The time it takes to make money. I have four years of poverty staring me in the face. There's a high emotional price for being on welfare.

• I have less time to waste.

• Being a conventional housewife, but that hasn't been painful.

• I gave up a relationship with a man, but I was ready to. I had to leave my home in the country, my house in the woods, and some good friends. But it had been a long time since I had felt really stimulated, and I felt that the city would be a good place for me to be.

• Having a lot of free time and not accomplishing very much. I was glad to give that up.

• The housework. It's been five years since I've done much of that sort of thing. I always think next spring or next winter I'll get to some of these things, but I haven't.

- Sleep!

- I've had to give up my feeling of being a perfect mother. Many times I have to study when my kids have to study, and they want my help. I haven't time to give it to them and study my assignments, too, so they get angry with me.

- Most of my social life. Rarely a weekend would go by that we didn't have people over, but I'm so exhausted by the time the weekend comes around, and I use the weekend to catch up. Sometimes I spend four to five hours in the library, and there's no time to do other things.

- I had to temporarily shelve certain friendships. I had to give up being free to choose how I would spend my time, because it was no longer my own. I frequently felt very angry that I was required to do certain things—attend certain classes, turn in papers that seemed like mere busy work. I thought some of the work we were required to do was worthless.

- A lot of time with my daughter when she was young. When I got my master's degree, it was an incredible investment of time. I was working full-time in a program that demanded at least 80 hours a week. On top of that, I went to school three nights a week and over some weekends. The time demands were really hard to combine with parenting.

- An image of myself as a free spirit. That was a pretty hard thing to give up.

- Sanity! The opportunity to enjoy myself. Social life. There's not a lot of time to be friends with people. It takes time and effort to make friendships, and to sustain them. People aren't willing to wait three years until you get out of school.

- If it wasn't for school, I'd be working so I'd have some money. I've given up a social life although I'm not that interested in it any longer, not as much as I used to be. I've given up new clothes, a stereo, I've given up everything except the bare essentials, but I feel really good about it. After you've had just about everything you could think of when you're growing up, it's kind of neat to realize that you can get by on very little. I think it will make me a more thrifty person when I get out into the working world.

- Not having the same kind of time with my daughter that I did before. It's not that I don't spend time with her. It's that when I am spending time with her, it's usually on things that have to be done. Before, I'd take a day and we'd be together and do our own thing. There's no time for that anymore. If we are together, we usually shop for something that has to be bought.

CONFUSING MESSAGES FROM SPOUSES

• He was very happy when I decided to go back to school. But once I started, it immediately became a problem. Whatever I had to do for school was fine, as long as I did it when my husband wasn't home. He was very proud that I was going, but he didn't want it to interfere with his time with me. He made it very difficult. We did come to one crisis period about a year ago, when I had an exam coming up and he was ready to go on vacation. I went with him and missed my classes, but I did all my studying on the trip. He really resented it, and we both blew up. He has a good friend who really spoke to him, who made him see how important it was for me to be doing what I was doing. I think that was the point when his attitude changed. *He* became easier to live with, and then I began to try to understand his point of view. We had a meeting of the minds about it, and things have been much better since then.

• My husband was verbally very enthusiastic, but there's a big difference between someone who likes the idea that you're doing something and someone who is willing to live with the mechanics of its happening. He was very supportive on a conscious level, but he had a lot of difficulty when I became really absorbed in what I was doing.

• They were all quite positive about it on an open level. But the underlying current was definitely negative. And it was difficult for them to confront the negative aspects. They kept saying: "Oh, no, no, no, it's fine." But I became very persistent with them at one point because it obviously was not fine, and I resented the facade they were presenting because they were trying to please me. My husband was very supportive on one level. But on other levels, I felt that he was trying to sabotage the effort. He would suggest that we go away for two or three days. I would say that I couldn't because of school. "Aw, you can skip it," he would say. It was like dangling a carrot in front of a donkey's nose. Who wouldn't like to get out of a stuffy classroom? It was a kind of insidious sabotage, I felt. My husband even suggested that my desire to go to school was a temporary lapse in sanity and that he was merely going along with it to humor me. That didn't sit very well with me, as you can imagine.

• My husband said if that's what you want to do, fine, as long as nothing was disrupted in his life. He still wanted dinner on time. There have been a lot of irritations for both of us, possibly because I've had difficulty expressing what I was going through, and possibly because he's so tied up in what he's doing, he doesn't want to become involved with all the interim phases.

• My husband was generally very supportive both emotionally and economically. That's what he said, and we both bought it. But his subtle "Why aren't the dishes done?" and "I don't like making my own dinner," and "You sure like to spend money on tuition," gave me the feeling that he wasn't as supportive as he claimed to be.

• He's very supportive. That is, he's very encouraging, but I feel he doesn't understand the complications involved for me. He just says to go ahead and do it and that the details will work themselves out. But they won't just work themselves out. The details are overwhelmingly complicated—housing, schools for the children, money. He has pat answers for all of these. If I'm worried about money, I should take out a loan. I tell him that won't solve the problem of the rent. He then suggests that I get a part-time job or try for a scholarship. I feel as if I have to work out all these details even though he says he's supportive. It's all my responsibility if I want to do it.

• They gave me a lot of trouble about it, but when they talked to other people, they were proud of me. My children have said many times: "You don't love me."

• My husband complains when he doesn't have a terrific meal on the table. His theory is that if I can't do both well, then drop school, because the family shouldn't be affected in any way.

ADVICE FROM HUSBANDS OF REENTRY STUDENTS TO OTHER HUSBANDS

• You have to recognize that what counts is not the ups and downs of the studying, but the goal at the other end. And what you have at the other end is a partner who is a person in her own right, who has activities in her own right. You have to recognize that you will have to sacrifice a great deal. You have to be prepared to work around the house. A man's activities and a woman's activities are defined largely by culture. If your wife is going to have her own career, you have to work toward it and support her, and you've got to do it with more than just words.

• When anyone takes on an added responsibility or activity that consumes a significant amount of time, something has got to give somewhere. There are only a certain number of hours in the day. And you can't do everything, so something's got to change. If you have any particular goals, aspirations, or important needs that you feel have to be met, you'll have to take into consideration how they might be affected.

• If the husband and children go down to the school and see what she's doing, see some of the classes, it might make a difference. Get as many things in your life as you can lined up to be as ordinary as possible so that you are ready for all the surprises that the transition makes.

• It's taken us years to realize what now seems to be some very simple formulas that would have avoided a great deal of hassle. It's important to have a little fun together once in a while, for instance. You need rewards at the end of a long stretch of work, a sense of frivolity sometimes. Be sure to set aside time for the relationship. It probably doesn't make any difference whether the degree comes in two years or three. Have a little flexibility to make compromises.

• No matter how poor you are, borrow the money to have someone else do the laundry and cleaning. Don't underestimate the degree of determination and intensity your wife might have about trying to make up for "lost years." If the accusation is made that you have somehow retarded your wife's career, look at it squarely, and don't let it fester or simmer, because in a sense it's true. Maybe when you got married, it was part of the deal that you worked and she stayed home and took care of the kids. You've given up incredible amounts of yourself, too, to come through with your end of the deal. Talk with each other about your changing goals and needs.

• Everyone has demands. The biggest thing about going back to school has to do with time demands and attention demands or needs, and a potential problem of competitiveness. How does one really view bright women getting really good jobs with really high degrees? How does a man really feel about that? It can be a problem. Many men feel that they should be on top of the heap, so to speak. He should be the one earning all the money, not the one who's running the house, whether it be his shirts he's ironing or her skirts or both. There's always been this feeling among men that they are supposed to be more competitive and excel more than the woman and that is definitely something that has to be reckoned with. It becomes a far greater problem if you don't feel you are succeeding in what you are doing.

• You are going to have to do more work around the house. Even your wife will feel that she is doing more around the house because her time will be so compressed. You might try to discover how your time will be used and then plan for the use of it. But you won't be able to do that too well until you get into it, because each person's time problem is subjective and each person has different demands. Expect to have things happen differently, and cultivate flexibility. It's pretty easy to get upset with each other because of a lack of attention or a lack of getting things done the way one or the other feels they should be done.

• I would encourage a mate to approach it positively, but also to look downstream five to ten years to see where it's going as far as the relationship goes. Try to work out a plan that doesn't just stop with the two years of school, and some sort of understanding about what the future's going to bring after that.

GENERAL COMMENTS

• It really helped me to have the women in my women's group supporting me and providing me with role models of people who were more than just housewife/mothers. It gave me a whole new frame of reference. I can't imagine how a woman isolated in a real suburban, homey setting, where her only contacts are other housewives, can establish whatever it takes to go back to school. I had people who would at least let me cry on their shoulder when I felt conflicts and confusions.

• So very often our lives are defined by the needs of others to the extent that we don't really develop our own potential. Women really haven't been encouraged to be serious about a career, and the consequences can be disastrous. Going to school is one way to become independent and to grow and develop confidence. Most schools have career counseling which can be very helpful. Women have to be serious about a career. You may never marry, you may divorce, be widowed, or experience the empty-nest syndrome. Be prepared. After all, Prince Charming may never show up! Men know that they need to be able to be independent and responsible. Women need to know that, too.

• Do your best, but don't make yourself sick. Don't work to the point of sheer exhaustion. Set up special guidelines like: "I'm not going to work at all this weekend but I'll work 100 percent of the time during the week."

• Use as many shortcuts as possible. Go out to dinner, use packaged foods, paper plates, and buy a lot of underwear so that you don't have to do the laundry very often. We only clean the house when company is coming. Sometimes, we intentionally schedule in company so that we can find the living room again.

• Recognize that if you are a busy person you're going to have a hard time budgeting time for everything. Eliminate those things that don't matter. You have to overlook some things. You can't have a clean house, a good job, a perfectly groomed child, and all A's. Establish your priorities.

• The best thing to do is to seek out other people who have gone through some of the same problems. Look to them for support. If women tell you that their children have suffered, they're probably feeling guilty. Children are flexible. They adjust if you don't make a big deal out of it.

• Don't get too grimly earnest about it. Just relax and try to enjoy it. Think about what you know you're good in, and start with those subjects. If you start with things you're too out of tune with, it can be demoralizing. I started taking statistics and realized that I couldn't even remember how to do fractions. I'll pick up statistics later, but first I'll take a remedial course to get the background. Take advantage of remedial courses and tutors.

• Get ready for a lot of hard work and self-discipline. Know what your goals are and go after them. Set goals that you can reach without frustrating yourself.

• The most important thing that's happened to me is the realization that my home is not my entire life and that I can't live my life through my husband and children. I honestly always thought that my place was in the home, no matter how trite that sounds. I was brought up to think that you got married, stayed home, you had children, you raised them, did volunteer activities, you helped further your husband's career, and you kept your house neat, clean, and impressive. You did everything you could to make the lives of your husband and children better. Now I realize that our house is where we live. We sleep there, and we eat there, and it's ours, but there's no reason to spend a lot of time mopping and scrubbing and fixing up and putting away. It's much more important to do something for myself that makes me feel better, because then everyone else feels better, too.

• The hardest part is actually registering. Once you get past that, it's not too hard. Take something you're really interested in that will help you make a smoother transition. You can always change your mind about a class. Just go and change your schedule—it's just one more form. If you've been home for many years and are anxious about being in school, take a women's course. It gets you used to being in school, and the people in class will most likely be like you.

• Don't expect to do as well the first semester as you will later. It will take you a while to get your study habits.

• Laugh at yourself along the way. It's ludicrous to think that you have any less ability than the next person who's coming along. The first thing you need to do if you're thinking about going back to school is be willing to be light-hearted. Just because things don't go perfectly, so what? When it's all in perspective, it will be fine.

• Everyone I know who has gone back to school has stayed in school and done well. We all had visions of everyone being smarter than we were, but then they opened their mouths! You'll always find people who are brighter than you are—and people that aren't.

• Get as familiar as you can with the admissions process and what your program is going to be like. Find out all that you can in advance so it won't be a big mystery. Talk to some professors. The support group was really important to me. You may not want to go to a professor and say: "Hey, I'm really scared," but a support group would be really understanding about it.

• You take on a new set of problems when you are a student, and you have to learn how to solve them. Your conflicts will be different, and there's always fear when you try to do something different. Be prepared to be nervous. Things *will* be different—you'll have to schedule your time differently, and it will be harder to meet people's needs. You'll have more questions about yourself, your identity. A big question will be: will it have been worth it? When I have the degree in my hand, will I be able to get the job I want? You'll have fears and worries, and all you can do is live with them. Take the plunge and hope that it's worth it. It's definitely been worth it for me and everyone else I know who went back to school in order to change careers.

• It's okay to take it slowly, to take one class at a time. Start out by taking what you really like. If you like the first class, you'll probably enjoy the second. By the time you take something you thought you'd never care for, you'll be ready to deal with it. Get your feet wet. Get the feel of the school and how it runs. You'll feel more secure.

• Don't be afraid to ask questions. I was because of my conditioning. But there are plenty of people who can help, who can explain the regulations, what courses you should take. If the people you ask don't know, they'll send you to someone who does.

• Talk about it a lot with the people you're involved with. Have everyone understand what you're feeling and what you're hoping to do and where everyone fits in. How do they feel about it? You have to be committed, and you have to understand that it means giving up a lot of things.

• If you are returning to school to prepare for a job, do research on the job market. What can you expect to earn? How do you go about getting the job once you are out of school? You'll go in feeling much more armed for the whole process if you know these things. It will give you a much better sense of direction.

• There is no way after being a wife and mother for 20 years that you're not going to get any flack from your family when you all of a sudden return to school. Don't let it affect you. Do the best you can. Don't try to cover all jobs, all areas of being wife/mother/student. Don't try to be perfect in everything. You can't be all things to everybody. Your family, in the long run, will appreciate you more and will be a source of help to you before long. They will be shocked and surprised themselves about what they can handle.

• A proverb that I think about a lot is that the pessimist sees difficulty in every opportunity and the optimist sees the opportunity in every difficulty. When I tend to get down, I realize that the next time I'll know a better way. It takes a lot less energy to be positive about life than negative. Any woman who has even the germ of the feeling that she'd like to go back to school, for whatever reason, should take the chance. It may be the opening of a whole new life.

Chapter 11

The Options:
What Sort of College?

If you are fortunate enough to have several possible colleges or universities in your area to choose from, it is important to begin by asking several questions:

1. Can I get in?
2. Can I afford it?
3. Is it within a feasible commuting distance?
4. Does it have a good program in my field of interest?
5. Do classes meet at a time that fits my schedule?
6. Will I feel comfortable there?

The selection process may turn out to be quite simple, once you've asked these questions. By the time you've eliminated those schools whose entrance requirements are so strict that you haven't a chance, or that are too expensive or too far away, or that don't have a good program in your field of interest, or that simply don't "feel" right to you, the choice may have become perfectly obvious. Don't assume, though, that it's obvious without taking note of the options that may be available to you as a returning student. Some of these have been mentioned in connection with getting admitted. You'll find others in Chapters 13 and 14, on finances and on other areas related to earning a degree.

In this chapter you'll find information on the major categories to be considered: two-year colleges, four-year colleges and universities, and graduate or specialized schools.

TWO-YEAR COLLEGES

The number of people attending two-year colleges has skyrocketed over the past 30 years. In 1948, 150,000 students were enrolled in junior (community) colleges in the United States. In the academic year 1984-85, 1,660,000 people in California alone took at least one course at a junior college! Nationally, over 50 percent of all freshmen attending college for credit are enrolled in community colleges.

Junior colleges serve to satisfy the needs of a wide variety of students. For example:

If you want to get a four-year university degree, many of the courses offered at a junior college will be accepted for credit if you transfer to a four-year school. Usually your academic experience is evaluated course by course at the university of your choice, and if the courses you took at the junior college are comparable to ones offered at the university, you will receive credit. With conscientious preplanning, it is certainly possible to enter a university as a junior after spending two years in a community college transfer program.

Go through the annual catalog to see if courses in the field that interests you are available. If you want to get a B.A. in something esoteric like Italian Renaissance literature, you may find very few junior college courses in the subject. Nevertheless, you could get many or all of your general education requirements out of the way. Most junior colleges offer courses in the following subjects, among others, that would transfer to a four-year school:

agriculture
business and commerce
education
engineering
foreign languages
health
humanities
mathematics
computer/informational
  sciences

fine and applied arts—music, drama, photography, art appreciation, studio art
home economics—family relations, child development
physical sciences
social sciences—anthropology, economics, geography, government, history, political sciences, psychology, sociology

biological sciences
communications
ethnic and women's studies

• *If you want to qualify for a specific job or career,* two-year colleges offer a large number of options for obtaining concrete, marketable skills while earning a college degree. With some of the trade and vocational programs, you can earn an A.A. or A.S. degree, and *then* decide whether or not to transfer on to a four-year school. Another option is to earn a certificate of completion, which may take less than two years and indicates you have developed the necessary skills for a particular occupation.

Some of the career-oriented programs which might be available through a junior college year are:

AGRICULTURE

farm management
animal science
horticulture

ARTS

architectural technology
applied design
photography/cinema
graphic arts
interior design

BUSINESS

accounting
hotel and restaurant management
management and administration
office management
marketing and purchasing
secretarial studies
banking operations
merchandising
real estate
broadcasting
paralegal assistant
court reporting
legal secretary
computer programming
data processing
computer operating

HEALTH

dental assisting
medical or lab technician

nursing—R.N., L.V.N.
X-ray technology
inhalation therapist
medical office assistant
dental hygienist

PUBLIC SERVICE/SOCIAL
    SCIENCES

law enforcement/correction
parks/recreation management
social work
fire science
teacher's aid
library assistant
recreation worker

TECHNICAL/SKILLED
TRADES

automotive technology
printing
carpentry/construction
drafting
electronics
radio/TV repair
welding
solar technology
aeronautics
machinework
engineering technology—electrical, civil, mechanical

• *If you aren't sure of what direction to take,* a two-year college will usually be well equipped to offer career, academic, and psychological counseling.

In addition, junior colleges place special emphasis on such self-development courses as these: "Psychological Adjustment to Maturing Years," "The Psychology of Personal Growth," "Assertiveness Training," "Career Planning," "Orienting Yourself to College," "Coping with Change." Junior colleges, at least the public ones, are very receptive to community residents who want to take only one or two courses at a time. This kind of gradual reentry is great for building confidence and sorting out long-term goals.

• *If you did poorly in high school or college or are in any way anxious about getting good grades,* two-year colleges are known for their excellent remedial courses. If you are not eligible for the four-year college of your choice because of a poor academic performance in the past, you can attend a two-year college long enough to prove to the university and yourself that you're able to make the grade. And if you do find along the way that your study habits are rusty, you are in a great environment for polishing them up. Junior college students report that the faculty and staff involved with the remedial programs, in general, tend to be extremely supportive and concerned about their students.

THE ADVANTAGES ARE MANY

• The two-year colleges are usually *very* receptive to reentry students. There are often reentry offices and programs which specifically cater to the needs of students who have been out of school for a long time. If you are at all concerned that you will be the oldest in your classes, don't be; many of the students at the two-year schools are reentering. In California, for example, the average age of students at public two-year colleges is 31.

Counselors are usually available to help you with registration and to fill you in on child care (there are often excellent low-cost centers right on campus), learning programs, the various curricula, the possibilities of vocational interest testing, and reentry rap groups. Tutors are, as a rule, very accessible, and most reentry programs have peer counselors, to answer any questions you might have.

Many reentry students who have transferred to four-year colleges think that spending time at a junior college is a "great way to get your academic feet wet." Whereas a four-year college can seem overwhelming at first, the atmosphere at a junior college is much more encouraging.

• Exclusivity is *not* an attribute of the public two-year colleges! All public two-year schools have an open admissions plan—you are automatically accepted if you have a high school diploma or its equivalent. (However, acceptance does not automatically guarantee admission into the program of your choice.) Private junior colleges require a certain high school class standing and/or a minimum combination score on an aptitude test (see Chapter 12 for information about A.C.T. and S.A.T.).

Women who are intimidated by the admissions procedures at four-year institutions find that at junior colleges these procedures are usually painless. When the admissions policy is open-door, essentially all you have to do to take a few courses is sign up and dive in. Many two-year schools have set up extensive outreach programs, and you may wind up registering through a mobile unit parked in front of your library or shopping mall. Some junior colleges even publish an application form in the daily newspaper to make it as easy as they can for community residents to sign up.

If you are registering to be a full-time student in a degree program, a formal application is usually necessary. In addition, you might be required to submit proof of residence and your high school transcripts—neither of which takes very long or is very complicated to get.

The admissions policies just described do not apply to private junior colleges, which are sometimes as hard to get into as four-year private colleges.

Tuition—or lack of it—is a huge plus at public two-year colleges. The average cost of tuition and fees at public two-year colleges for the academic year 1985-86, according to *The College Cost Book*, was $659. The cost varies widely by region. For example, the average cost in the West is $342, $461 in the Southwest, and $1,127 in the middle states. The cost of tuition and fees is likely to be far less at a community college than at a four-year institution.

Financial aid is available to community college students, and counselors at each school can explain how to apply for it. The low tuition cost applies only to the *public* two-year schools. The average tuition and fees for the academic year 1985-86 at private junior colleges was $3,719. At one private school in Massachusetts, the cost was $6,250!

If you plan to attend a junior college that is outside your state or region, the tuition will almost certainly no longer be free, so be sure to prepare yourself for the extra cost.

• Classes are usually offered at times convenient for working people. If you work, it should not be necessary to rearrange your life completely in order to take classes at a junior college. Classes are usually offered in the evenings, so if you need to work full-time during the day, it is still possible to squeeze in a class or two.

• There is most likely a two-year college near you. Traveling to and from school becomes an important factor when you are trying to juggle home, school, and work. You will be grateful for every mile you *don't* have to travel.

SOME DISADVANTAGES

•Not all the courses you take at the junior college level may be transferable for credit to the university of your choice. If receiving a degree from a four-year institution is important to you, keep in close contact with your counselor or academic adviser about which courses will give you transferable credit. In fact, once you have decided on a program, it is a good idea to talk with someone in the admissions office of the university you plan to attend about transfer policies.

• If you develop an interest in a specific academic area while you are at a two-year school, you may find yourself exhausting the courses in that subject in far less than two years. The choice of courses in liberal arts and the social sciences is often quite limited, and the ones that exist fill up with students very quickly. So if you decided that you want a bachelor's degree in anthropology, you may have trouble finding enough courses to take until you transfer to the four-year school. Be sure to look through the catalog for course offerings in your field of interest.

• Some students report that they spent two years in the classroom in order to obtain a credential that really wasn't necessary for the kind of employment they wanted. If you have a specific vocation in mind, be sure to investigate *before you enroll in school* whether a degree or certificate is required or even helpful. Talk with potential employers about this, and with people who are doing the kind of work you want to be doing. How did they get their jobs? What kind of experience did they have? Obviously, going to school for two years to learn office management is not the *only* route to a good job in office management. What are the advantages of getting a degree in office management? Find out before you waste precious time!

If you live in an area where there are many junior colleges to choose from, you can save time by doing some initial research in the reference section of your local library. There are many good reference books. Two helpful ones are:

The College Handbook, published annually by the College Entrance Examination Board. For each junior college included in the book, you can find out how many students attend, the curriculum, remedial services available, admissions requirements, what percentage of students choose what programs, cost, financial aid, and whom to correspond with.

College Planning/Search Book, published by the American College Testing Program. This book gives good tips on what to look for when selecting a school and how to go through the process. It has specific information about almost all the junior colleges in the United States.

FOUR-YEAR COLLEGES

There are nearly 2,000 public and private four-year institutions in the United States with programs leading to a bachelor's degree. The private ones usually cost much more than the public. Four-year schools can be divided into three basic types:

1. *The liberal arts colleges.* These are often privately supported and tend to have small enrollments (under 5,000). At a liberal arts college, you are exposed to a wide variety of subjects through required courses during the first two years. Subjects you might be required to take include sociology, political science, English, history, philosophy, art history, and one of the sciences. Usually by the end of the first year, you choose an area of emphasis (a major). Then, in order to graduate with a bachelor's degree, you will be required to take certain courses in that field, along with others that are elective.

There are some distinct advantages to being an undergraduate at a small school. For one thing, it is less likely that you'll be lost in the shuffle than at a larger university. Classes are often small, and there is more opportunity to know your professors personally. The same kind of interaction is possible with counselors and academic advisers as well. At larger schools, meetings with such people tend to be fairly impersonal. At a small college, you will be more likely to find someone who will follow your college career with genuine interest and concern.

2. *Universities.* The words *college* and *university* have been used interchangeably in this book, but there is this difference between them: a university offers graduate programs beyond the bachelor's degree. The degrees most frequently offered are Master of Arts (M.A.), Master of Science (M.S.), and Doctor of Philosophy (the coveted Ph.D.). Degrees in law, medicine, and other professions are often earned at schools that are part of a university.

Universities are usually composed of several schools or colleges, and each may have its own entry requirements. For instance, if you wanted to get a master's degree in psychology, you might have to be admitted to the university *and* to the program in psychology.

Like the liberal arts colleges, the university system aims to expose you to a wide variety of subjects by requiring you to take entry-level courses in many different areas. You then choose a major and take the required courses plus any others you have time for.

Being at a university whose student population may be as high as 50,000 has its advantages. You will have the chance to choose from many more areas of specialized study than you would at a smaller college. There will also be a much wider selection of courses *within* your field of interest. The faculty is highly diversified at a larger institution. You can take courses for ten years and still not encounter all the professors in your department! To be able to pick and choose your professors is definitely a luxury. If you hear of one who has a bad reputation, you can probably arrange it so that you never have to run into him or her.

Another advantage of being at a university is that if you decide to go on to graduate school, you can often begin taking graduate-level courses while you are still an undergraduate. This can be a real time-saver, and the transition from undergraduate to graduate school will be much easier.

University libraries are usually much larger than those at liberal arts colleges, and if you are pursuing a laboratory science, the facilities available are also usually better.

3. *Specialized colleges.* These colleges also offer a bachelor's degree, but there is much less emphasis on exposing the student to a wide selection of liberal arts courses. If you want to become an engineer, a college that specializes in engineering may be perfect for you. But if you are also really interested in studying Shakespeare, you may be disappointed by the caliber of the literature courses there. Students at specialized colleges are usually preparing for a career. There are, for example, schools that emphasize music, art, engineering, business, and home economics, just to mention a few.

GRADUATE SCHOOL

Many women who contemplate going to graduate school have put in a considerable amount of time in the world of work. Some feel that they have climbed as high as they can on the career ladder, given their current credentials. Others have grown to dislike their jobs and want a complete change.

Some returning students enter graduate school for the sheer joy of learning. A master's program in English literature is a good chance to do some critical reading in an atmosphere conducive to study. The number of women who return to school as graduate students just for the sake of learning is quite small, however. Most are very much career oriented and the graduate school is the most direct route to a more satisfying, higher-paying job.

Graduate programs involve an impressive amount of time and devotion. A master's degree usually takes one or two years; it often includes a master's project or thesis and sometimes a third year doing an internship. A doctorate can involve anywhere from three to seven years of study, a dissertation, and a written and/or oral examination.

One problem for the returning student who has roots in her community is that only 947 accredited academic institutions in the United States offer master's degrees, and only 320 have doctoral programs. You will probably not have much trouble deciding which university has the best program. It will be more a matter of doing everything possible to make sure you are admitted to the one and only program near you that suits your needs.

FINDING A GOOD PROGRAM

Remember that there are often several different routes that can take you to the same place. For example, if you have your heart set on being a social worker, but there are no programs for a master's degree in social work (M.S.W.) near you, look at the master's programs in psychology or counseling. You may discover that half of their graduates find jobs with the welfare department.

The following suggestions might help you to find a program that will be right for you:

1. If one of your professors during your undergraduate days was particularly supportive, reestablish contact and ask him or her for advice on how best to pursue your interest. If there is a graduate adviser at your alma mater, perhaps you are still eligible for some counseling.

2. Try to track down the names of some recent graduates in whatever program you are considering. What do they think of the program? What kind of work are they doing?

3. Visit the college placement office and ask for information on what recent graduates from that department are doing. If you are contemplating an M.A. in psychology in order to be involved in some aspect of counseling, and you find that all the graduates have jobs doing research, that's a pretty important clue.

4. One way to discover the orientation of a department is to look at the theses and dissertations that have been turned in over the past few years. The department will have these on file. Is this the kind of work you want to be doing? Which faculty members are involved with projects that reflect your interests?

5. The descriptive material that a department gives out concerning its program usually includes biographical sketches of the faculty. Decide which faculty members might have interests similar to yours, and see if you can make an appointment with one or more of them. By this time, you will probably have several questions that need answering, and most often a professor will be delighted to help anyone entering his or her field.

6. Talk with as many current graduate students as you can. If you can blend the impressions you get from faculty, students, and alumni, you should begin to have a realistic picture of the program.

7. Read the graduate school catalogs thoroughly. Do the courses look interesting? Do you have the necessary prerequisites? Do you have time to apply before the deadline?

8. Choose two or three possible employers that appeal to you, and try to make an appointment with someone there. Ask this person what kind of academic route he or she would recommend for

someone interested in finding a similar job. This may sound like an outrageous approach, but few of those who have tried it have met with a cold shoulder.

PROFESSIONAL PROGRAMS

If you are planning to enter a profession such as medicine, law, dentistry, or management, you are probably already well aware of the stringent admissions requirements. Just about all the programs in these specialized fields will require you to take a special entrance examination similar to the Graduate Record Examination. (See Chapter 12 for information about this.)

No matter what you plan to study in graduate school, be sure to review the entrance requirements for each program to see if there are special exams that are required.

Chapter 12

Getting Admitted

How students are selected varies tremendously from school to school. The first thing you need to do is find out the admission requirements at the schools which interest you. Remember that the policy may be different for older students, so do not rule out a college because of the requirements listed in the catalog. Some colleges, for instance, will let in anyone over age 30, no matter what their qualifications are. This is done because the university has figured out that your life experience is worth more than where you stood in your high school class however many years ago. And they're right!

Other colleges have requirements that older students have to meet, but they are different from the requirements for the younger students. If you truly want to attend a particular college, go talk to the director of admissions about it. Through a personal interview you may be able to convince him or her that you have a lot to offer as a student, and that your grades and test scores do not reflect your real assets. Even if you do not qualify for admission through an accepted program, the director of admissions has it within his or her power to make exceptions. So don't let yourself be overwhelmed by the formalities of applying.

If you have no idea how strict the entrance requirements are for a school that interests you, these will be spelled out in the school's annual catalog. Finding out the number of students who apply and the number of students accepted will also give you a good indication of your chances. Some schools accept everyone, and others reject three students for every one that gets accepted! (See the table on pp. 141–142.)

ENTRANCE REQUIREMENTS—THE FIRST HURDLE

The more traditional requirements you can expect to confront include:

1. *High school transcripts.* These consist of the official record of courses you took, grades you received, your grade-point average, and your rank in the class. Usually you can expect to be charged a small fee (about $1) for sending a transcript, and you should allow about three weeks for the process to be completed. The time it takes to get your transcript can vary considerably, however—from a few days to three months (if the high school is completely shut down during the summer).

If you have not graduated from high school, you can take a high school equivalency test to submit in place of a transcript. This is known as the General Educational Development Test, or G.E.D. This exam often requires no fee, or only a minimal one (under $25). The test consists of five segments, each lasting between an hour and an hour and a half. Subjects include: writing skills; social studies; science; reading skills; and mathematics. The department of education in your state can tell you where to take the test. You usually have several options about when to take the test—one day, two days, five evenings, etc. You can prepare for the G.E.D. by using review books or taking a special preparation course through an adult education program.

2. *Aptitude Examinations.* As part of the admissions process at a good two-thirds of the colleges and universities in the United States, students are required to take either the Scholastic Aptitude Test (known as the S.A.T. or "college boards") or the American College Testing assessment (known as A.C.T.).

The S.A.T. is usually given seven times a year, in thousands of high schools and colleges throughout the country. It consists of a verbal and a mathematical section, separately timed and each made up of multiple-choice questions. The verbal section aims to measure your reading comprehension, vocabulary, and verbal reasoning. The mathematical section measures your ability to solve problems involving arithmetic, algebra, and geometry. The exam is three hours long, costs $11.50, and can be taken more than once.

The A.C.T. Assessment Program is generally considered easier than the S.A.T., and includes four tests, made up of multiple-choice questions in English, mathematics, social sciences, and natural sciences. It strives to measure your current level of educational development and your ability to perform tasks frequently required in college courses. It is usually given five times a year, takes three and a half hours, and costs $10 ($12 in New York).

Should you study for these tests? If you have not been required to use algebra and geometry since high school, you are probably pretty fuzzy about them by now. If you read for pleasure, on the other hand, you may be surprised to find how well you do on the reading comprehension and vocabulary sections.

There are review books available for the S.A.T. and the A.C.T. If you can spare the time, just becoming familiar with the *kinds* of questions that are asked can be a big help. The announcement bulletins for both tests give sample exercises which can easily give you an indication of what you need to bone up on. You may discover that an afternoon spent with a high school geometry book makes the questions on that subject seem less foreign. Any high school guidance department or college testing center will have plenty of extra copies of the announcement bulletins, or you can write directly for a copy to: A.C.T. Registration, P.O. Box 414, Iowa City, IA 52243; S.A.T., c/o College Board ATP, CN6200, Princeton, NJ 08541-6200.

How these tests "count" varies from school to school, but the more highly selective a college is, the better you are expected to do on them. A college can tell you the average combined scores its freshmen got on their S.A.T. or A.C.T. On the S.A.T., scores for each of the two tests range from 200 to 800. According to the *College Planning/Search Book*, at a school which accepts all high school graduates, the combined S.A.T. score ranges from 750 to 900. At highly selective schools, the students averaged combined scores of 1,100 to 1,300.

Some colleges also require you to take one or more of the S.A.T.'s one-hour achievement tests, which are given in subjects such as English composition, literature, a selection of foreign languages, American and European history, mathematics, biology, chemistry, and physics. These achievement tests, most of them given five times a year, can and should be studied for, and review books are available. The cost for a morning of testing is $18.50. You cannot take the S.A.T. and achievement tests on the same day.

Any high school or college can give you information about these S.A.T. and A.C.T. tests, along with the necessary application forms. Be sure to register at least five weeks in advance of the test date. It will take another five or six weeks to process your tests; then the results will be mailed to you and to four colleges of your choice. Some private institutions will not accept S.A.T. scores taken after January for students planning to enroll the following September. This means that you will have to register to take the test in November.

College and university officials are beginning to understand that being away from test taking a long time can affect your performance on the A.C.T. or S.A.T. At some colleges this part of the admissions process may be waived or altered. Be sure to find out whether this is possible at the college you're considering.

If you are really anxious about your performance on the S.A.T. or A.C.T., remember that you can take it more than once. Also, there are probably remedial classes available through your local junior college or high school adult education program.

3. *A formal application.* Filling out a college application can be a fairly quick procedure or it can require a great deal of thought. Even the schools that ask for written commentaries are looking for answers to questions that you have probably given a lot more thought to than the younger applicants. A fee (typically ranging from $15 to $40) is charged for processing most college applications.

4. *An interview with an admissions officer.* Some of the more competitive colleges strongly recommend an interview with someone in their admissions office. The admissions people are looking for sound investments and serious intentions. Your intentions, especially if you plan to pursue a career, are probably a lot more serious and specific than those of most younger students. See the admissions officer if it is suggested to you at all. This may be your *only* chance to get some personal attention for your application. Life experience is a valuable asset to a student, so spend some time talking with the admissions officer about it.

GETTING ADMITTED IF YOU'VE ALREADY BEEN TO COLLEGE

If you have had some college or received a degree and now want to go back to school, the admissions process will be somewhat different from what's involved if you have never been to college. You will probably not have to take the S.A.T. or A.C.T. again if you are seeking a second bachelor's degree. You will be expected to supply transcripts from your first college, and a certain grade-point average may be expected. If yours falls short of the mark, go see the admissions officer—who is likely to be receptive to the idea that poor grades the first time around can be irrelevant.

If you dropped out of college, the admissions process applying to you will probably be the same as for transfer students. You will be required to submit your college transcripts. If you have under 30 units of credit, your high school transcripts will probably also be required, and you may have to meet freshman admissions requirements—by taking the A.C.T. or S.A.T., meeting a minimum standard in your high school G.P.A., and so on. A minimum G.P.A. is sometimes required of *all* transfer students, and there are some colleges that want A.C.T. or S.A.T. scores, no matter how much undergraduate work you have done.

"Transfer" students and people going back for additional undergraduate degrees have one thing in their favor: there is no way you can be automatically processed! Even if admissions are handled by a computer, you will probably put the machine on "tilt" by the number of years of education you've listed on your application form. This means you will almost certainly receive someone's individual attention. If you're at all worried that your performance before may disqualify you now, be sure to have a personal interview with the director of admissions. There's a good chance that you can talk yourself into the school. Admissions people are fast becoming familiar with how well reentry students can do, given the chance.

GETTING ADMITTED TO GRADUATE SCHOOL

When you apply to graduate school, the admissions process can be a real psychological hurdle. Even women with incredible ability can become instantly intimidated. Just settle yourself down and decide whether it's really important to you to get this degree. If it is, then no matter how long it takes is how long you'll spend doing it. Get tutored in math for the G.R.E.'s if you need it. If it takes two or three years to get in, that's not long out of a lifetime. Once you're in, it's really worth it. If you make a firm decision to get the degree, you will be able to do it.

—ADVICE FROM A 40-YEAR-OLD
MASSACHUSETTS WOMAN WHO JUST
COMPLETED A MASTER'S DEGREE
IN FINE ARTS

Some of the more traditional entrance requirements for graduate school include:

1. *Transcripts.* You will need to have an official record of all the courses you have taken, your grades, and your grade-point average from each of the colleges you have attended, even if you only received credit for one course. Address your request to the Registrar's Office, enclose the fee (usually between $1 and $4), and allow three weeks for processing (although it probably won't take that long).

2. *Prerequisites.* Most programs have set ideas about courses that you needed to take as an undergraduate. If you majored in the subject that you plan to do graduate work in, you will probably have fulfilled all the prerequisites. Otherwise, you may have to take some undergraduate courses before you are officially admitted to the program. To save time, try to take these along with your graduate courses.

3. *Letters of recommendation.* Most graduate programs consider these letters to be quite important in their evaluation of you. Usually, applicants ask three or four people to write letters for them, and the letters are sent directly to the university. You should select people who know your potential as a scholar or your experience in the field you are considering.

Don't make your letter writers work too hard for you. Give them plenty of time to get their letters done. Provide them with written information about the school, the program, and your reasons for applying. A copy of your employment resume would be helpful, and you might ask each writer to emphasize a different aspect of your ability. Give each writer a stamped envelope addressed to the graduate school, and make sure each one knows when the deadline is. A thank-you note is appropriate when the letter reaches the school.

4. *Test scores.* Many programs require you to take the Graduate Record Examination (G.R.E.) General Test, which is usually given five mornings a year at colleges throughout the country. The exam, which takes three and a half hours, measures verbal, quantitative, and analytical ability. It costs $29. Some programs no longer require the G.R.E.; others use it only for placement and research purposes.

Eight Special Administration Service test centers across the country give the G.R.E. tests more frequently. Their application deadline is shorter, but the fee is $20 extra. See the G.R.E. Information Bulletin and the Special Administration Service Supplement for additional information.

No advanced mathematics is required for the General Test, but if it has been a long time since you last used math, you may want to bone up on basic algebra and geometry before the test. The G.R.E. application booklet (available at any college) includes a full-length sample test. Take it to see what you need to review.

Some programs will also require you to take a Subject Test as well. These exams, which take 2 hours and 50 minutes, are given on the same days as the General Test, in an afternoon session. A Subject Test costs $29 and tests 17 subjects: biology, chemistry, computer science, economics, education, engineering, French, geology, history, literature in English, mathematics, music, physics, political science, psychology, sociology, and Spanish. Some of the tests have subscores—for example, history is subdivided into an American and a European section. Going on to graduate school in one of these subjects does *not* mean that you will be required to take the achievement test.

If you do have to take an achievement test, however, you should certainly spend some time reviewing for it. Your notes and texts from college can be a big help in this process. There are also review books for most of the subjects mentioned.

5. *Statement of purpose.* This is your personal statement on why you want to participate in this particular program and your reasons for wanting to enter the field. This is your chance to discuss how you feel your life experience could help you as a student in this program.

6. *Portfolio/audition.* If you are applying to graduate school in art, music, drama, photography, or filmmaking, you will probably be required to submit samples of your work.

7. *Interview.* A graduate school interview is a lot like a job interview—both parties looking each other over to see if getting together would be a good investment. Before the interview, spend some time thinking about the assets you would bring to this particular program. Study the catalog to determine what the authorities are looking for in their graduate students. Think of good questions to ask that show you are genuinely interested in the program.

8. *Application and fee.* If you belong to a racial or ethnic minority, you can take advantage of the Graduate Record Examination Minority Graduate Student Locater Service—at no cost to you. By

filling out a form enclosed in the G.R.E. announcement bulletin, you ensure that your biographical data will be placed into the locater service, which is examined three times a year by more than 200 graduate schools. If a school is interested in students with your major, belonging to your ethnic or racial group, and living in your state or region, or any combination of these, you will hear from someone there. This is a *free* service, and you need not take the G.R.E. in order to participate. During the academic year 1984-85, approximately 19,000 students enrolled for the locater service, and 230 graduate schools selected names for use in their applicant mailings.

FINANCIAL AID FOR GRADUATE STUDENTS

One hitch for reentry students who need financial aid is the deadline for applications, which can be as early as December for the term beginning the following fall.

Another problem is that many government grants, such as Pell and SEOG, are not available to graduate students. If you are a reentry student who has recently received aid for undergraduate work, you may be shocked by the lack of funding available for your graduate education.

As an undergraduate, almost all of your discussion about financial aid was centered around the financial aid office. This is not the case with graduate school. Fellowships, traineeships, teaching and research assistantships are probably located through the graduate department you will be affiliated with. The first two are usually grants, awarded on the basis of competition, and require no service to the school. Teaching and research assistantships can provide you with invaluable experience, earn you credit toward your degree, and provide you with funds. Ask the department secretary for the name of the person to talk with about them, and watch the bulletin boards for announcements of positions.

Other resources available to graduate students—work/study, loans, scholarships—are discussed in depth in Chapter 13.

Peterson's Annual Guides/Graduate Study are an excellent source of information on all aspects of specific graduate programs, including financial aid information. They cite the types of aid given, the average amount, and how many students in the program receive aid. Another excellent resource is the *Directory of Graduate Programs*, a four-volume set put out by the Educational Testing Service. More good resources are listed in Appendix D, Section 4.

DEADLINES

There are many deadlines involved in the application process. Be sure you are aware of everything you need to do! It is crucial that you make up a checklist of all the deadlines for each of the colleges you plan to apply to—and keep it up to date. A sample checklist is given at the end of this chapter.

For students planning to enter in September, the deadline for applying is often the first of February and sometimes as early as the preceding December.

Some colleges and universities, especially those that are privately operated, admit students only once a year, for the fall term. They let applicants they have accepted know their decision by March or April—six months before school opens. This means, of course, that if you were to decide in February that a particular private college is the one you are determined to get into, you will have virtually no chance of being admitted—as a regular student—for another 19 months! Some private colleges do not even take part-time students. There are others, however, that have come a long way in recent years toward accommodating returning students. This means that you should make a point of finding out whether any exceptions are made for older students.

While you are going through the selection process, talk with as many people as you can—students, faculty, alumni, college staff, potential employers, friends—to find out what they know about the school and the department you are considering. The questions at the end of Chapter 14 can serve as a preliminary list of the ones you should be asking yourself and others all along the reentry route.

The process of sending for catalogs, deciding, and applying can be tedious and frustrating—even overwhelming at times. But it will also be stimulating. If you do a thorough job of your research, you will be meeting interesting new people and exploring new places. Making a decision that can have a real effect on your future is exciting in itself. Doing it in an organized, well-thought-out way can be deeply satisfying.

A CHECKLIST OF THINGS TO BE DONE

Once you have done all the research and it looks as though you have a reasonable chance of getting past the various hurdles, you are ready for the next step: drawing up a checklist to ensure that everything gets done when it's needed.

There are just too many factors involved to make any generalizations about how far in advance each step in your campaign needs to be taken. The sequence of events is pretty straightforward, however. The times given below will allow you to go through the necessary steps without feeling as though you are doing the 50-yard dash.

Each school will have different requirements, so draw up a checklist for each one.

Name of school:_____

Application for admissions due: _____

Application for financial aid due: _____

About six months before the admissions or financial aid deadline (whichever comes first):

Investigate schools of interest by answering the questions posed in Chapter 14.

Talk with family members about wanting to return to school.

About five months before the deadline:

Pick up admissions and financial aid packets or request them by writing or by telephone. Date: _____

Pick up or request A.C.T. or S.A.T.* announcement bulletin if exam is required.

Take the S.A.T. or A.C.T. sample test in the announcement bulletin, and begin to review whatever is necessary.

If the college grants credit for life experience or C.L.E.P., start preparing.

About four months before the deadline:

Register for A.C.T. or S.A.T. and any other necessary tests. (Send six weeks before test date.) Sent: _____

Begin gathering the necessary material for the financial aid packet.

Continue to review for A.C.T. or S.A.T.

GRADUATE STUDENTS: Begin preparation of portfolio or for audition if required.

* Graduate students: Just substitute G.R.E. every time you see A.C.T. or S.A.T.

About two and one-half months before the deadline:
   Take A.C.T. or S.A.T. and achievement tests (allow six weeks
   for processing). Date: _____

GRADUATE STUDENTS: Ask three to four people to write letters of
recommendation. Get the necessary material to them. Draft statement of purpose, if required. Sent: _____
   Continue to exchange feelings with family members about the
   whole reentry process.

About two months before the deadline:
   Send for high school and college transcripts. (Allow about two
   weeks, include fee, and have them sent directly to the school.)
   Requested: _____
   Fill out admissions packet and send. (Don't forget to include
   fee.) Sent: _____
   Other admissions requirements (proof of residence, short essay
   on goals, etc.). Sent: _____
   Interview with admissions officer. Date:_____

   _____

   _____

   _____

Graduate Students: Statement of purpose. _____
Portfolio? Audition? _____

About one month before the deadline:
   Call the admissions office (Have transcripts, S.A.T. or A.C.T.
   scores, application materials arrived? *Is application complete?*)
   Date: _____

Graduate Students: Be sure letters of recommendation have
arrived.
   Call the financial aid office (Is financial aid packet complete?).
   Date: _____

Some additions for public junior college applicants:
   Part-time students: If you graduated from high school, you
   probably only need to appear on registration day and sign up
   for classes you want. However, go to the school *now* and find
   out if there is anything you need to do before registration day.
   If there is advance registration, try to get in on it because you
   will be more likely to get the classes you want.
   Full-time students. It is unlikely that the school will ask you to

take a national test except for placement purposes. If you begin classes in September, you should probably take the exam in May or June, and there's no real need to study for it. If no tests are required, investigate schools of interest by answering questions on pages 154–156. Then use this checklist beginning at two months before the deadline.

Once you have been accepted:

Discuss school schedule and anticipated changes with family members. Listen carefully to their reactions.

Investigate child-care possibilities and register.

Set up a study area.

Deal with the transportation issue.

Get together with other returning students.

Find someone to help you go through the registration process.

Take a tour of the library.

Borrow a study guide, and begin to think about a study schedule.

Arrange for parking at school.

Spend time at the reentry office.

Have family meetings to discuss dividing up household tasks.

Talk with financial aid. Date: _____

Talk with faculty adviser. Date: _____

Register. Date: _____

Buy textbooks. Date: _____

Chapter 13

Financing Your Education

Many returning students assume that they will not be eligible for financial aid, or that if they do apply, what they receive won't be sufficient. However, the following facts should help reassure you that there really *is* money out there for students:

• At many colleges, over half the student population receives some form of financial aid.

• For the academic year 1984–85, more than 5 million students received more than $16 billion in various forms of student assistance for postsecondary education and training.

• At least $6.6 billion of student financial aid from the private sector has gone unused each year.

If your income is low, or if returning to school will cause financial hardship for you and your family, you are just as eligible for most kinds of aid as any younger student. The key to getting it is that *you must apply early.* Many colleges want you to apply for financial aid as soon as possible after January 1 for the academic year beginning the following fall.

Even if you are only *thinking* of going back to college, you should lose no time in getting a need analysis form from the place you are most likely to attend. It is not necessary to have been admitted in order to have a needs assessment processed.

Finding funds for going to college is *not* a lost cause. It may take a certain amount of hard work to track down an aid plan that is the right one for you, especially if you attend only part-time. But it *can* be done. Here is the advice of Tamara, whose experience is described in Chapter 2, and who has worked as a full-time counselor at a community college in California: "There is a lot of money out there. You just have to know how to get it. Go to financial aid and get them to work for you. Find a teacher to help you. You will discover that all kinds of people will be willing to help."

The people you should talk to about funding prospects are: (1) the staff at the campus financial aid office; (2) students who have traveled the same route that you are about to go; and (3) professors, department chairpeople, and the department secretaries in your field of interest. Talk to as many people as you can.

The financial aid office will give you an application packet, including the needs-assessment form. Even if you have been supporting yourself (and others) for years, you will have to prove that you are self-supporting, and it takes time to gather all the essential documents.

When the financial aid office has received the results of your needs assessment (it usually takes six weeks to process) and all other needed documentation, you will be told how much money you would be expected to pay for your education, and other avenues available for funding will be explained. Usually several funding sources are combined into a "package" for the student. Since almost all forms of financial aid are limited and given on a first-come, first-served basis, the sooner you process the forms the better.

Several need analysis forms are used nationwide. If forms automatically make your eyes glaze over, try filling one out item by item according to the instruction booklet; you'll find it is much easier than you first thought. As you fill out a financial aid form, write down any questions you have as you go along. When you have completed as much as you can, ask the financial aid office to help you with those questions.

Even though financial aid is definitely available, it is often difficult to find out about. The following resources should be helpful.

AID FROM THE FEDERAL GOVERNMENT

The information in this book is current for the academic year 1985–86. However, the only thing constant about the student financial aid picture is that it keeps changing. The national administration has been urging Congress to reduce the federal role in postsecondary education funding. To be sure that you have up-to-the-minute information about federal financial aid, consult a financial aid office on a college campus, or write for the free pamphlet, *The Student Guide: Five Federal Financial Aid Programs*, from Consumer Information Center, Department B, Pueblo, Colorado 81009.

1. *Pell Grant Program* (formerly the Basic Educational Opportunity Grant Program). This is the largest need-based student aid program. In 1984–85, nearly three million undergraduates received grants from $200 to $1,670. How much a student receives depends on: (a) need; (b) the cost of the academic program; (c) the length of the program; and (d) whether enrollment is full-time or part-time (you must attend at least half-time). This grant, which does not have to be paid back, is for undergraduates only. If you are enrolled in an undergraduate program and have already received a bachelor's degree, you are not eligible.

Any college financial aid office will have a Pell Grant application form. The forms are also available through all high school guidance offices. Application for Pell Grants should be made before you are enrolled, and takes about six weeks to process.

2. *The Supplemental Educational Opportunity Grant Program (SEOG)*. Undergraduates who are enrolled at least half-time at an accredited college or university and are U.S. citizens are eligible to apply for this grant. Awards are based on need and range from $200 to $2,000. The funds come from the federal government, but the colleges take care of distribution. These funds do not have to be repaid. This program is designed to supplement other sources of financial aid. You can get application forms for the SEOG from college financial aid offices.

3. *The National Direct Student Loan Program (NDSL)*. Undergraduates and graduate students who are enrolled at least half-time may be eligible to borrow $3,000 per year for a total of $6,000 for undergraduates and $12,000 for graduate students. Graduate students must include any NDSL funds for undergraduate years in their figuring.

The NDSL provides the lowest interest rate of any of the educational loans—5 percent in 1985. Repayment begins six months after a student graduates or leaves school. Regular payments may be spread out over ten years. These federally funded loans are obtained through colleges and universities.

4. *The College Work-Study Program (CWS)*. This federally funded program is run through college financial aid offices and provides employment opportunities for students with demonstrated need. Undergraduates and graduate students who are enrolled at least half-time are eligible to apply. Work-study positions are almost always located on the campus itself.

Students generally earn at least the minimum wage for work-study jobs. A work-study job can be a fine way to do something useful and earn money at the same time. Positions can involve anything from janitorial to library work. You can earn money through the work-study program while gathering marketable skills in your particular field of interest. For example, if your career goal is to be a student personnel worker, you might get a work-study job in the student employment office. Work-study students average about 15 hours per week at their jobs during the school year, although you can work as many as 40 hours per week if your financial need is great enough.

To qualify for work-study, go to a college financial aid office for an application.

Any college financial aid officer can tell you all about these avenues for obtaining federal financial aid. You can also write for the free pamphlet, *The Student Guide* (see page 132 for information).

AID FROM THE STATE GOVERNMENT

The kind of assistance offered varies widely from state to state. Be sure to check out the resources your state has to offer. Often really good scholarships, grants, loans, and fellowships are available.

For instance, it is possible to qualify for state scholarships that will cover the full cost of your tuition at a public *or* private university. In addition, there are state grants that will cover your living expenses, if you qualify.

California, for example, has an impressive variety of state grants for undergraduates. One is Cal Grant A, which helps with tuition costs for students—selected on the basis of financial need and grade-point average—who plan to attend a college in California. For the academic year 1984–85, awards ranged from $600 to $3,740 at independent colleges, and from $300 to $972 at the University of California; for the California State University system, they averaged $291.

The key to success is to find out about opportunities in your state and apply for them before the deadline. This may mean planning very far in advance. In some cases, you have to submit Scholastic Aptitude Test (S.A.T.) or American College Testing (A.C.T.) scores as far ahead as nine months before the next academic year begins. This means that if you decide in March that you want to return to school, some forms of state funding would not be available to you until the academic year that begins 18 months later. If you are remotely interested in returning to school, pursue your potential resources *right now.*

The financial aid office on your campus will probably have a detailed listing of state resources for financial aid, or you can contact the state education department or higher education coordination agency. There are also many good books and pamphlets that can help. See Appendix D, Section 4.

THE GUARANTEED STUDENT LOAN PROGRAM and PLUS LOANS

The Guaranteed Student Loan Program (GSL) makes it possible to borrow money for educational expenses from banks, credit unions, savings and loan associations, and, in some cases, the college itself.

The GSL is subsidized by the federal government, with a 1985 interest rate of 8 percent. In most states, a state agency insures the loans. If the state has no such agency, the federal government does the insuring. In such a case, the loan is called a Federally Insured Student Loan.

Most states require GSL recipients to attend school full-time. Undergraduates may apply to borrow up to $2,500 per year, to a maximum of $12,500. Graduate and professional students can apply to borrow $5,000 per year to a maximum of $25,000, including undergraduate loans. However, the federal government is reviewing its policy on loans for students in graduate and professional schools, and is discussing eliminating these opportunities.

You pay a 5 percent service charge for borrowing money through the GSL. This amount is taken from the loan funds before you receive payment. The usual length of repayment time is between five and ten years. Payment begins within six to twelve months of leaving school.

The GSL is definitely in a state of flux. Be sure to get the most current information before you plan on this type of loan.

PLUS loans are also made by a lender such as a bank, credit union, or savings and loan association. Unlike the GSL, PLUS borrowers do not have to show need, although they may have to undergo a credit analysis. PLUS loans are available to both undergraduate and graduate students, and the interest rate for 1984–85 was 12 percent. Repayment must begin within 60 days after graduation.

AID FROM ACADEMIC INSTITUTIONS

1. *Scholarships and grants.* Many scholarships and grants do not depend in any way on your area of interest and are awarded only on the basis of academic achievement and/or financial need. For general scholarships and grants, you will probably have to file an application through the financial aid office, which will be well versed in the various opportunities available. The financial aid office will probably know about scholarships and grants awarded in specific fields of interest, but you might also consult the head of the department in which you plan to major or the department secretary.

2. *Loans.* The academic institutions you are interested in may have their own arrangements for long-term loans, so be sure to look into this possible resource. In addition, many schools can provide short-term loans of up to $200 at no interest. These generally have to be repaid by the end of the semester or quarter. Such a short-term loan could mean the difference between being able to buy your books or not.

3. *Deferred-tuition plan.* Some universities will let you attend even if you are unable to pay the tuition immediately. The financial aid or admissions office will be able to tell you whether or not this is possible at the school you are considering.

4. *Opportunities through the student employment office.*

a. JOBS IN THE COMMUNITY. Most academic institutions maintain an employment bureau which lists jobs available in the community. Anyone in the community who uses the service realizes that students have many other obligations. As a result, quite a few of the jobs listed are part-time or at odd and flexible hours. There is usually a big demand for house cleaners, gardeners, babysitters, and salespeople.

The student employment office is also a good resource for finding full-time or part-time summer jobs.

b. COOPERATIVE EDUCATION. Almost 1,000 schools have programs where local employers take on students, usually full-time, for one or more semesters. During this time, you earn academic credit and/or money while being involved with a job that is directly related to your major. For example, if you are majoring in child development, you may be able to get a job in a child-care center through your department which will permit you to earn money, experience, and credit toward your degree.

The chairperson and secretary of your department will probably know about these jobs, and they will also be posted at the student employment office. Although participating in cooperative education programs may mean taking longer to get through college, when you graduate you will have a degree *plus* valuable job experience.

If you have any ideas about employers who might be willing to cooperate, there is no harm in trying to channel them through the academic mill and creating your own job. For a list of colleges that are involved with cooperative education, write to the National Commission for Cooperative Education, 360 Huntington Ave., Boston, MA 02115.

c. ASSISTANTSHIPS AND INTERNSHIPS. Teaching assistants, graders, and resident advisers can all receive credit or funds for their work. An internship is something like a cooperative education job except that the employer is within the university. Internships are often unpaid, but the work experience can be valuable in landing a job once you have a degree. Assistantships and internships are often listed through department heads as well as the student employment office. Department heads and secretaries will often also know about temporary jobs for students in their department.

OTHER SCHOLARSHIPS AND GRANTS

Scholarships usually involve competition based on merit and financial need, whereas grants place more of an emphasis on need. There are many scholarships and grants available; it's a matter of finding the right one for you and then applying for it at the appropriate time. Both are available through so many different channels that it becomes a feat of organization to sift through all the resources.

There are national and state scholarships as well as those that originate with a particular academic institution or individual. Fraternal organizations, religious groups, local and national businesses, racial and ethnic groups all offer funds for higher education. What is involved is tracking them down.

To find out about scholarships and grants:

1. Check with the financial aid office. It may publish lists of noninstitutional scholarships and grants.

2. Check with people in your own field of interest. They may know of funding that is available.

3. If you have a specific career in mind, write to the appropriate national organization to inquire about possible resources.

4. Find out about commercial scholarship agencies which locate potential sources of funding for a fee. An example of a good scholarship search agency is The National Scholarship Research Service, 86 Belvedere Street, Suite E, San Rafael, CA 94912. For $45, you will receive a detailed listing (usually between 30 and 50 resources) of funding possibilities most appropriate to your background and educational goals. Your financial aid office should have details about others.

5. Keep a close watch on campus bulletin boards and newspapers for announcements about scholarships and grants.

6. Take full advantage of the resource books in the reference section at your library. *The Scholarship Book: The Complete Guide to Private Sector Scholarships, Grants and Loans for Undergraduates* will give you a good idea of the impressive variety and quantity of funds that are available. Other very helpful books are listed in Appendix B and Appendix D, Section 4.

AID FOR FAMILIES WITH DEPENDENT CHILDREN
(A.F.D.C. or Welfare)

Welfare recipients often report that it is a confusing and harrowing experience to be a student. If you attend school full-time, you do not qualify for a work registration exemption. Welfare recipients are only supposed to attend school part-time.

One returning student was in her final year of nursing school when her youngest turned six, and the welfare authorities insisted that she stop school and go to work. She finally had herself declared mentally incompetent, thus qualifying herself for an exemption that allowed her to stay on welfare and finish school.

Another problem is that there is a lot of rigamarole about the blend between welfare money and financial aid. For example, welfare does not deduct federally funded financial aid but can sometimes deduct other financial aid sources, such as privately funded scholarships.

On a more positive note: if you are on welfare, you are probably eligible for Federal Day Care Funds. Your caseworker may not be aware of this, so be sure to bring it up.

If you are on A.F.D.C. and plan to return to school, or if returning to school will mean going on welfare, the best thing to do is to talk with other welfare students to be sure you know the ropes *before* discussing it with a caseworker. Welfare students are usually able to find acceptable and legitimate ways of avoiding the major conflicts, and you can profit from their experience.

EMPLOYER SUBSIDIES

According to the College Board's useful guide, *Paying For Your Education: A Guide for Adult Learners*, employers have more than $10 billion available in educational funds each year, but only a small fraction of these funds are actually used. It is certainly possible that your employer, or your husband's, might allocate funds for higher education. The federal government, for example, is generous about subsidizing the education of its employees. Many universities also encourage their employees to take courses. You might keep both these employers in mind if you are thinking about changing jobs or are looking for work.

Quite a few private companies, both big and small, are willing to reimburse you for some of your educational expenses if you can convince them that the expense will prove beneficial to them. If you are currently employed, do some homework on how a return to school can benefit your employer.

If you or your husband is a member of a union, be sure to find out whether it would be willing to subsidize your education. The degree you are pursuing does not have to be related to the interests of the union—one returning student who is getting a master's degree in reading and learning disabilities is being subsidized by her husband's electrical union.

OTHER APPROACHES

1. *Personal savings and loans.* Take a deep breath and then delve into personal savings, take out a loan, or ask someone close to you for one. If you are returning to school in order to pursue a career, you should have no trouble justifying the expense as a sound investment. A Colorado woman who received her master's degree in urban planning was astounded that she could pay her entire tuition bill for graduate school with her first two-week paycheck. Another student, age 64, was offered financing by her 28-year-old son.

Even if you are ineligible for any of the loans that have already been described, you might be able to take out a loan from your own bank. The interest rates will be higher than for the other loans, but it is still an investment in your future.

2. *Get a part-time or summer job.* Jobs found through want ads often pay more than the ones that are listed through the student employment office. Keep in mind that there are jobs—waitress, nurse's aid, or telephone operator, for example—that require round-the-clock shifts and thus could fit a student's schedule.

3. *Veterans' benefits.* If anyone in your family is or was a veteran, check with the campus V.A. office to see if you are eligible for educational benefits.

4. *Take courses at a community college.* You can often take basic or required courses at a community college, where they are free or a lot less expensive than at a four-year institution.

5. *Try the College Level Examination Program.* You can get college credit without going to classes by participating in the CLEP. See Chapter 18 on other access routes to earning a degree. More than 2,000 educational institutions are now willing to grant credit based on your results on these national exams which are given monthly. For a free copy of "Moving Ahead with CLEP," write to CLEP, CN6600, Princeton, NJ 08541.

6. *Food stamps.* This form of financial assistance is available to far more college students than are aware of it. If you cook your own meals or share cooking responsibilities with other members of your household, you may be eligible, depending on your combined household income. It would mean buying food stamps each month at a discount, and thus increasing your purchasing power. To find out how to apply, talk to the campus financial aid office or the Welfare Department's Food Stamp Office in your city.

7. *Inexpensive or subsidized child care.* Form a babysitting co-

op or exchange babysitting services with one other student. Many child-care agencies have sliding scales which students can afford. State agencies often subsidize your child's care completely if you can demonstrate a need. For more details, see Chapter 15 on child care.

8. *Buy used books.* Textbooks can cost you an incredible amount of money. You can sometimes buy them used or borrow them from the library.

John Bear's *Finding Money For College* comes up with an amazing array of unusual and common-sense ways to find or save money for college. *Paying For Your Education: A Guide for Adult Learners* is another excellent resource. Be sure to consult these useful books.

WHAT WILL IT COST?

According to *The College Cost Book,* for commuting students at public four-year colleges across the nation, the average cost of tuition and fees for the academic year 1985–86 was $1,242 for a nine-month school year. At privately supported colleges and universities, the average for tuition and fees over the same period came to $5,418! Attending college during the academic year 1985–86 cost students an average of 7 percent more than in 1984–85.

This may sound discouraging. But remember that financial aid is available, even at the most prestigious of privately run colleges. At Harvard, for example, where the tuition was $11,340 in 1985, 67 percent of the students that year qualified for at least some financial aid.

What follows is a sampling of four-year schools, both public and private; their tuition for in-state and out-of-state residents; the number of students who applied in 1985 and the number who were actually accepted; the number of students who were judged by the school to have need of financial aid; the number who were offered at least some aid; the number who were offered the full amount that they needed; and the financial aid application deadline. There are several things worth noting as you look at the table on pp. 142–143.

1. The cost of these schools varies beyond belief. A bachelor's degree in English can cost you $2,736 (for four years of tuition) at one of the public schools or $44,000 at a private one. The cost varies not only from public to private school, but among the various schools in the same category. Don't assume that a school is too expensive until you have actually checked it out.

2. If you live across the state border from a good public university or state college, you might seriously consider moving, since there are considerable savings involved if you are an in-state resident. First, however, you should check out the residency requirements because some states require you to reside in-state for a minimum of a year.

3. There is *no* way for you to tell what your chances are of being admitted to a school if you just know how many students got in. You also have to know how many students applied! One school accepted all but 41 of its 2,136 applicants, while another rejected 9,721 of the 12,035 students who wanted to go there.

4. The number of students who receive financial aid varies from college to college, and you should make no generalizations until you have checked that particular college. Find out how many of these students were judged in need of financial assistance by the school, and how many received some or all of the assistance they needed. Don't pass by a school as too expensive until you explore these particular figures.

5. Each school has its own deadlines for filing the financial aid forms. If you are applying to several schools, be sure to keep careful records of deadline dates so that you don't pass them by. See the section at the end of the previous chapter about creating a checklist.

The information for the table on the next two pages was taken from the 1985–86 edition of *The College Handbook*, put out by the College Entrance Examination Board in New York. Published annually, it consists of over 1,800 pages, and covers over 2,800 colleges and universities.

INFORMATION IN THE APPENDIX

Appendix B is a selected listing of financial resources specifically for women students. Many of the scholarships, grants, and loans now available are aimed directly at students over the age of 25. Appendix D, Section 4, lists general handbooks and directories that are useful in tracking down financial aid.

INSTITUTION PUBLICLY SUPPORTED	TUITION & FEES*	APPLYING & ACCEPTED FRESHMEN 1984**	ACCEPTED & NEEDING FINANCIAL AID***	APPLICATION DEADLINE, AID
U. of Central Arkansas at Conway	$900	2,136	980	April 15
	$1,750	2,095(98%)	850(87%)	priority
Humboldt State U., Ca.	$684	1,600	200	March 1
	$4,464	922(62%)	176(88%)	priority
U. of California at Los Angeles (UCLA)	$1,290	8,143	1,866 1,866(100%)	February 11
	$5,106	5,782(71%)	1,800(96%)	
U. of Colorado at Boulder	$1,453	9,164	1,420	March 1
	$5,635	7,321(80%)	1,264(89%)	priority
Southern Connecticut State College	$1,088	5,943	1,100 900(82%)	March 15
	$2,558	4,206(71%)	230(21%)	
U. of Florida	$910	10,579	1,100	March 1
	$2,440	6,349(60%)	700(64%)	priority
U. of Georgia	$1,560	7,510	752	April 15
	$4,104	5,440(72%)	708(94%)	priority
Boise State U., ID	$1,044	2,950	875	March 1
	$2,944	2,800(95%)	800(91%)	priority
Winona State U., MN	$1,610	1,800	700 700(100%)	April 15
	$2,784	1,700(94%)	700(100%)	priority
Montclair State College, NJ	$1,340	6,818	980 680(70%)	March 15
	$1,940	3,475(51%)	0(0%)	priority
State U. of NY at Binghamton	$1,500	11,627	975	April 1
	$3,350	6,584(57%)	975(100%)	priority
Ohio State U. at Columbus	$1,641	14,760	4,800 4,000(83%)	March 1
	$4,251	13,820(94%)	400(80%)	priority
U. of Texas at Austin	$705	13,448	2,000	March 1
	$3,945	9,347(70%)	1,750(88%)	priority

INSTITUTION PUBLICLY SUPPORTED	TUITION & FEES*	APPLYING & ACCEPTED FRESHMEN 1984**	ACCEPTED & NEEDING FINANCIAL AID***	APPLICATION DEADLINE, AID
U. of Virginia	$2,036	12,070	1,400	March 1
	$4,886	4,580(38%)	1,400(100%)	
U. of Wisconsin at Madison	$1,279	12,580	1,270	March 15
	$4,191	10,383(83%)	1,140(90%)	priority
PRIVATELY SUPPORTED				
U. of Chicago, IL	$9,906	4,301	1,254	January 15
		1,926(45%)	1,254(100%)	
Mass. Institute of Technology, MA	$11,000	5,960	928	January 9
		1,820(31%)	928(100%)	
New England College, NH	$7,110	1,010 968(96%)	266 266(100%) 218(81%)	April 1 priority
U. of Pennsylvania	$10,400	11,603 4,671(40%)	1,866 1,866(100%) 1,866(100%)	January 1
Reed College, OR	$9,000	798 666(83%)	252 236(94%)	March 1
Smith College, MA	$9,990	2,160 1,284(59%)	502 502(100%) 502(100%)	February 1
Tulane U., LA	$9,080	5,373 3,976(74%)	1,200 1,200(100%)	March 1
Yale U., CT	$10,520	12,035 2,314(19%)	970 970(100%) 970(100%)	January 15

* *Top figure is in-state tuition and bottom figure is out-of state.*
** *Top figure is number who applied; bottom figure is number accepted and percentage of those who applied.*
*** *Top figure is number judged to have need of financial aid; middle figure is number offered at least some financial assistance and percentage of number in need; bottom figure is number offered full amount needed and percentage of number in need.*

Chapter 14

Other Factors to Consider

FINDING A GOOD PROGRAM IN YOUR
FIELD OF INTEREST

If you have a specific major or a definite career in mind, it is important to be sure that the school of your choice has a good department in your field of interest. Being sure about this may call for extensive investigation beforehand. Will the courses teach you what you want and need to know? What kind of reputation does the department have? How well do its graduates do when it comes to looking for work? Do the jobs that they get sound appealing to you? There are ways of arriving at some preliminary answers to these questions before you make your final decision about which school to attend. Here are some clues:

   1. People like to talk about their jobs. For example, if you are considering a social service career, visit as many people as possible who have jobs in this field. Talk with the head of a family planning clinic, the director of a recreational program for the elderly, a coordinator at a juvenile center, a welfare worker, and so on. Ask these people how they got their jobs and what kind of training they think is necessary. Ask them especially what they know about the social services or welfare departments at whatever schools you are considering. Do they know people in the field who were educated

there? What kind of reputation does the faculty have? Comments such as "Our best employees come from that department," or "I haven't found anyone yet who knows anything about social welfare coming out of that place," are pretty important clues. See if you can get the names of people they know who received their degrees from these schools, and talk with them about the department. This kind of extensive research can be done for any area of interest you might be considering.

2. Talk with current students in the department. What do *they* know about how recent graduates are doing in the job market? What are the department's strong points? What are its weak points? Suppose you were to major in library science, and your special interest is libraries for children. If the department you are considering has an "adequate" curriculum but places *no* importance on children's literature, you're probably in the wrong place.

3. The campus placement office is another good resource. It may publish the results of a survey concerning what recent graduates are doing in the way of work. Are the graduates working in jobs related to their major? If 80 percent of the graduates are employed, that looks impressive. If 50 percent of them are working as dishwashers, that should give you pause.

4. Credentials certainly aren't everything, but in the college catalog there is probably a section on the educational background of the faculty. What kinds of credentials do the faculty members in your department have? The department itself may draw up a more elaborate sketch of its faculty, so ask the departmental secretary if such a thing exists. Try to find out whether faculty members are involved with community-related activities and research events outside of the school. If many of the department's faculty members are called in as consultants within the community or are being published in academic journals, this is a good sign.

5. Make an appointment to talk with the chairperson of the department. He or she will be impressed by your serious intentions. Ask him or her what becomes of recent graduates and which faculty members are particularly involved with your field of interest.

Feeling good about your department may not be crucial. If you have a definite career in mind, and all you need is the credential, you may want to pick the *easiest* route. But considering the close association you will have with faculty and students for however long it will be, it certainly *helps* if you can have confidence in your department and its mentors.

FINDING A SCHOOL THAT *FEELS* RIGHT

If you've done your research well, your decision about whether a school is right for you should be pretty clear-cut. But one important set of questions you have to ask in selecting a school is a lot more nebulous and can't be answered by doing the traditional research. Will I feel comfortable here? School will consume a great deal of your time, and if you feel ill at ease on the campus you choose, this would really be unfortunate.

Obviously, the best way to get the feel of a school is to spend some time there. Take an organized tour for starters, and go back on your own to all the places that looked interesting. You can probably arrange to sit in on some courses through the admissions office or the department of your choice. It would be better to do this toward the beginning of the semester rather than at the end, when the material being covered will be harder for you to understand.

Spend some time in the student union and any other popular gathering places you can find. See if there is a reentry or continuing education office, and pay it a visit. Wander around the library. Browse through the bookstore. Talk to as many students as you can, particularly those in your field of interest.

What kind of impression does the college *want* to give? You can figure this out by carefully studying the annual catalog. The college newspaper is also an excellent resource, so try to read at least several copies of that.

In order to gather as much information as you possibly can, you would be wise to develop a list of intangibles that you should be sure to explore.

You want to find out what the students are like. Do they seem, in general, serious? Friendly? Bored? Relaxed? Enthusiastic? Rowdy? Are there other returning students? Does the student population seem diversified? As you wander around, do the students make you feel like an outsider? Do you think you could blend in? What do the students think of this school?

You will want to explore what the campus environment is like. Would this be a pleasant place to spend your time? How much cultural activity is there? Are there good places to have lunch or coffee? Are there areas conducive to studying? Does the campus feel safe? Does the campus look as though people there care about it? Is it neat and attractive? Does it feel good to be in this rural/urban setting?

You will want to pay particular attention to the department that interests you. Is there a group spirit among the students, or is the atmosphere businesslike? Which would you prefer—do you want to get involved with other students or just with the course work? Do the students look alert and enthusiastic? Are there other students your age in this department? Do you feel welcome? Do the faculty members seem friendly, accessible, involved with their students? Are the classes large or small? How do you feel about large/small classes? Do the classroom procedures seem comfortable or conducive to learning?

Spend some time thinking about the intangibles. You may want to get a degree at a school even if it *doesn't* "feel right" to you because getting past the other hurdles is far more crucial to you. By taking a reading of the atmosphere beforehand, however, you will be in for far fewer unpleasant surprises once your student role actually begins.

KNOWING YOUR PRIORITIES

As a returning student, you will be continuously called on to know what your priorities are. If you have your heart set on studying medieval history and the university one or even four hours away has the absolutely best department around, and it looks as though you can get in and qualify for financial aid, perhaps having to commute is not too high a price to pay. But maybe it is. How do you feel about this much time away from your family and other responsibilities? How do you feel about settling for less than the best medieval history department, knowing that the one you want is just out of reach? These are not easy questions to answer. Don't *immediately* reject a school because it is "just out of reach." In the same way, don't take on a school four hours away without coming to grips with the problems it will create.

TIPS ON COMMUTING

Returning students have adapted in miraculous ways to the problems of getting to and from a school that is just too far away. They have arranged their classes on two consecutive days and spent the night near the college. They have created car pools—making the commute a lot more economical and enjoyable. They have decided that time spent on the road by themselves is a luxury for someone who is constantly involved with relating to people. They have bought cassette tape recorders and listened to their favorite music and learned foreign languages. And they have moved their entire troupe closer to school.

Living within a 20-minute commute from school is a blessing to students who have other responsibilities in their lives. Distance is a subjective matter—even if you are only 10 minutes from school, if it feels like light-years before you even start, beware. The days may become all too frequent when *two* trips to school are necessary, and you and/or your car may start to rebel.

If you will be attending classes on a full-time basis, get your transportation plans ironed out beforehand. Make sure your car is in good running order or that your car pool is foolproof or that the public transportation system is available. There is nothing more frustrating than wasting valuable study and class time trying to figure out how you're going to get home.

REGISTRATION—ADVICE FROM WOMEN WHO WENT THROUGH IT

• Don't be intimidated by the officials at registration! Just because someone sits behind a desk doesn't make a god out of them. They are performing a function, and they would be out of a job unless you as a student came to them. It takes *two* people to make the situation work. That person behind the desk needs you as much as you need them! If you're not willing to be the student, they have no role either, so use them!

• I was accompanied through registration the first time by a close friend, and it helped so much. Really try to find someone to go through it with you! Make contact with the school and see if there is an office that might have students volunteering to help register. And spend time with someone who can look at your schedule and tell you if you're taking what you need to take.

• You figure out registration from watching other people. Just keep asking questions and you'll feel comfortable with it in a semester or two.

• It wasn't all that much of a problem to register. I made it into more than it actually was. It's just that the younger students come through their high schools and are cued right along, step by step. If you're older, you have to do it on your own, so you feel at a disadvantage. Figure out the specific questions that need answering and then find the right person to ask.

• When you register for classes, unless you have to take a class because it's required, the most helpful thing is to find people who have taken these classes and get their opinion of the professors. I've come to realize that the professor who's teaching the class is often much more important than what he's actually teaching.

• If you're worried about getting into the classes that you want, take a counseling or orientation class, and they'll give you hints about it. I was told that if I really wanted to get into the art classes, all I had to do was switch my major to art, and the classes would open up.

• If a class is closed out, don't give up until you have personally asked the professor for special permission to take his or her class. It's worked a lot for me. When the instructor sees how serious you are about the class, you get in.

• You will be amazed by how many younger students drop classes just a few weeks after the semester begins. Attend class even if you're not on the rolls. Hand in the homework assignments. Once the ranks begin to diminish, then ask the teacher if you can add the class. It works for me!

• The secret is if you scream loud enough and long enough, someone will hear you and either cart you away or say "Okay, don't carry on. We'll get you into this class."

• Registration was amusing and overwhelming at the same time. I couldn't believe what you had to go through to register. Stick with it. You'll get used to it. Ask for help, and you'll get it.

• After being out of school 38 years, I was very apprehensive about speaking to the dean of admissions. As it turned out, he was very understanding and encouraging. He carefully explained the registration process to me, so that was no problem either.

• I requested special permission to get requirements waived and to take courses out of sequence. You can do it if you approach it properly.

• They simply lost my transcripts! Even reapplying to the same school you went to 10 years ago can be a mess. My papers were under my maiden name all along. One of my old professors finally had to go down to see what was going on, and they found all the necessary papers. It was a purely mechanical foul-up, but it could have held me back.

• I had horrible memories of the whole registration scene left over from 30 years ago—of being shuffled and pushed around. It turned out that it was far worse in my mind than it was in reality. Schools have made it a lot easier now.

SCHEDULING—A MAJOR HURDLE

If you plan to go to school part-time, or if you can only attend at certain hours, these considerations will be high on your list of things to check out when you consider a school.

If classes are scheduled for times when you can take them, you should also look into the current semester's schedule of classes to see if courses in your own major are well represented during your available time slots. If there is the least bit of doubt about whether the courses you'll need will be available, make an appointment to see the head of the department. Ask him or her if there will be any trouble about getting your degree, given your time limitations. If you are planning to go to school part-time, you might also ask the department chairperson how he or she feels about part-time students majoring in that field. If it is a highly specialized major and only a small number of students are involved each year, you may meet with some resistance because you will not be part of the cohesive group.

It is not uncommon for some classes to be offered only every other year or during particular quarters each year. It is essential for you to know the class-scheduling quirks of your department if you have only special times that you can take classes. Probably the departmental secretaries are most aware of the mechanics of class scheduling, so be sure to talk with them about this. Departments have their class schedules done far enough in advance to have them printed up, so check well ahead. You don't want to wind up unable to graduate because one of the necessary courses isn't being offered your last semester.

Generally speaking, the larger public colleges and universities hold evening classes more often than the small private colleges. And it is more likely that you can attend a larger school part-time, although the private schools are now admitting part-time students as well. One Ivy League school invited any high school graduate to apply to take courses part-time—to the tune of $950 per course! Other private schools are *a lot* more reasonable, however.

SCHEDULING—SOME COMMENTS FROM WOMEN WHO WENT THROUGH IT

Going to school and working full-time meant I had to postpone some courses for many semesters. Some courses I missed out on completely. Talk with your professors and ask them to offer the classes at times that are better for working people. Mine were surprisingly receptive.

In order to give myself some time off, I took all my classes on one day. I really don't recommend it. By 5:30, I was bowlegged, cross-eyed, and cranky.

Class scheduling for me was completely determined by my children's school hours. I would get the catalog and circle the classes that interested me between 10:00 and 3:00. My major was actually determined by my scheduling needs! A lot of upper-division English courses were offered at night when I wasn't free. Sociology classes met at better times, so I chose it as a major.

IS THERE DISCRIMINATION?

The women interviewed for this book were asked to rank the difficulties they encountered along the reentry route. Only 7 percent mentioned discrimination against women, and these were all enrolled or hoping to enroll in graduate school. According to statistics from the American Council on Education, as recently as the school year 1969–70, only 13.3 percent of the doctorates awarded in this country went to women—a percentage that had actually *declined* since 1920! However, by 1983, the number of women earning Ph.Ds had risen dramatically to 34 percent. It is also reassuring to know that by 1982, over half of the bachelor's and master's degrees were awarded to women. In fact, more women than men attend college today. This is a sharp turnaround from as recently as 1970, when there were 1.4 million more men than women on college campuses.

One reason for the imbalance in the number of men and women working toward doctorate degrees is sex-role socialization. This inhibits the aspirations of women from the time they are children and leads to many forms of conscious or unconscious discrimination. For example, in one state that subsidizes child care for needy students at state colleges, legislation was actually being considered that would deprive graduate students of this service. Would male graduate students be as hard hit as female graduate students if this kind of law were passed? In fact, almost a *third* of the children who were being cared for on the campuses of this particular state college system came from families without fathers in the home! Happily, the legislation did not pass.

Another example is the woman whose husband was in law school, and who was turned down for financial aid in order to enter law school herself. She was told that she could, after all, wait for three years, and then her husband could support her. Other women applying for graduate school while their husbands were enrolled received the same answer. One woman who applied for graduate school was lucky enough to know someone on the admissions committee, who told her privately that there had been a decision not to admit her because she had said that she intended to work while she was studying for her degree. She knew that men had been accepted into the program who likewise planned to hold full-time jobs at the same time. She wrote a letter to the committee saying that she had reconsidered her plans, and would not be working after all. A few weeks later she received a letter notifying her that she had been accepted.

On the undergraduate level, it is unlikely that you will run into a blatant case of sex discrimination. If you do, you should be aware that most campuses now have an affirmative action officer to advise anyone with a grievance. Such cases should also be brought to the attention of the office dealing with reentry students, or to the campus ombudsman whose job is to mediate disputes.

Despite all the good news, it would be incorrect to say that you will not run up against the subtler forms of discrimination. Anyone who has personally encountered this kind of bias knows how extremely difficult it is to be definite about it. As often as not, you wind up feeling that it is *you* who did something wrong. The bias may be so commonplace that you accept it without question.

If you have been feeling enthusiastic about your new role as a student, and then suddenly you're aware that the wind has been taken out of your sails, you should think carefully over what might have caused it. Have women been the subject of a "joke" in one of your classes? Has some professor asked why you're going to the trouble of getting a degree when you don't have to work? Such things can drain away precious motivation.

In 1969 a group of women students at the University of Chicago collected statements illustrating their contention that "some of our professors have different expectations about our performance than about the performance of male graduate students—expectations based not on our ability as individuals but on the fact that we are women." Here are some of the comments they heard or overheard:

"Any girl who gets this far has got to be a kook."

"The admissions committee didn't do their job. There isn't one good-looking girl in the entering class."

"You have no business looking for a job with a child that age."

"You're so cute. I can't see you as a professor of anything."

Most of the professors who make such statements are not aware of being discriminatory. But they do tend to discourage graduate students who already have enough social pressures to contend with. If you're feeling discouraged or undervalued, you should stop and think about whether you've been hearing things of this kind, and letting them affect you.

One of the good things about going back to college now is that there's an antidote to many of the negative attitudes toward women: becoming involved with a supportive group of people. Many campuses have a reentry or women's center, where you can have professional counseling or join a rap or discussion group that can help by sharing the burden. Departments of women's studies offer a wealth of courses that rely on small discussion groups as an aid to learning. A course on the psychology of women, if it's available, can be a help in coping with the attitudes of those around you. You will learn there that a lot of your own discouragement is culturally produced and can be *unlearned.* A list of articles and books on sex-role socialization and discrimination against women in the academic world is given in Appendix E, Section 7.

WATCH OUT FOR DISCRIMINATION IN FINANCIAL AID

Returning students do report that they have experienced discrimination either because they are older or because they are married. One woman who was in college at the same time as her husband and several of their children was told by a financial aid officer that if there were younger students who needed financial aid, they would get it before she did. The rationale was that she had enrolled in school only because she "thought it would be a nice thing to do." "I accepted that," commented the student, who went on to receive a B.A. in sociology, "but now I know I deserved financial aid as much as anyone else did."

Many women whose spouses are in school meet with resistance when it comes to seeking additional funds for themselves.

You might find that a university will want you to hold off on your education until your husband has finished his.

How do you approach an obvious example of discrimination, when there never seems to be enough time to do everything that you already have to do? At least talk with the person in charge of the financial aid office if you encounter resistance that seems inequitable.

QUESTIONS YOU'LL NEED TO ASK

The following questions are some of the ones you should keep in mind as you decide whether or not a particular school is right for you. Which other questions do you need to add to this list?

Am I eligible for admissions?—the first hurdle
Do I have the necessary prerequisites?
Is there a formal application and fee?
Are there other forms required?
Does the college require the A.C.T./S.A.T.? Achievement tests? Any other tests?
What is the average combined score on the A.C.T./S.A.T. for this year's freshmen?
Are my high school/college transcripts needed?
Is an interview with the admissions officer recommended?
How many students apply here and how many get accepted?
Is credit given for life experience?
Are there any special admissions plans for reentry students?
Are students only admitted for the fall quarter?
What is the deadline for application?
When will I find out if I've been accepted?

Can I afford this school?—the second hurdle
How much does it cost to go to school here?
Is there a residency requirement to qualify for the low tuition?
What kinds of financial aid are available?
What percentage of the students are receiving financial aid?
What is the average amount of financial aid given?
Am I aware of all the financial aid options? (Read Chapter 13.)
When is the financial aid application deadline?

Is this school conveniently located?—the third hurdle
Do I need to arrange a car pool, buy a new car, get my car fixed, or check out public transportation?

Is there a good program in my field of interest?—the fourth hurdle
   Are there courses that will teach me what I want and need to know?
   Do the courses look interesting?
   Does this department have a good reputation?
   What kinds of jobs do the graduates from this department get? Are the jobs related to the major?
   What do potential employers, alumni, current students say about this department?
   Has a survey been done on what jobs the graduates have gotten?
   Do the faculty members have good credentials? Are they involved with research? As consultants to the community?
   What is the student/teacher ratio?

Am I available when classes are scheduled?—the fifth hurdle
   Does this school allow part-time students?
   How does the head of the department I'm considering feel about part-time students?
   Even though classes are scheduled when I'm available, does this mean that classes in *my* major are well represented then?
   Are the required courses offered when I can take them?
   Which classes are offered every other year? Only once a year?
   What kinds of scheduling quirks does this department have?

Do I feel comfortable here?—the sixth hurdle
   What kind of impression do I get from the catalog? The student newspaper?
   What are the students like? Do they look glad to be here? Troubled? Bored? Enthusiastic? Alert? Am I made to feel like an outsider?
   Is there a reentry office? Does the school seem receptive to reentry students? Do I see many reentry students here?
   Is this a pleasant place to be? Are the grounds neat? Safe?
   Are there good places to have lunch? Coffee? For study?
   Is there a group spirit in the department I'm considering?
   Do the students in the department look approachable? Enthusiastic? Bored? Friendly?
   Are there other students my age in the department I'm considering?
   Am I made to feel welcome by students, staff, faculty in the department I'm considering?

Is the faculty friendly? Involved with the students? Accessible?

Are classes large or small? Does the classroom experience seem comfortable?

Some additions for junior college applicants:

Are courses available in my field of interest?

Are there enough courses to keep me busy and earning transferable credits while I earn an A.A.?

What are the *university* policies about transfering units?

What percentage of the student body transfer to four-year schools?

What percentage of the students in my major transfer to four-year schools?

If in a career-oriented course—What kinds of jobs have the graduates of my department gotten? Is it really necessary to get this degree in order to find a job in my field?

Some additions for graduate school applicants:

Do I have to take the G.R.E.?

Can I fulfill prerequisites while I'm already taking graduate courses?

How many letters of recommendation are needed?

Is a statement of purpose required?

Do I need to submit a portfolio? Have an audition?

Whom do I talk to about financial aid?

Is there anyone at my alma mater who can give me some advice?

Would a degree in a different subject get me to the same goal or job?

Don't forget to ask—

Are there child-care facilities on campus? How are they? Can I afford them? How and when do you register?

Are counselors/academic advisers readily available?

Are there remedial or refresher courses? Tutors? Courses in self-development?

Is the school accredited by one of the regional associations of colleges and universities?

Chapter 15

Child Care

For any mother who goes back to school, finding child care is sure to be a major anxiety. Since this is so, mothers who have been through the process of finding it are the best source of information. Seek out mothers who have been back in school for a while and who have children about the same age as yours. If there is ever a problem that a harried student mother would take the time to discuss with you, it would be this one about quality care. If you don't know any returning students, it would not be hard to track them down. On campus, try the reentry and continuing education offices, the women's studies department, and the secretary in the department of your field of interest. Your children, if they are of school age, are almost sure to have classmates whose mothers are students.

The whole point is to find a situation for your child that frees you from worry as much as possible. It is hard to become involved in your school-related activities if you are continually uneasy about your child's well-being. If you begin by thinking about your own child's particular needs, and spend some time exploring possible arrangements, you should be able to find an environment that your child will enjoy and that will set your own mind at rest.

As a first step, spend some time considering whether you'd prefer to have your child in a one-to-one situation, in a structured learning environment, or as part of an extended family.

These alternatives may all be possible in your community. Making up your mind about just what kind of situation you want can eliminate a lot of steps right at the beginning. For instance, if you are adamant about placing your child in a one-to-one situation, preschools and day-care centers are eliminated right away.

Child-care referral service centers are becoming more common throughout this country. You should find out whether there is one in your community. Usually such a center can provide you with a listing of available child-care services. There are often counselors to help you make a decision about what type of service would be most suitable, and funds are sometimes available to help mothers who are trying to pursue a career or education.

BABYSITTERS

Even though day-care centers and preschools are springing up at an amazing rate, as recently as 1982 fewer than 15 percent of the children under age five of full-time working mothers were involved in group care. The rest were being taken care of by friends, relatives, or babysitters.

If it is important to you to have your child in a one-to-one relationship, and if you are going to feel most comfortable knowing that your child is being cared for at home, a babysitter is probably the best solution to the problem. It will certainly cut down on a lot of transportation headaches, especially if you have more than one child who will need to be rounded up. Another advantage of having a babysitter come into your home is that you may find one who will agree to start dinner or do other household tasks. This would free you to give some undivided attention to your children when you get home.

What are the disadvantages? Good sitters are usually very expensive or very hard to find. Also, if your sitter gets sick or quits, you will find yourself in a terrible jam. And it means that you will have to be solely responsible for interviewing and assessing the prospective sitter, and this is not an easy job.

Before you interview anyone, try to think very carefully about the kind of person you hope to find, and the kind of arrangement best suited to your child's needs. If you like the idea of having your child feel that he or she is part of an extended family, it's worth remembering that many sitters are themselves mothers who would prefer to take a child into their own home. Do you want someone to be just in your home to make sure all is well, or do you want someone who will be giving actively to your child? Either arrangement can have its advantages. But don't consider a grandmotherly type if you're expecting someone who will take your child on long, arduous hikes after school!

As you think about what kind of person and arrangement you want, write down some of the qualities you will be looking for in the people you interview, and refer to notes while you are in the process of interviewing. You should also write down beforehand all the questions you will be asking. After the interview has ended, jot down the answers and your impressions.

Be sure to ask each person about his or her babysitting experience and get the names of people you can call as references. Find out what kind of activities each person enjoys doing in the company of children. You may find that his or her idea of a great afternoon is reading comic books together. If the sight of a comic book puts knots in your stomach, this is probably not the person you want.

You owe it to the potential babysitter, to your child, and to yourself to explain as thoroughly as possible what *you* expect in the way of activities and discipline. If you want your child to be read to, or taken on walks, or encouraged to work with clay, be sure to make this clear. If you never spank your child, or if you punish him or her only after three warnings have been given, that is essential information for a potential sitter.

It is just as important to talk about what you do *not* want to be happening while you are away. How do you feel about a babysitter having friends over? Making telephone calls? Watching TV? Smoking? Taking your child out without consulting you first? All of this needs to be settled beforehand.

One of the best places to find a babysitter, if no child-care referral service center is available, is the campus student employment center. More than likely it will have a list of students who are interested in babysitting, complete with their schedules, where they live, and whether or not they need transportation. Many students find that they can work out an exchange of services with other student/mothers. This is an excellent arrangement, especially if you are strapped for funds. Sororities and high schools also often have the names of students looking for babysitting jobs. Sitters often advertise in newspapers and place notices on bulletin boards in grocery stores and laundromats.

PUBLIC AND PRIVATE DAY-CARE CENTERS AND PRESCHOOLS

If you want your child to be in a learning situation and exposed to a wide assortment of children and adults, a day-care center or preschool could be an ideal choice.

You are really in luck if the college you're attending has a preschool or day-care center. The quality of care at these centers is usually good; but since it can range from fantastic to no more than adequate, check out the place first. The chances are that you will be delighted by what you see—enthusiastic teachers with a genuine interest in children, a clean, attractive, and safe location, and up-to-date toys and equipment which are conducive to learning.

One reason why these centers provide such good care is that they are strictly regulated by their major source of funding—in many instances, the state. In addition, there are usually some parents on the board of trustees, giving you a chance to have your say on the kind of care the center provides.

If the school you plan to attend does not have child-care facilities, visit other schools in the area; your child is very likely to be eligible there even if you are not enrolled.

One great advantage of having your child in a day-care center or preschool is that the staff have to be on their toes in order to pass the scrutiny of the funding source. Also, since there is a *group* of teachers, help is always available for handling difficult children. When a babysitter gets up on the wrong side of the bed, there is usually no one there to help her through the day. But if a teacher is having a bad day, she has a good backup team to help share the load. And if one teacher at the day-care center gets sick, your child can still attend; but if a single babysitter or caretaker gets sick, you will be left in the lurch.

The fees charged by public day-care centers are usually on a sliding scale. If you have limited means, you may be able to get the entire cost of your child's care subsidized. Unfortunately, having a moderate income *can* work against you at a public center—your child may be given a low priority because you supposedly can afford more expensive child care. And, as it turns out, private centers are often prohibitively expensive. Since hours at both public and private centers are usually geared more toward working mothers than toward students, few of them remain open during the evening when you might have classes.

Each center will have its own philosophy of child care, and it will usually be fairly obvious when you visit. One returning student remembers visiting two centers in one afternoon. At the first, all five teachers were huddled in the kitchen while chaos reigned elsewhere. At the second, the director was saying "No" to every child with whom she came into contact. It was immediately apparent to the student that she would not feel comfortable about leaving her children at either of these places.

Before you begin to explore day-care centers, take some time to decide what are the most important things for you to observe at each one. Make a list of these, and jot down your impressions as soon as possible after leaving each place. Here are some of the items you might want to have on your list:

- Do the children seem to like the teachers?
- Do the teachers seem to like the children?
- Is the program well planned?
- Do you feel welcome?
- Does the center seem safe?
- What kind of food is served?

Think about the kind of environment you want your child to be in—emotionally, physically, socially, and academically. What kinds of feelings do you get from each center in these realms?

Several good publications on how to assess child-care centers and preschools are listed in Appendix D, Section 6. One of the handiest is *Some Ways of Distinguishing a Good Early Childhood Program*. This free pamphlet includes the kinds of questions you will want answered when exploring programs for your child. To receive this pamphlet, send a self-addressed stamped envelope to National Association for the Education of Young Children, 1834 Connecticut Avenue NW, Washington, DC 20009.

FAMILY DAY-CARE HOMES

Family day-care homes range from marvelous to miserable, depending entirely on the caretaker and the kind of environment that is provided. The state is responsible for assessing these homes.

However, licensing does not guarantee that the home will satisfy your child's particular needs.

There are some strong advantages to having your child in a family day-care home. It means that your child will be in a home environment and will have other children to play with. Also, unlike the day-care centers and preschools, these homes often have very flexible hours—a fact that may make all the difference in whether you'll be able to attend evening classes or not.

One important disadvantage of family day-care homes is that they don't expose children to the varied activities that are offered at day-care centers and preschools. And, as with babysitters, if the caretaker is ill, you may have to miss class unless you have established a really strong backup system.

It is certainly possible to find a first-rate family day-care home for your child, but to do so will take a lot of telephoning and interviewing in person. In choosing a suitable home, the same advice applies as does for finding a good day-care center: have a clear picture of the kind of care that you want for your child, know what aspects are particularly important to you, and write down your impressions of a few key issues after each interview. (See Appendix E, Section 6a for books and pamphlets that will help you draw up a checklist.) Unlike the public centers, these homes are not generally assessed for the social, emotional, and academic environment they provide. You will have to rely on your own judgment, although you can find out a lot by talking to other parents whose children are being taken care of there.

You can find out about family day-care centers from a child-care referral service center, as well as by talking with any other student and working mothers you may know. The Department of Social Services or the state or county licensing agency will also have a listing of licensed homes. Like babysitters, caretakers often place ads in newspapers and on bulletin boards in grocery stores and laundromats.

PARENT COOPERATIVES AND BABYSITTING POOLS

In some cooperatives, several parents pool child-care responsibilities on a rotating basis. Under such an arrangement, there would be essentially no cost. On a larger scale, as many as 20 parents might get together, hire a main teacher, rent a space, and donate their time and energy on a regular basis. Again, the cost would be minimal.

There are many advantages to forming a co-op, aside from its minimal cost. Most student/parents are very enthusiastic caretakers. In addition, it will appeal to you if you like having firm control over your child's activities. Your child will also be exposed to many different children and adults.

If you take part in a co-op, you must be prepared to spend an enormous amount of your time and effort to keep it going. In addition to caretaker responsibilities, you will be obligated to attend meetings regularly. If you are interested in group dynamics and in exchanging ideas with other parents, the experience can be stimulating and productive. Unfortunately, many student/mothers find that such things take up too much of their time.

If you're interested in the possibility, check with various departmental offices and bulletin boards on campus to see if any other students are trying to form a co-op. Co-op organizers often leave notes on bulletin boards in laundromats, grocery stores, and women's centers.

LIVE-IN SITTERS

If you can afford the price, it is feasible to find a college student who would gladly take on child-care responsibilities in exchange for free rent. This kind of child care allows your child to stay at home, and is obviously a very inexpensive arrangement. Nevertheless, adding a new member to your family is a major step that should be taken cautiously. A potential conflict you should anticipate is whether the student's schedule, which meshed with yours perfectly the first quarter, will do so the following quarter.

If you are a single parent, you might consider sharing a house with another single parent who is a student. Being able to split the child care is often very comforting for everyone, since it gives children more than one person to bounce off of. This kind of situation can work beautifully or miserably, depending on how good your assessment techniques are. Once again, you should have a clear picture in mind of the kind of person you are looking for. Make a list of the traits that you consider most important. Talk with a prospective housemate about the way you like things to be in your home and about the kinds of things that make you uncomfortable—e.g., dirty floors, junk food, leaving all the windows closed at night, or whatever. Discuss the living situations you have both been in. Which ones went smoothly? Why? Which were rocky? Why?

To find someone who might want to share a home, put up notices on bulletin boards in women's centers and in reentry and continuing education offices, and run an ad in the newspaper.

CHANGE YOUR LIFE-STYLE

If you feel that returning to school will mean spending too much time away from your child, but you still want to try it, it may be possible to take your classes when close friends or relatives are available to watch your child, and do all your studying late at night or early in the morning. Your body rhythms may dictate going to sleep at 11:00 P.M., but if your maternal rhythms dictate that you will have peace of mind only if you study with your child asleep in the next room, you will be tired a lot of the time, but you may find that you can manage. You will have to decide how much time you are willing to spend away from your child, and then fit in studying when you can. The way to begin is by taking only a few courses at a time.

CREATE YOUR OWN DAY-CARE CENTER

Do not pass this suggestion by! Creating your own center is not at all an impossible dream. One returning student was concerned about the quality of child care in her county, and she wound up heading a staff of 45 people who incorporated a state-funded child-care council.

Your involvement in setting up a center need not be quite so elaborate. If you can pull together a committed group of people, the process of forming a center is pretty straightforward. Publications are listed in Appendix D, Section 6 that can give you a great deal of basic information.

Band together and apply pressure at your university if there are no child-care facilities there. One university in California created a $10,000 Drop-In Doggie Day-Care Center! If *that's* possible, anything is!

ABOUT YOUR SCHOOL-AGE CHILDREN

Returning students often mention feeling concerned about having their children come home to an empty house, and finding no one there to greet them is something that children often do complain about.

Many schools offer excellent after-school programs. In addition, the Department of Parks and Recreation and your local Y may offer courses on subjects such as pottery, drawing, or swimming that are inexpensive or entirely free.

Though an organizational feat of transportation may be involved, scouting, music lessons, or team sports can certainly keep your children busy and happy. Another mother may be grateful to have your child over for a few hours each afternoon—two school-age children are usually less of a bother than one who is looking for something to do.

Don't let lack of available child care for school-age children deter you from a return to school, because you can usually schedule your classes during the hours that they are in school.

Chapter 16

Developing Good Study Habits

Although returning students are often anxious about how they will do academically, it should be clear from the experiences described in this book that they tend to get better grades than they expected.

If you are still worried about being able to study, you will probably find that there is a learning-skills program at the college or university you plan to enter. Typically, it will consist of a series of workshops—on using the library, on preparing for and taking exams, on term papers, and on improving reading skills. Many returning students find these workshops invaluable, and recommend them highly to anyone who is at all dubious about being able to study well.

If you haven't the time to attend a workshop but feel that you need guidance, you'll find some useful books on developing study skills listed in Appendix D, Section 5. These books will probably be available at your campus library or at the learning skills center. An excellent resource, specifically geared to reentry students, is a 31-page pamphlet called *Academic Skills: A Handbook for Working Adults Returning to School* by Rebecca Thatcher ($2.00 from ILR Press, New York State School of Industrial and Labor Relations, Cornell University, Ithaca, NY 14851-0952). It discusses how to organize an effective study place, participate well in class, take exams, and write papers.

Don't neglect to find yourself a tutor if you are having trouble with a specific subject. The campus learning center will probably be able to recommend a tutor, though the most reliable recommendation is likely to come from a faculty member in the department concerned.

One good way to build confidence in your study skills is to start your reentry slowly. Most universities now offer more self-development courses than they once did. Taking one of these can help you build confidence, learn more about the direction you are taking, and polish up on your study habits. Begin by looking through the catalog and picking one course on a subject that especially interests you.

The following suggestions might make your stay in the academic world more comfortable. Obviously, what works for someone else may not work for you; but the intention is to expose you to some ideas that might help you set up a system of your own.

ESTABLISHING A SPACE AND A TIME FOR STUDY

You would be astounded by the number of women who have tried to study at the kitchen table, and found that it just doesn't work. You will need a special space in your home that is used just for studying, in a room that is neither a family-gathering place nor an access route. You won't need an entire room—an out-of-the-way table that is yours and yours alone should be sufficient.

You will also have to set aside specific times for studying. Because of all your other obligations, it will be far too easy to push your schoolwork completely off your list of things to do unless definite and inviolate time slots have already been arranged.

After you have been in school a few weeks, you should have become aware of how long it takes you to read your assignments and review your notes—information that is essential for a realistic study schedule. If you average two hours to read each assignment for your English class, for example, you will know to allow that much time for studying for that particular class. When you make your study schedule, you will need to be specific about what subject is to be studied when.

Many students treat time as a motivating factor. Suppose, for instance, that you have given yourself a certain amount of time to read an assignment. If your attention starts to wander, divide up the material into smaller allotments of time, so that you have intermediate goals on the way to the long-term one of finishing the whole reading assignment. A short-term goal—"I'll have five pages read in 20 minutes"—really helps to keep you going.

Speaking of motivation, there have to be some payoffs for all the hard work you are doing, and the rewards have to be more immediate than the grade you will receive three weeks after studying for an exam. You will find that the luxury of reading a magazine or telephoning a friend can serve as an impetus for finishing an assignment. A 59-year-old graduate student (who maintained a 3.89 grade-point average) devised this system of rewards: "I decided that for every hour of studying I'd take five minutes to do something just for me—a cup of coffee or a run around the block. Every hour, there needs to be something for you that's fun."

Arrange your study hours at times when you have the best chance of not being interrupted—after the children are asleep, for example. For some women, a method that works well is to study every night for two hours and as much as necessary on Saturdays. Some students find that they get their best studying done by waking up at 3:00 A.M. Judith, a 54-year-old sophomore with a 3.8 G.P.A., says:

> I discovered I don't need much sleep. I can get up at three and read for four hours before breakfast. It's the best time for me to read and study and learn. Of course I'm tired at the end of the day, but I don't care. So I don't watch TV!

Most study guides tell you that you'll have to study two hours for every hour that you are in class. A full load of classes is about 15 hours a week. Thirty hours of study per week is almost certainly much more than you will ever have to do even if you are compulsively conscientious. According to research by David Yarington, freshmen at a university in Ohio averaged 14 hours of studying per week. Two hours a day isn't a whole lot of time to set aside.

When it comes to dividing up your study sessions, you will be most efficient if you spend no more than two hours at a time on a particular subject. It is generally best to start a study session by approaching your hardest subject first, while you are most alert and your motivation is strongest. If you must study when you're exhausted, choose the subjects that are easiest.

Before and after class is a great time to do some quick but important reviewing. If the course involves group discussion, review what you have read before you go to class. If it is mainly a lecture course, review the notes you have just taken immediately after class, annotating them a bit, so that what you wind up with will be coherent when you need it to study for exams.

How much time you need to devote to studying will soon become apparent to you. When it is, work out your schedule, and stick to it.

This is probably a good moment to talk about the wonderful invention of Alexander Graham Bell that drains returning students of their precious time. Stay away from that telephone when you are supposed to be studying! Many older students mention it as a major stumbling block to keeping on their schedule. Don't be reluctant to tell friends and relatives that you're studying. Use telephone calls as a reward for getting an assignment done, not as an excuse for homework that is incomplete.

When all is said and done, you can *still* get good grades even if your life is too busy to set aside a regular time for studying. A 55-year-old mother of five, who had a 3.2 G.P.A. as a returning undergraduate and a 3.75 as a graduate, recalls: "I studied French while I was ironing and stirred the soup while I memorized my lessons."

LEARNING TO TAKE GOOD NOTES

There are two main reasons for taking good notes. One is to help you learn valuable material. The other is so that you will do well on tests. Often the two are not mutually exclusive.

You may be enrolled in classes where what is discussed is not covered by the exams, but this will rarely be the case. You should be able to tell what points are important in your reading assignments by what the professor emphasizes in class. Therefore, good class listening and good note taking are important steps for doing well on exams.

One way of making sure that you are taking good notes *before* you actually have to take an exam is to ask one or two particularly alert-looking students if you can compare your notes with theirs. If theirs make more sense or include more important points than yours do, you'll want to revise your technique of note taking.

Try to find out beforehand from other students how much emphasis a particular professor places on class discussion in making up his exams. One 40-year-old graduate student in New York, who had a G.P.A. of 3.9, regards notes as so crucial that she writes down everything. "If the professor laughs," she says, "I write down 'laugh.' I leave out nothing. I feel that while I am writing, I am learning. When I have to study for a test, it's all there."

Essentially, your class notes should build on and clarify your reading assignments. As the process of taking notes becomes more familiar to you, you will be able to pick out the important points that the instructor is making, see how those points are related, and weed out the rest.

STUDYING FOR AN EXAM

When the time comes to study for an exam, you have to be sure that you have converted the material from your textbook or the instructor's lectures into a language that you understand. There are various ways of doing this, but the most common seems to be by underlining the important points in your text and then making an outline of these.

Be sure to underline from your reading as you go along, from assignment to assignment. Successful students often try to have an outline based on what they've underlined ready about a week before an exam, so that they can spend the rest of their study time reviewing the outlines and their class notes.

There are many variations on how to translate the material from textbook and instructor into something you feel comfortable with. One straight-A student finds an empty room in the library before each exam and writes down important points on the blackboard. Then she turns her back to see what she can remember.

It is a good idea to start studying for an exam well in advance—though some reentry students mention that they actually enjoy the frenzy and excitement of colliding with a deadline. Certainly many younger students do wait until the last minute to study for tests and still write good exams. But you have to remember that in your case, the chances are a lot greater that an emergency can keep you from studying the night before an exam—a child with an upset stomach or a debut in the class play, a meeting that can't be canceled.

Should you study in a group? Some returning students have mentioned this as a helpful technique. Research shows, however, that people who study in groups do less well than those who study alone—probably because it is so easy to get distracted in a group.

Well in advance of an exam, be sure to talk with students who have taken classes from the professor who is giving it, to find out what to expect. This information can save you enormous amounts of study time! For example, you may find out that the instructor only asks questions based on the review questions at the end of a chapter, or that the material included on the test will all have been covered in class.

Also, you should be sure to ask the professor what kind of exam he or she will be giving, and specifically what material will be covered. Find out as much as you can from the ultimate source. The aim of a good exam is to find out how much you know, not to trick or frustrate you. Unless your professor is some kind of sadist, he or she will be ready to guide you toward what is most important for you to learn.

One good technique for being well prepared is to decide for yourself which questions should be included on the exam, and then emphasize those when you study. You'll be surprised by how adept you'll become at judging which material is worth putting into an exam.

Finally, take good care of yourself! Don't stay up all night when you're not used to it, or your body will rebel. It is far easier to learn material by studying two hours every day than to assimilate it all in an eight-hour session.

TAKING AN EXAM

On the day of the exam, try to keep the following points in mind:

1. Be sure you know exactly how much time you have to take the exam. The test may not take the whole period, or you may be allowed to stay as long as you want. Knowing how much time you have is crucial.

2. Read through the entire test before you answer any of the questions. Different questions may be worth a different number of points, and you don't want to wind up spending all your time answering a question that is only worth a few points. Set a limit in advance on the time you allow yourself per question. If the exam includes both essay and objective sections, be sure you know how much each section is worth. For example, the objective section may count for as little as 25 percent of the total exam or as much as 75

percent. You must know how much each is worth in order to allot your time correctly. Assume nothing!

3. Be sure you understand the instructions. If you have any doubts, ask right at the beginning. Read the instructions very slowly and carefully. Underline the important words in the instructions, as for example: "Choose *two* out of the four *essay questions* numbers one through four. Everyone is required to *answer* question *number five.*" Don't risk the sinking feeling that comes with discovering you have spent precious time answering one too many questions.

4. Begin with the questions that seem easiest to you, and don't allow yourself to get upset about any difficult ones you may have spotted. You will feel more comfortable about the difficult ones after you have warmed up on the others. That may sound implausible, but it does seem to work. As your anxiety lessens, you will find that what looked like hard questions become easier.

5. If the exam is an objective one:

On *multiple-choice questions,* first read the statement and try to anticipate what the answer will be without looking at the choices. Always read *all* the choices before you actually select one. If you aren't sure of the answer, narrow down the possibilities as much as you can, devise a system for marking questions you plan to come back to, and go on to the next question.

On *true-false questions,* watch out for universal words such as *always, never, all,* and *none.* They are usually an indication that the answer is false. Absolute statements are not very popular in academic circles.

Should you change answers on objective tests after your first time through? Research indicates you should go ahead and do it. According to Raygor and Wark (*Systems for Study*), students tend to change twice as many answers from wrong to right as they do from right to wrong.

6. If the exam includes essay questions:

Most professors will give you a certain amount of choice on essay tests, so be absolutely sure about how many essays you are expected to write and how much each one is worth.

As you read over the questions, jot down any ideas that immediately come to mind. Then, before you begin to respond to each question, make a careful outline of the points you want to make: otherwise it is all too easy to go off on tangents. If *you* had to read essays from a class of 40 students, you would not want to have to delve for the answers.

Be sure to look for crucial words such as *define, compare, discuss*, and *prove* on the instructions, because each of these words requires you to take a different approach. In *Systems for Study*, Raygor and Wark have developed exercises to familiarize students with the meanings of the words most frequently used in exams and writing assignments. Being fully aware of the meanings of these frequently used words can save you a lot of confusion and anxiety during the first round of exams.

ABOUT WRITING PAPERS

If you are able to pick your own topic, be sure to select one that is fairly specific. A common mistake of students is to pick topics that would take years of research to cover properly. You would not want to write a 20-page paper on child-care opportunities in America, but one covering child-care opportunities in a town of 25,000 would certainly be feasible.

Try to allow yourself more than enough time to get your paper done. Often a paper or a part of one may have to sit for a day or so before you know where to go next. You'll do better when you allow the time for this process to run its course.

If your paper is to involve research, be sure to go to the library as soon as possible, since the books or periodicals that you will need may be signed out. If a book has been out over a certain length of time, the library will probably get it back for you. If your library does not have the book or periodical you need, they may be willing to get it for you through an interlibrary loan; but this can take several weeks.

When you sit down to write, don't spend time worrying about how the ideas actually look on paper. If you become self-conscious about style and grammar, you may bog down. Let the ideas flow, and worry about editing later.

Ask a friend who is interested in your subject to read your paper and give his or her honest reactions. If you can get your paper done early enough, try bringing it to your professor for his or her reaction and guidance.

MORE POINTERS

1. *Knowing how to use the library can save you a vast amount of time.* Be sure to take a thorough tour of the library facilities *before* you get loaded down with research papers. Do you know about

microfilm? Interlibrary loans? Abstracts? There is a wealth of material available—if you find out about it and learn how to use it.

2. *Ask your professors for help.* Returning students usually find that professors appreciate their serious intentions. If you are having trouble understanding something, talk to your instructor. Part of his or her job is to hold office hours so that students can receive individual attention.

3. *Make a calendar of your academic obligations for the quarter or semester.* If your professors are doing their jobs right, they will let you know as early as the first or second class when any exams will be and when papers are due. By putting all these obligations on a calendar, you will be able to see very quickly which weeks are going to be bad ones for you—e.g., if you have an exam and a paper due all in one week, you'll have to plan further ahead than usual.

4. *Know how to reach at least one student in each of your classes.* The chances are that you will be thrown off balance in your juggling act from time to time, so accept the fact that you will be missing some classes. Make sure you have at least one reliable contact per class, who can tell you about homework assignments and from whom you can borrow notes.

SOME THOUGHTS ABOUT BUDGETING TIME

Is it possible to be a good student/mother/wife/friend/ worker/human being without losing your sanity? How do you put it all together?

Most returning students, when asked how they are able to get so much done, say that their success has to do with the energy that comes from feeling good about the way they are spending their time. The essential element in managing your time effectively is to think carefully about what your priorities are, what activities are really meaningful to you. There is a very delicate balance involved here: on the one hand you must have the self-discipline to stick with the priorities that you have established; on the other, you must remain flexible enough to adjust your schedule to unexpected situations as they come up.

It is important to accept the fact that items low down on your priority list may not get attended to. Try to cultivate a relaxed attitude about this. If it is truly upsetting that this particular thing is not getting done, you can always move it up on your priority list.

Things that you consider really important have a way of getting done if you don't waste time in panic over what isn't getting done.

You will be surprised at how easy it is to decide on your priorities and stick to them. If you have been raising children or working outside your home, you will already have had quite a bit of practice in deciding what is important to you. Going back to school will be a matter of adding a rather odd-shaped ball to your already elaborate juggling act.

It is important to get used to sticking to a schedule. One step in that direction is to find out how you are spending your time now. Try keeping a record of everything you do for one week. Leave nothing out. Draw up a kind of appointment book, with hourly slots where you write down your activities at the appropriate time. After a week, go over the record to see where you can pick up extra time. Ask yourself the following questions:

1. Which activities on this list are most important to me?
2. Am I spending enough time on the things I consider meaningful or top-priority, or is that time going to other things?
3. Which activities would I miss least? Where can I borrow some time from?

When you do start school, keep careful track of how much time it takes you to accomplish school-related activities, such as reading assignments, writing papers, and studying for exams. Then incorporate these, along with your class schedule, into your overall scheme of things.

As you work out your daily schedule, first put down all the obligations that don't vary—classes, Scout meetings, and so on. Then put down the other things that you consider to be essential, such as studying and time with your family. As you find out about dental appointments, exams, papers due, plays that your children are in, or a movie you especially want to see, write them in at the appropriate time.

Things like getting your shoes repaired and writing a letter to a friend may have to wait a while. You may actually become very adept at running errands before and after class—making five stops in 10 minutes if you have to. Keep the shoes that need mending in the trunk of your car. You will be amazed at how well you keep up with your correspondence if you decide to write one note before each class. Keep a list of all such obligations; when a spare half-hour happens to come along, you can take advantage of it by pulling out your list.

While you are a student (and it will be, after all, only a small percentage of your life), try to forget about the days of spontaneity you once knew. You will miss being able to do things on the spur of the moment, but mostly you will be too busy even to notice. Every once in a while, if your schedule seems just too rigorous, you may have to shut down your system temporarily. One 47-year-old returning student, the mother of four, commented, "Sometimes, when there's not enough time for me, I cut class to hide under a bush for an hour and a half. Sometimes, you just have to steal time."

Believe it or not, the kind of planning that is essential in order to include school in your life can be extremely liberating. Once you have committed yourself to your priorities and have eliminated all the uncertainty about what you will do with your time, you will waste less of it, get more done, and wind up feeling very good about yourself.

Here are a few time-saving tips:

1. *Stay away from the telephone when you are supposed to be studying.* Being in school usually does mean less time for socializing, and you may wish you saw more of your friends. A lot of precious study time can be wasted on the telephone. Use telephone calls to your friends as a kind of reward system for getting your assignments done (When I finish reading these 20 pages, I'll call Patty on the phone and talk for 10 minutes).

2. *Rewards for studying are important.* Planning special treats for yourself will keep up your motivation, make you work faster, and save you time. Planning to take a bath or fix a snack or go out to dinner with someone special can certainly serve as impetus for sticking with your studying goals.

3. *Ask for help.* The returning student as juggler *extraordinaire* already has enough ammunition to satisfy any martyr urges she might have. Allow yourself to ask those close to you for help. Your professors are paid to hold office hours so students can receive individual attention. If you are confused about material in the textbook or about what was discussed in class, get help right away, since an understanding of these things may be essential to what follows.

4. *Don't worry about how your house looks.* Many women who return to school drastically change their expectations about

how important it is to have a spotless home. You can free an incredible amount of time if you decide that your house does not have to be what one woman calls "the showplace of the neighborhood."

Many returning students talk about "letting go" their immaculate houses with a definite gleam in their eye. In the words of one graduate student, "The floor no longer gets up and says, 'I feel so nice and clean, thank you.' Nobody eats off it anyway. I used to run in and make beds. Now I just condemn rooms and close the doors. I don't care anymore whether their beds are made or not. My values have changed."

Another woman, a 39-year-old senior, agrees: "I was such a stickler for cleanliness. My husband used to joke that if he had to get up in the middle of the night to use the bathroom, the bed was made when he got back. So what if every pin isn't in place? It just doesn't have the importance anymore."

Encourage the members of your family to share equally in household chores. You are not helping your children by sparing them responsibilities around the house. Have a family meeting where you all decide what chores need to be done and who will do them. Post a list on the refrigerator door, and plan things you will do as a family when the system runs smoothly.

5. *Do your hardest assignments when you are most alert.* Everyone has times during the day or night when she is most alert and productive. In order to save time, try to arrange your schedule so that the work requiring the most brain power gets done during the time that you are most alert. There will be times when you feel particularly tired, often right after lunch. Don't try to study statistics then. Run errands instead.

Chapter 17

Services for
Reentry Students

Thanks to the rapid increase in the number of older students, there is hardly a public college or university that does not offer at least some degree of support for students of nontraditional age. The private colleges have been a bit slower, but things are changing there, too.

Here is the way a brochure issued in 1984 described the Center for Continuing Education of Women at the University of Michigan: "CEW is for everyone—especially those thinking about resuming interrupted educations, entering, reentering or changing employment, managing family, job, and educational commitments, and dealing with transitions in their lives." And at College of Marin in Kentfield, California, a brochure describes their Re-entry Services as being for both students and nonstudents. "The staff of our program provides support and the opportunity to know and utilize the resources of the campus and the community." Some of the services that are offered include:

- Assistance with admissions procedures
- Peer counseling and support

- Professional career and personal counseling
- Child care assistance and information
- Financial aid information and help in completing the forms
- Workshops, special events
- Personal growth and awareness groups
- Math clinic and tutoring assistance

If these aims and services sound at all relevant to you, and you decide to track down an office involved with reentry students, remember that it may be housed under a completely different name from the one you are expecting. Try Reentry, Continuing Education, Adult Services, Special Student Services, The Women's Center, or any combination of letters you see that look vaguely suspicious such as: ENCORE, WIN, ACE, ABLE, WREP. Asking the first older-looking student you see on campus should also get you immediate results.

Even if the campus does *not* have a reentry office, it may have a network of administration, faculty, and staff who are committed to helping meet your special needs. The University of California at Davis, for example, lists 16 people working in various campus offices who are in tune with the barriers that reentry students might confront.

What kinds of services might help make your academic reentry easier? Even if the reentry "office" consists of only *one* receptive person who does not have reentry as his or her only responsibility, some of the following on-campus services may be available to you.

COUNSELING

Individual counseling may be available on a drop-in basis, or by appointment, or both. Group-counseling and "brown bag lunch" sessions are often part of the program. REAP (Re-entry Advisory Program) at San Jose State University in California had a brown bag lunch series in 1985 that included the following topics: math anxiety, stress on relationships, staying organized, relating effectively to the faculty, superperson syndrome, time management, test anxieties, and sharing survival strategies. Even if there isn't a center for reentering students, the campus counseling office will often take the responsibility for organizing group counseling sessions and/or coordinating brown bag lunch groups.

INFORMATION/REFERRAL SERVICES

The staff at a reentry office should be able to provide you with answers to all major questions about registration, academic programs, financial aid, career development, and child care, or they will direct you to the person who can.

Some reentry offices are working toward having the entire admissions/registration/financial aid process all happen in their own office. Even if this is not the case at schools near you, being referred to the *right* person on the *first* try will be very reassuring to you.

Since policies concerning returning students are changing so rapidly, information that you find in the current catalog may already be obsolete. Check with the reentry office about anything major— a campus child-care center may be about to open, CLEP tests may now be accepted, etc.

Also, see if there is an educational brokering center in your area. Educational brokers can serve as the important go-betweens for adult learners and the enormous array of educational resources that they confront. These impartial brokers help people make personal and career decisions, select appropriate educational resources, and embark on learning programs. Brokers are not involved with recruiting students for individual institutions. There are over 1,100 educational brokering-type programs listed in the *1985 Educational and Career Information Services for Adults Directory*. To find out what programs are in your area, call the National Center for Educational Brokering, 415-626-2378. To receive a copy of the *Directory*, send $4.00 to NCEB, 325 Ninth Street, San Francisco, CA 94103.

ORIENTATION

Returning students report that the mechanics of registration, finding the proper parking lot, standing in endless lines to buy textbooks, become old hat after a while. But the first time is usually remembered as a truly bewildering experience. To make it easier for you, many campuses offer a special orientation for their older students.

For example, the Returning Students Program at the University of Maryland, College Park, offers an invaluable all-day program for people who are thinking about or in the midst of applying to the University. Peer counselors, Returning Students Program staff, faculty, and personnel from the various services of interest to reentry students are all on hand to provide information and answer questions. You can even initiate *and* complete the admissions process right then and there, if you come prepared with transcripts and other necessary forms. What do faculty expect from students? What types of experiential learning activities are available? What if you have no idea what you want to major in? These issues and countless others are addressed.

This kind of orientation session can help you to start some initial friendships, make contact with the reentry office staff, plus provide you with valuable information that you will be using immediately.

SELF-DEVELOPMENT COURSES

Some colleges and universities offer courses for credit that deal specifically with the kind of transition you are going through. A woman who enrolled in a course called "Psychology of Personal Growth" at Oakton Community College in Des Plaines, Illinois, after 21 years out of school, declared that "it opened up all kinds of worlds I never knew existed." A course called "Options For Women" is offered at Montgomery College in Rockville, Maryland. One woman who enrolled, after 15 years away from school, said that the course "helps you decide what it is that you want to do— either return to school, get a job, or just clarify your mind." "Guidance for Women," a very popular class at Cabrillo College in Aptos, California, addresses such topics as how to deal with guilt, working on your self-esteem, planning study time, focusing in on your interests, and how to build a network.

Special career and life planning classes are taught for reentry students, and workshops which address the specific career and job-hunt needs of the reentry student are given frequently. The Center for Continuing Education of Women at the University of Michigan has a Job Hunt Club that meets weekly. It also offers a four-session workshop called "Step Before the Job Search."

REFRESHER COURSES

Many reentry programs offer workshops and classes which help students improve their reading, writing, and study skills. The Reading and Learning Skills Center at the University of Michigan offers a six-week course, "Updating Reading and Academic Survival Skills," at the beginning of each semester; it is held at times convenient for older students. The Center for Continuing Education of Women there offers a panel discussion on taking the Graduate Record Examinations, a session for brushing up on basic mathematics, and a workshop called "How to Do an On-Line Library Search." And the University of California, Santa Cruz, has writing courses specifically geared for reentry women—composition and research writing techniques. Most reentry offices also keep a current list of available tutors.

SPECIAL-INTEREST LIBRARY SERVICES

Reentry centers often set up libraries on subjects of special interest to older students. Some are putting together publications of their own: for example, the Program on Women at Northwestern University in Evanston, Illinois, offers a 26-page booklet, *Re-entry: A Handbook for Adult Women Students*. WREP (Women's Re-entry Program) at University of California, Santa Cruz, publishes a 44-page booklet for and by reentry women students.

Several offices involved with reentry are committed to encouraging research projects. In 1977, the Center for Continuing Education of Women at the University of Michigan, under the direction of Jean Campbell, was awarded $100,000 by the Ford Foundation for research purposes. A major study was conducted there on the transition from education to employment by returning women students. A second Ford Foundation grant in 1980 provided funds to focus on issues of career development. This center is an exceptionally productive place. It has published a number of books in the field of research on women, and the list of its published research papers is truly impressive. For a copy of the list of publications and research papers, write to Center for Continuing Education of Women, the University of Michigan, 350 S. Thayer Street, Ann Arbor, MI 48104–1608.

FINANCIAL AID

Although most reentry offices are not in the business of providing financial aid, they are often a knowledgeable source of information on special grants available to older students. As the link between reentry offices and their communities becomes stronger, more special scholarships may become available. At the University of Michigan, once again, the Center for Continuing Education of Women listed over 40 scholarships ranging from $500 to $2,000.

Even the prestigious Seven Sisters are making major commitments to reentry women. Mount Holyoke in South Hadley, Massachusetts, is a good example. There were 71 reentry students involved with their Frances Perkins Program in the academic year 1985–86. Finances are *not* a barrier. If you qualify for admission and need financial aid, Mount Holyoke will put together a financial aid package from a variety of sources, up to the full amount of tuition. (In 1985, tuition was over $10,000 per student!)

ADVOCACY

Reentry offices try to initiate changes on campus that will benefit the students they serve—such as applying pressure to provide a campus child-care center, or to establish different methods of evaluating older students for admission. San Jose State University, for example, has a Special Adult Admission Program for people who are over 25 and have been out of college for at least five years. The motivation and successful experiences of these potential students are definitely taken into consideration. The Returning Students Program at the University of Maryland, College Park, holds workshops for faculty and staff in order to increase their awareness of the characteristics and special needs of returning students.

In California, people committed to improving the quality of reentry education have formed a group called California Advocates for Re-entry Education. Since 1978, they have been working to improve admissions and administrative policies, to develop responsive program design and class scheduling, and to institute adequate support services for the returning student. For a free copy of the "C.A.R.E. Resource Review," published several times a year, write to Ceiny Carney, Special Programs, Admissions, University of California at Santa Cruz, Santa Cruz, CA 95064.

A CHECKLIST OF SPECIAL SERVICES
FOR RETURNING STUDENTS

When you are investigating schools, check to see if the following services are available. If a campus is receptive to older students, it will either have many of the following services or be willing to consider instigating some of them.

- A space where returning students can gather informally
- A reentry office (even if it's only one person) who can serve as a major resource and advocate
- Good on-campus child care that is affordable
- Counseling, both individually and in groups, on a drop-in basis or by appointment
- Special admissions procedures that take life experience into account in addition to a realistic attitude toward transfer credits and assessment of prior learning
- Flexible class scheduling that is realistic for working people and parents
- Availability of part-time study
- Updated guidelines for handling prerequisites and the challenging of courses
- Receptivity to earning credit through correspondence, television, newspaper, summer, and extension courses
- Scholarships specifically designated for older students
- Special orientation for returning students and help through the registration process
- Self-development courses specifically geared to the issues that most concern older students
- Exposure to good role models
- A solid informational service on the issues that most concern reentry students (financial aid, child care, etc.) *or* an infallible referral system
- Refresher courses
- Special-interest library services

For hundreds of years, universities and colleges have been investing in the special needs of their younger students. Now that older students make up more than one-third of the student population, your special needs must be and are being taken seriously by the academic community as well. This is an exciting time to be in school!

Chapter 18

Other Access Routes to a College Degree

Imagine earning credit toward your college degree while commuting to work on a train! If you happen to ride the Speonk and Port Jefferson lines of the Long Island Railroad, you are probably eligible for the Adelphi-on-Wheels Program. Instead of dozing or reading newspapers, commuters in special classroom cars are busy earning bachelor's and master's degrees in business. Anything is possible!

Adelphi University in Garden City, New York, is a good example of the many universities that have responded to the special needs that adult learners often have. University administrators throughout the country are beginning to realize how important getting credit for past academic performance and life experience is to people who have interrupted their education. Adelphi, for instance, allows up to 90 semester credits (comparable to three years of college work) toward a bachelor's degree based on previous college work, life experience, CLEP/CPEP, and other college-level examinations and experiences.

Colleges are also responding to the special time demands placed on older students by holding classes at times that might be most convenient. Students in Adelphi's ABLE (Adult Baccalaureate Life Experience) program can choose courses worth two or four credits each which usually meet once a week for 15 weeks on weekdays, weekends, or in the evenings.

How common are colleges which hold weekend sessions? Can you really get college credit for what you know? For knowledge gained from paying and nonpaying jobs? For experience as a homemaker? What is CLEP? Life experience?

It's hard to find a returning student who doesn't feel the pressure of time. Many would give anything to be able to speed up their academic years so that they can get on with their careers. Others can't figure out how to take away precious time from their already fully committed lives in order to attend class. Some of the ways you can get through college *in your own time*—whether you need to take less or more—follow.

CREDIT FOR LIFE EXPERIENCE

Some colleges now offer credit for what you've learned outside the classroom. Many other colleges still won't consider such a thing. The principle behind this kind of credit is that what is important is not the number of hours you've spent in class, but what you know. One accredited university will give you as much as 50 semester units of credit for a life-experience portfolio, which you are given six weeks to prepare. Fifty units means that you're well on your way to skipping two years of classroom experience!

What counts as life experience? Volunteer activities, work on the job, community involvement, travel, noncredit courses, workshops and seminars, and self-directed study are all included in the category of prior learning. Some of the experiences you have had may be related specifically to what you would learn in a college course. Others may have involved a tremendous amount of learning that is in no way traditionally academic.

On the one hand, it would be hard to imagine anyone requiring a woman who has been mayor of a town for five years to take an introductory course in political science or government. Similarly, if you have written a book, it would seem foolish to put you into a basic English composition class. On the other hand, should the cosmic insights experienced by way of psychedelic drugs be translated into college credit? At some colleges they are!

The issue of granting credit for experiential learning is a controversial one for all concerned. Nevertheless, more and more universities are granting at least partial credit for prior off-campus learning experiences. There are sure to be a lot of policy decisions in the next few years about how life learning ought to be assessed.

Some universities now offer a course that guides students through the process of putting together a portfolio on their life experiences. At Humboldt State University in Arcata, California, for example, a course called "Conceptualizing Prior Learning" earns you four units of academic credit in one quarter. During the second quarter you prepare a portfolio that includes an autobiography, definitions of learning, identification of competencies, and validation of knowledge and skills. This is assessed by a special committee, and you can earn up to ten more units of credit.

At the Educational Testing Service, Ruth Ekstrom, Marlaine Lockheed, and Abigail Harris have prepared a text and workbook to help women assess their homemaking and volunteer experience for college credit. It is called *How to Get College Credit for What You Have Learned As a Homemaker and Volunteer* and is available for $5.00. This book can guide you through the process of identifying the academically accreditable competencies which you have acquired from your volunteer work and homemaking experiences. The kinds of skills you develop as a volunteer or homemaker, the kinds of information colleges will want from you, and how to go about documenting your own experiences are all included in the publication. You can get a copy from: Publications Order Department, Educational Testing Service, Princeton, NJ 08541.

The Council for Advancement of Experiential Learning (CAEL) is a national association of 500 institutions, agencies, and individuals who are dedicated to fostering quality experiential learning and its valid and reliable assessment. Through taking their Comp-Activity Inventory ($22.00), you can get a good idea of how much credit you might be able to earn for your educational experiences and accomplishments. Write for more information to CAEL, 10840 Little Patuxent Road, Columbia, MD 21044.

Earn College Credit for What You Know, by Susan Simosko under the auspices of CAEL, explains how to put together and present a portfolio for assessment. It also gives the names and addresses of nearly 600 prior-learning assessment programs. The book costs $8.95 and is published by Acropolis Books, Ltd.

As you investigate any college that interests you, you will want to find out: (1) whether or not it grants credit for experiential learning; (2) if so, exactly what kinds of information and documentation are required; and (3) the acceptable format for presenting your material.

COLLEGE-LEVEL EXAMINATION PROGRAM (CLEP)

The College Entrance Examination Board (CEEB) initiated these exams in 1965. Over 2,000 colleges and universities across the country now give varying degrees of credit, depending on how well you do on these exams.

There are five general tests available through CLEP—English composition, humanities, mathematics, history, natural sciences, and social studies. Each test consists of multiple-choice questions and has a time limit of 90 minutes. An optional English composition exam offers the opportunity to write a 45-minute essay in addition to 45 minutes of multiple-choice questions. The general tests are designed to measure the kind of broad-based intellectual experiences you might have accumulated during the first two years of college.

In addition, over 30 subject examinations, also multiple-choice and having the same time limit, are comparable to final exams in courses that might be required of college freshmen or sophomores. The subject areas include: history and social sciences; foreign languages; composition and literature; science and mathematics; and business. There is an optional 90-minute essay section for almost all the subject exams that you may be asked to take as well.

The fee for each of the general and subject exams is $30.00.

Like the S.A.T. ("college boards"), these tests are scored on a scale of 200 to 800 (20 to 80 on the subject exams). There is no standard passing mark. It is up to the college or university administering the test to decide what score is acceptable. A college usually grants the same amount of credit to students who earn satisfactory scores on CLEP tests as it does to students who successfully complete the course in the classroom. The CEEB does not itself grant college credit; it simply provides a vehicle for academic institutions to do so.

How much credit you may earn through CLEP will vary from school to school. Some schools allow only a few CLEP credits; at the other extreme, a few may allow you to earn enough credit for an entire degree through examinations. The norm is somewhere between 30 and 60 credits. If you are considering earning credit this way, be sure first to ask each college you investigate what its policy is. You may be able to earn a whole year's worth of credits before you even attend your first class. Or you may be able to get credit for general education requirements by taking CLEP tests *after* you begin classes.

CLEP makes things as comfortable and convenient as possible for the reentry student. There are no prerequisites for the tests, you do not need a high school diploma, and no one cares how or where you learned what you know.

CLEP tests are given ten times a year at more than 1,000 centers across the country. If you are over 150 miles away from the nearest center, CEEB will arrange for you to take the exams at some place closer to you. Exams may be retaken after a waiting period of six months if you are not satisfied with your scores.

The following material is available at no charge by writing to CLEP Publications, CN6600, Princeton, NJ 08541-6600:

Moving Ahead with CLEP, giving a brief description of each exam, registration information, and an application form
CLEP Colleges: Test Centers and Other Participating Institutions, telling you about the test centers in your area

If you are considering taking CLEP tests, you will find *Guide to the CLEP Examinations* ($5.00) a very valuable resource. The book gives a complete description of each test, including sample questions. You can take practice tests to see how you will perform. Copies can be ordered from College Board Publications, Department B10, Box 886, New York, NY 10101. California and Pennsylvania residents need to add sales tax.

OTHER EXAMINATIONS

Several other exams are used by colleges in granting credit. One well-known example is the Proficiency Examination Program (PEP), offered in the State of New York by Regents College Examinations and everywhere else by the American College Testing Program. There are 55 exams which have been developed by the faculty of The University of the State of New York. About 700 colleges and universities accept the PEP tests. To find out more about these exams, write to ACT-Proficiency Examination Program, Box 168, Iowa City, IA 52243 if you live outside of New York State, or to Regents College Examinations, Cultural Education Center, Albany, NY 12230 if you live in New York State.

By studying on your own for these exams, you can earn college credit at your own pace without any obligation to be at a certain place at a certain time. And you will have saved valuable time by cutting down the number of courses you are required to take.

CHALLENGING COURSES

If you feel that you could pass a certain course without attending class, some colleges will allow you to take an exam designed by the professor who teaches the course. Suppose, for instance, that there is a course in group dynamics and you have done extensive work with groups; you might buy the textbook and find out from the professor whether you can get credit by taking either the regular final exam or one made up specifically for challengers.

Some universities have blanket policies about challenging courses, and so do particular departments and/or professors.

Before accidentally stepping on anyone's toes, ask some of the students who are further along in your field of interest whether the department is receptive to challenging courses. If so, approach the department chairperson or the specific professor with your proposal—depending on which one appears more likely to agree.

Like the CLEP tests, this procedure allows you to review the subject at your own pace, meanwhile gaining precious time by not having to go to class.

EXTERNAL DEGREE PROGRAMS

Through most such programs, it is possible to earn a bachelor's or associate's degree without ever attending a single class. Special examinations, correspondence courses, assessment of life experience, independent study, on-the-job experience, and previous college work all contribute toward the degree.

The best-known external degree program is offered by The University of the State of New York—although anyone, regardless of residence, age, or academic background, is eligible to enroll. The program is fully accredited by the Board of Regents of the State of New York and by the Middle States Association of Colleges and Schools. Since 1970 more than 27,000 people have earned associate's and bachelor's degrees through Regents College Degrees, and 16,000 others were in the process in 1985.

Even if you have never gotten any college credit or had any relevant job experience, you can earn all the credits you need by taking approved examinations that earn anywhere from three to thirty credits each. A fee is charged for every exam you take, and the average cost of a degree taken entirely in this way will be between $400 and $1,000. You can also earn credit by transferring the credits you have already received at accredited colleges and approved educational programs of the military, business, and industry. Students may be eligible for Pell Grants and other forms of financial aid. To send for a free copy of a 20-page view book describing the ways of earning credit, academic policies, and the 16 degree programs in liberal arts, business, nursing, and technology, write to Regents College Degrees, Cultural Education Center, Albany, NY 12230.

The State of New Jersey offers a similar program through Thomas A. Edison College. In fact, over 100 institutions now have external degree programs on the undergraduate and/or graduate level. Charter Oak College in Connecticut offers bachelor of arts and bachelor of science degrees to residents of Connecticut, Maine, Massachusetts, Rhode Island, New Hampshire, and Vermont. The Fielding Institute in Santa Barbara, California, has accredited doctoral programs in addition to their master's degree programs.

The external degree program lends itself nicely to the life-style of someone with major nonacademic commitments. Many students involved in external degree programs are working full-time; many are also parents. You should certainly consider one of these programs if there is no way for you to rearrange your life to include classroom experience.

Guide to External Degree Programs in the United States is an excellent resource concerning the various external degree programs that exist nationwide. Other resources can be found in Appendix D, Section 3.

MENTOR/STUDENT RELATIONSHIPS

A number of colleges and universities offer very individualized programs for earning degrees. These programs emphasize an assessment of competence rather than the number of credit hours. Usually, there is no set time for completing degree requirements. The most important feature of these programs is that students have the opportunity to establish a one-to-one relationship with a professor/mentor, without the restrictions imposed by class scheduling. This type of individualized programming is sometimes known as the "university without walls" approach.

An example of a program that relies heavily on the student/ mentor relationship is Empire State College in New York, where the average age of the students is 37. Together, each student and his or her mentor draw up a degree program, composed of individual learning contracts that will meet the student's educational objectives. What is to be studied, the resources to be used, what the end result will be, how it is to be assessed, and how much credit is to be given are all spelled out in great detail.

Ninety-six units of advanced standing are allowed—including credit from previous college work, CLEP tests, college-level learning experiences, and so on. This material is assembled in a portfolio and evaluated by a committee. The program that is then set up makes use of employment, internships, and extensive independent study.

Being able to earn up to 96 units of credit based on previous learning experiences means that you can enter Empire State with the equivalent of three years of college behind you even if you have never attended college before.

At Empire State, you can enroll full-time or part-time during any month of the year except August. You can arrange your studies to realistically fit your lifestyle. One great advantage to anyone with major nonacademic commitments is that there is no penalty for interrupted study.

Empire State College also provides degree programs and a variety of courses for students seeking structured learning opportunities with absolutely no classroom attendance or travel. The Center for Distance Learning offers students guidance and support from course tutors who maintain contact through regular telephone conferences and mail exchanges. There are associate and baccalaureate degrees in Interdisciplinary Studies, Human Services, and Business. In addition, a full range of courses is available in other subject areas.

Many other colleges across the country offer degrees primarily through independent studies, with little or no on-campus attendance required. Check with colleges and libraries near you to find out about them. Be absolutely sure to find out whether or not the school is accredited—and by whom! If you want a bona fide college degree and the school you choose isn't accredited, you will wind up deeply disappointed over precious time lost. Be especially careful of "diploma mills" that guarantee you a degree in exchange for your money! If you have any doubts about the accreditation of a school you are investigating, check with the Council on Postsecondary Accreditation's *Accredited Institutions of Postsecondary Education*, which should be available at your local library. See Appendix

C for further information on accreditation.

For more information on external degree programs, the "university without walls" approach, and other programs where independent study is emphasized by accredited schools, consult the references listed in Appendix D, Section 3.

CORRESPONDENCE COURSES

You can select from over 12,000 academic courses at more than 70 schools and earn college credit without ever leaving home! Home-study courses can serve a multitude of purposes:

• You can take them for college credit, although almost all universities place limitations on how many units you can earn this way. For women who are unable to spare the time to attend classes, this is an ideal way to start accumulating credit without the restrictions of a fixed schedule.

• If you have decided to pursue a certain subject and you don't have the necessary prerequisites, fulfilling these requirements through home-study courses may be the least disruptive route to take.

• There are correspondence courses specifically geared to preparing for CLEP tests.

• If you are considering a specific field, you might want to take a course or two through correspondence *before* you change your schedule dramatically by entering an on-campus program.

When you are shopping for a correspondence school, be sure that it is accredited. The National University Continuing Education Association, Suite 360, 1 Du Pont Circle NW, Washington, DC 20036, puts out *NUCEA Guide to Independent Study* (Peterson's Guides, $5.95). This publication lists all courses, both credit and noncredit, that are offered by the more than 70 institutions accredited for this type of home-study. For vocational courses, the National Home-Study Council, 1601 18th Street NW, Washington, DC 20009, can provide you with a number of helpful bulletins.

One major advantage of taking a home-study course is that you can usually begin it at any time of the year and take up to 12 months to complete it. You can go at your own pace.

When you enroll, you will receive a study guide which contains all of your assignments. After completing an assignment, you mail it to your instructor. Assignments are usually processed very quickly—the University of Wisconsin Extension Program, for example, allows less than two weeks to receive, read, grade, and re-mail an assignment. Correspondence teachers *do* give individual attention through their corrections and comments on your assignments.

Most correspondence courses for college credit have a final exam, which has to be proctored by an educational officer (such as a librarian) who has been approved by the school.

EXTENSION AND SUMMER COURSES

Taking extension or summer courses for credit is a great way to introduce yourself or reintroduce yourself to the college class-room without having to bother with admission requirements and registration. Usually, anyone can register for courses at any time through the extension department (or the continuing education office) or during the summer, provided the necessary prerequisites for advanced courses have been fulfilled. Courses are often offered at times that are convenient for working people and parents—in the evening and on weekends.

Recently, because of the decrease in enrollment of matricu-lated students, nonmatriculated students have been encouraged to take many of the courses offered during the university's regular session, provided space is available and the prerequisites are met. Un-fortunately, extension students still have to pay the extension fee for the courses, and this fee is often fairly steep.

Certainly many extension and summer courses can be applied as transferable credit when you do enter college as a matriculated student. But almost all schools set limits on how many such trans-ferable credits they will accept. The California state system, for in-stance, accepts twenty-four semester units of extension credit to-ward a bachelor's degree, and nine semester units toward a master's degree. Be sure to find out from any university that interests you how many extension units will be accepted as transferable.

Aside from the traditional academic course offerings, you will probably find self-development courses are available through exten-sion and during the summer session. An added advantage of at-tending during the summer is that the courses are often condensed into six or eight weeks.

If you are not within commuting distance of the nearest university that offers extension courses, contact its continuing education office anyway. Extension courses are often available in outlying areas. You may discover classes being held at your local library that can earn you college credit.

A really enjoyable way to go back to school is to combine it with a family vacation! Quite a few American colleges and universities offer special package deals to families: a one-week stay in a dormitory, a variety of course offerings for the adults, and fun activities for the children. *Learning Vacations* (Peterson's Guides) by Gerson Eisenberg describes 500 such programs.

FLEXIBLE SCHEDULING ARRANGEMENTS

It is possible to earn a bachelor's degree by going to school only on weekends. If you work full-time, weekend college can be an excellent opportunity for you to get your degree. You might be able to get through college in the same amount of time it would have taken you if you had quit work to become a full-time student!

Colleges offering weekend programs are springing up all over the country, as administrators realize how much precious time is wasted by allowing classrooms to be vacant two and a half days every week. The 1985 *Bear's Guide to Non-Traditional College Degrees* (Ten Speed Press), an excellent resource concerning innovative access routes to a college degree, lists 50 schools that have well-established weekend degree programs.

At C. W. Post Campus of Long Island University, New York, for example, six Saturdays and six Sundays or three intensive weekends can earn you three credits toward a degree. At Alverno College in Milwaukee, Wisconsin, it is possible to earn a bachelor's degree in management or communications over a period of four years if you go to school every other weekend during the school year. There may be a school near you that has a weekend program. Those that do will become a lot more common in the near future.

Many older students have found it easier to arrange time away from their other responsibilities if classes occupy one big block of time rather than being spread out over five days of every week. An example is Adelphi's ABLE program, mentioned earlier in this chapter. More and more universities are initiating adult programs which offer comparable schedules.

BRINGING THE CLASSROOM INTO YOUR HOME

Who would have imagined 30 years ago that you could earn college credit by watching TV in the comfort of your own home? Television is becoming an important educational medium, especially for adult learners. *Roots, The Ascent of Man, Civilization,* and *The Age of Uncertainty* were all offered as credit courses by many universities and colleges across the country. Programs that originate locally or regionally are used by schools as well.

Since 1981, the Public Broadcasting System has offered "telecourses," a series of programs aired on television each semester which can be used by colleges and universities as part of their curriculum. According to PBS, over 900 institutions offer telecourse options to their students.

With television courses, there is usually an initial seminar, at which attendance is required, before the series begins. In addition, the programs are supplemented by a textbook, readings, and study guides. An exam or paper may be required of anyone receiving credit for the course.

Inquire of colleges and television stations in your area to learn whether any television courses are being offered for credit. Watch for announcements in your local newspaper as well. You should also be on the lookout for courses offered through radio stations and newspapers.

If you have an Apple or Commodore 64 home computer, you may be only a modem away from enrolling in one of seven degree programs. The Electronic University Network links students into colleges and universities around the country. Over 150 accredited courses are available, as well as a variety of noncredit self-improvement classes. For example, you can earn an M.B.A. from City University in Bellevue, Washington, through your home computer. For information about the courses and degree program options, contact Electronic University, 505 Beach Street, San Francisco, CA 94113.

Chapter 19

Choosing a Career

You have to take life as it happens, but you should try to make it happen the way you want to take it.

AN OLD GERMAN SAYING

If you think of returning to school as a stepping stone to economic advancement, job security, and/or a stimulating career, you certainly must be wondering if there will be a desirable position open for you when you are ready.

According to an article called "The Job Outlook for College Graduates Through the Mid-1990's" (*Occupational Outlook Quarterly*, Summer 1984), nearly 21 million college graduates will enter the labor force between 1982 and 1995. During the same time period, job openings for college graduates are expected to total about 17 million. Therefore, about 4 million college graduates will be underemployed or unemployed.

What does this mean to you? It means that finding a position that fits your particular blend of abilities and expectations may prove to be a challenge. Yet *another* challenge, that is. Reentry students quickly become familiar with facing uphill battles as they learn to juggle school with the major commitments in their lives! Finding a

job or career that is right for you, like the processes of getting yourself into and out of school, requires *effective planning*.

This kind of planning—for what comes after school— is not a
one-shot deal: it's something you ideally do before you resume your
studies and throughout your days as a student. As your needs, skills,
and expectations change and develop, so will your plans for a career
or job. Are you aware of some effective tools that can help you
answer the following questions involved with good career development?

1. Have you done a thorough investigation of the career(s) or
job(s) that interests you?

2. If you have no idea about the kind of work you would like
to pursue, do you know how to explore your interests, values, and
skills to find the necessary clues?

3. Are you only considering positions traditionally held by
women or are you expanding your options to include less obvious
fields that might be even more suitable to your particular blend of
talents and needs?

4. Once you've narrowed down your field of interest, do you
know how to go about landing a position that is fulfilling on as many
levels as possible?

This chapter will explore ways to focus in on your career or job
choices.

EXPLORE YOUR OPTIONS THROUGH READING

Once you have found one or several fields that are of interest
to you, it's time to do some extensive reading, keeping the following
questions in mind:

• How does someone in this field spend his or her time? What
kind of activities are involved in this kind of work?

• What are the various settings for this kind of employment?

• What kind of training is necessary? What other qualifications
are there?

• How much room is there for advancement in this field? Do
women advance at the same rate as men?

• What is the employment outlook like? Is there going to be more or less of a need for people in this field during the next five, ten, twenty years?

• How much money can I expect to earn? Are women paid at the same level as men?

• What factors affect job security in this field? Is employment steady, seasonal, or irregular?

• What are the working conditions like? Do workers spend a lot of time alone or with other people? If with other people, in what capacity? Do the working hours fit into my lifestyle? How much vacation time is there?

• How do you go about entering this field? Are there examinations? A union to join?

• Is there any particular part of the country where workers are more or less likely to be employed?

• Are the skills that I will acquire transferable to other occupations that would interest me?

Where can you go for answers? Here are several sources of information:

OCCUPATIONAL OUTLOOK HANDBOOK

The *Occupational Outlook Handbook* is a good resource to help you start answering some of the above questions. Your local library and the career development center at any nearby college will be sure to have this book, which is published by the U.S. Labor Department's Bureau of Labor Statistics.

The descriptions of occupations in this book include: the nature of the work, where workers are employed, training, other qualifications, advancement, employment outlook, earnings, working conditions, and where to go for more information.

You can learn a great deal from looking through the *Occupational Outlook Handbook*. For example, the 1984–85 edition indicates that employment is expected to increase significantly in engineering, legal, social, and accounting services as well as in the areas of data processing, computer programming, and personnel supply. In addition, job prospects for elementary school teachers have improved due to increased school enrollments during the mid-1980s. More positions should be available for secondary school teachers by the early 1990s. Jobs in insurance, finance, and real estate are expected to rise dramatically.

The following is just a sampling of employment prospects through the mid-1990s according to the 1984–85 edition of the *Occupational Outlook Handbook*, Bureau of Labor Statistics, Bulletin 2205.

PSYCHOLOGISTS	Employment expected to grow faster than average due to increased emphasis on health maintenance rather than on illness. Keen competition for academic posts. For nondoctorates, severe competition.
LEGAL ASSISTANTS	Job openings expected to increase significantly, but so will the number of people pursuing this career. Job prospects are good for graduates of highly regarded programs.
REAL ESTATE AGENTS	Employment expected to rise faster than average in order to satisfy the growing sales and rental demand for housing and other properties.
SOCIAL WORKERS	Employment expected to increase about as fast as average for all occupations, reflecting public and private response to the social service needs of a growing and aging population. Opportunities depend on academic credentials and geographical location.
DENTAL HYGIENISTS	Employment expected to grow faster than average because of an expanding population and increased awareness of the importance of oral health.
REPORTERS	Employment expected to grow about as fast as average, due to anticipated increase in number of smalltown and suburban daily and weekly newspapers.
COMPUTER SYSTEMS ANALYSTS	Employment expected to grow much faster than average, due to the increasing capabilities of computers.
HEALTH CARE ADMINISTRATORS	Employment expected to grow faster than average as the health industry expands and as management becomes more complex.

REGISTERED NURSES	Employment expected to grow faster than average, due to the health care needs of a growing and aging population. There are shortages in rural areas, in some big city hospitals, and in specialties such as geriatrics.
COLLEGE AND UNIVERSITY TEACHERS	Employment expected to decline, due to decreasing enrollment. Employment is better in community colleges. The number of Ph.D. recipients alone will exceed the number of openings for college faculty. There are shortages in such departments as engineering, law, computer science, and business administration.
SECONDARY SCHOOL TEACHERS	Keen competition through the early 1990s. Employment opportunities should improve thereafter.
COMPUTER PROGRAMMERS	Employment expected to grow much faster than average, due to increased use of computers.
BANK OFFICERS AND MANAGERS	Employment expected to increase faster than average. Competition for managerial positions expected to stiffen because of an increase in qualified applicants.
ACCOUNTANTS	Employment expected to grow faster than average. CPAs will have an even wider range of opportunities.
ENGINEERS	Employment expected to increase faster than average.

If the statement reads . . .	It means . . .
Much faster than average growth	50 percent or more growth
Faster than average growth	30 to 49 percent growth
Growth about as fast as average	20 to 20 percent growth
Growing more slowly than average	6 to 9 percent growth
Little change	No more than 5 percent growth or decline
Decline	6 percent or greater decline

Catalyst, a national nonprofit organization, has the goals of furthering the upward mobility of women, reconciling the needs of the workplace and the family, and expanding career awareness among undergraduates and high school students. The Catalyst Network is a group of 170 independent resource centers that provide career and educational counseling and programs for people wishing to advance their careers, change fields, or reenter the job market. All these centers are committed to meeting the career needs of women. Check out the services of the affiliated resource center nearest you. Be sure to explore their excellent publications.

The *Catalyst Career Opportunity Series for Women* is a really good place to begin finding out information about interesting careers. There are 40 roughly 10-page booklets in the series, each covering a different career. Each booklet is divided into two parts. The first section looks candidly at the occupation by profiling an individual in a specific job. The second section gives "fast facts" about the industry in general, including: salary levels; education and training needed to enter the field; strategies for joining the occupation; general employment outlook; opportunities for women; and resources for further information.

The series also includes two career-planning booklets, "Have You Considered Your Career Options?" and "Have You Considered Your Job Campaign?" These cost $4.00 each. Individual career briefs cost $3.00 each. The entire series should be available at a resource center near you. (Catalyst, 250 Park Avenue South, New York, NY 10003.)

The *Catalyst Career Opportunities Series* covers the following occupations:

architecture
arts management
broadcasting
  programming
  newscasting and reporting
corporate legal services
data processing
  computer programming
  computer sales
  systems analysis
engineering
  biomedical
  electrical
  industrial
  mechanical

finance
  accounting
  bank management
  economic
  insurance
  investment banking
  securities sales
geological sciences
  geology
  geophysics
government and politics
  city management
  politics
  urban and regional planning

health sciences
    health services administration
    pharmacy
    veterinary medicine
hotel management
industrial management
    purchasing
management consulting
marketing and communications
    advertising
    market research
    marketing

public relations
personnel
    benefits and compensation
    training and development
publishing
    book publishing
    magazine publishing
real estate
retailing—buying
small business ownership

PROFESSIONAL JOURNALS AND NEWSPAPERS

Most university libraries carry a number of professional publications. Be sure to read those associated with your own career options regularly. Do you find the articles interesting or do they leave you cold? Who is doing work that sounds interesting to you, and where? Are there meetings or workshops that you might want to go to? Most professional periodicals and newspapers devote a section to job vacancies in the field. Are you getting the necessary qualifications for the jobs that attract you? Reading professional journals can help you answer these questions.

COLLEGE PLACEMENT COUNCIL MATERIALS

Surveys conducted by the College Placement Council, Inc. are of interest to anyone who will be looking for a job after graduating from college. For example, a 1985 survey of 386 employers showed a projected 2 percent increase in demand for June 1986 graduates over those of June 1985. The hiring of business graduates was projected to increase by 7 percent at the bachelor's-degree level and 4 percent at the master's-degree level.

For science, mathematics, and technical disciplines (excluding engineering), there was a 3 percent projected increase in demand for those with bachelor's degrees and a 13 percent increase for those with master's degrees. For engineering graduates with bachelor's degrees there was a 5 percent decline, but a 7 percent increase for those holding master's degrees. For liberal arts graduates, a 3 percent decline was predicted.

You should be able to find College Placement Council survey reports and their other publications at college and university placement offices.

WORKING WOMAN SALARY SURVEY

Since 1980, *Working Woman* Magazine has been publishing a yearly salary survey in their January issue. What jobs are expected to grow fastest during the next decade? How do women's salaries compare with men's in various fields? What percentage of people involved with your field of interest are women, and what kinds of positions do they hold? The survey is of interest to all working women and any woman who is considering entering the work force.

For instance, the 1985 survey points out that women are definitely receiving more bachelor's degrees in traditionally male-dominated fields. Between 1976 and 1982, there was a 531 percent increase in the number of women receiving degrees in computer sciences, 524 percent in engineering, and 200 percent in business. Women earned 28 percent of the MBAs awarded in 1982—a 24 percent jump over the number they received in 1971.

The three jobs that are projected to have the most job growth by 1995 are: computer service technicians (97 percent); legal assistants (94 percent); and computer systems analysts (85 percent). The worst bets for 1995 are postal clerks (-18 percent) and college and university faculty (-15 percent).

BOOKS ON YOUR FIELD OF INTEREST

If the placement office at the university nearest you is worth its salt, it will have a good resource library. Even if books concerning your special interest are not available there, someone will probably be able to suggest where to go for more reading material. A women's resource center would also be able to give you leads on additional reading material. Or you can write to the national organization involved with the careers you are exploring. They will most likely be able to suggest additional resources.

EXPLORE YOUR OPTIONS THROUGH TALKING WITH PEOPLE

Reading can give you a general overview of the field. But it is crucial for you to talk with people who are involved directly with what interests you. Is the information you are gathering through your reading fairly realistic? What you read and what you hear may be very different from each other.

For example, in 1978, the *Occupational Outlook Handbook* stressed the keen competition that was expected to confront graduates seeking teaching positions at the elementary and secondary school levels. Yet thousands of teaching jobs went unfilled that year. According to an article in *U.S. News & World Report*, in 1978 urban school districts in New York City and Baltimore desperately needed English, math, and science teachers. Two education programs in New York even offered *free* courses to those who agreed to teach in the city's public schools! At the height of this competition for teaching positions, Ohio State University's College of Education managed to place 98 percent of its 1,200 education graduates *in teaching positions.*

The front page of the October 20, 1985, *San Francisco Examiner* announced "Teacher Shortage Worsens." This article cited a number of factors as the cause of the projected severe teacher shortage: school enrollment is rising; more than half the nation's teachers are approaching retirement; and teacher-training programs have had declining enrollment for nearly a decade. By 1992, the nation will need 1.4 million new teachers. At that point, there will be a 34.6 percent shortage of teachers!

An 8 percent shortage of teachers was projected for 1985. Inner city schools, isolated rural towns, and places in between have been looking for teachers. Such areas as math, science, special education, and vocational education have more openings than those that require the teaching of the "3 Rs." To get an accurate picture of the job market, you *must* talk with people in your specific area of interest.

Four different groups of people—employers, employees, professors, and students—will give you four different views of what it would be like to work in a particular field, and of how *you* can best prepare yourself. You should talk to *all* of them, and as many as you possibly can from each group.

How do you arrange to talk with an employer? Calling one out of the blue may sound intimidating, but you'll be surprised by how much people like to talk about what they do. If you are contemplating a job in social work, for example, it is *not* out of line for you to ask the head of your favorite social service agency for some of his or her time. If you were in charge of an agency, would you refuse to see a student who wanted to know whether he or she was on the right career track?

Explain that you are a student or about to be a student in this particular field, and that when you graduate, you think you would like to find work in an organization similar to his or hers. *But* you have some basic questions about the direction your course work should take, and about the jobs that might be available to someone who graduates with your particular training.

If you are truly intimidated by the process and are already in school, get one of your professors to give you extra credit for giving a report on your findings. Then you can think of this valuable research as a class project!

The information that employees can give you will be just as valuable. Ask people you know for the names of people *they* know in your field of interest, and arrange to meet those people. Your professors and colleagues are bound to have friends working in jobs of interest to you, so be sure to use them as resources. Also, the campus career development center or alumni office may have a listing of community residents willing to talk with students about their work.

The following are some of the questions you might want to ask an employer and/or an employee:

• What is a typical day at work like? How do you spend your time here?

• What education and training have you had, and which courses have helped you the most in your job? What kind of training and which courses would you recommend to someone interested in this kind of work?

• What special aptitudes and abilities do you think someone in this kind of work should have?

• What do you like most about the kind of work you do? What do you like the least? What are the most important personal satisfactions and dissatisfactions connected with your job?

• How much and what kind of competition is required for success in this field?

• What did you find most helpful to you when you were getting your first job in this field?

• What are the present opportunities for advancement here?

• Do you feel that your job is a secure one?

• What are top, middle, and starting salaries like here?

• Are women hired as often as men? Do they advance as rapidly? Are they paid the same?

• What are some of the other settings where people with your qualifications work?

• What other occupations are closely related to this one?

• What would a typical career path in this field be?

• What advice would you give to someone who was thinking about entering this field?

The people who take the time to talk with you about their careers will be providing you with invaluable information. Be sure to send them thank-you notes afterward. As you talk with people in your field of interest, you will be building up an important list of contacts that you can use when you actually start the job-hunting process.

While you are in school, it can be all too easy to forget about your long-range plans as you become totally immersed in meeting your short-term goals—such as surviving next week's midterm. Be sure that when you talk with your professors, it is not only about term papers and exams. Your professors should be able to provide you with a wealth of information about careers involving your special interest. Find out where their colleagues whose interests are similar to yours, and the alumni of your program, have found satisfying jobs.

The other students in your program may have friends who have recently graduated. What were their aspirations? Are they happy in what they are doing? Were there any gaping holes in their training? Perhaps an informal gathering could be arranged with some of the recent graduates and current students.

EXPLORE YOUR OPTIONS THROUGH WORK EXPERIENCE

The most useful "reality testing" of all is direct experience. Internships and part-time jobs, whether paid or volunteer, give you a chance to test out your career interests and to modify them while there is still time.

How do you go about finding a job in your field when you have little or no experience?

1. Consult the campus career development center or student employment office. One of these can usually provide you with a list of volunteer agencies in your area, and can also tell you about co-operative programs and internships, or direct you to an office that has information about them. It may be possible to land a work-study position related to your career objective. The office that handles student employment can give you direct referral to part-time, seasonal, temporary, and full-time jobs both on and off campus, but most of these tend *not* to be career-oriented.

2. Talk with your professors. Faculty members are often themselves involved with community organizations on a volunteer basis. One accounting professor, for example, set up a bookkeeping system for a senior resource center, but hadn't yet settled on who would then carry the project through. When a reentry student in one of his classes asked how she could gather some work experience, a match was made. She wound up in charge of the bookkeeping project, and the professor was delighted to lend his advice whenever necessary.

A counseling professor was called by a junior high school guidance counselor who wanted advice on how to start a discussion group for students whose grades had declined. A second-year counseling student offered to run the group and received field placement credit for the experience. In addition, she met with her professor once a week to discuss the group's progress.

3. Create your own volunteer job. Organizations love to be helped—especially if the advice is free! Find a group that interests you, and spend time uncovering a need which you might be able to fill. Draw up a plan and present it to someone in a position to give you the go-ahead. For example, if you are planning to go into advertising, you might spot a restaurant in town that is running an ineffective ad campaign. Propose a better one to the owner, and see what happens.

In a survey of graduates with bachelor's and master's degrees at a California state university, students said that their experience in working as volunteers was the most significant factor in helping them find jobs after graduation.

EXPLORE YOUR OPTIONS
THROUGH A CAREER DEVELOPMENT CENTER

Remember to take advantage of the Career Development Center's staff members as primary resources, not only when you start hunting for a job but while you are exploring the possibilities.

The counselors there can help you choose a career in keeping with your interests, skills, and needs. You can meet with a counselor as an individual or through workshops that focus on your particular field of interest. At one university, the following workshops concerned with career exploration were offered during a 10-week period:

women and careers
volunteer summer positions with state and federal agencies
careers in aquaculture
men in traditionally female occupations
careers in newspapers, magazines, and book publishing
careers in advertising and public relations
natural resources careers with law enforcement
nontraditional careers for teachers
civil service careers
careers in geology
careers in social service
careers for biological science majors
careers in radio, TV, and film
women and engineering

A career development center's library, if adequately funded, can be a valuable resource. It is certainly the most likely place for you to find literature on careers and graduate school, along with someone who can explain to you how to use it.

EXPLORE NONTRADITIONAL CAREERS FOR WOMEN

Even though there are laws to promote equal opportunity and laws requiring employers to take "affirmative action," the longstanding problem of occupational segregation of men and women still remains. There are still "men's jobs" and women's jobs," and a shockingly high proportion of the positions women are encouraged to take are marginal, low in pay, and low in status. In fact, in 1984, nearly 60 percent of employed women were clustered in jobs involving service, sales, and administrative support.

That same year, women age 25 and older working full-time who had four years of college education had a median annual salary of

$20,257. That figure was *less than* the average for men with no more than a high school education—$23,269! According to the Census Bureau, only 11 percent of the full-time workers who earn over $30,000 are women.

While you are exploring your career options, be sure to take a close look at jobs which have been male-dominated in the past. The only two professions that women have traditionally pursued are teaching (in elementary and secondary schools) and nursing. But some of the professions that have been traditionally dominated by men are showing some increase in the number of women. These include accounting, banking (management-level positions), chemistry, city management, dentistry, engineering, finance, general business, geology, industrial management, law, marketing, mathematics, and medicine. Women who enter these fields will have a chance for higher earnings and more room for advancement than the women who choose traditionally female occupations.

Never assume that a field is impossible to break into until you have done your research! And don't assume that you aren't cut out for a certain kind of work until you have explored the skills and interests of those already involved. What kind of lifestyle do women who are already in this field have?

According to the U.S. Census Bureau, in 1970 only 3.5 percent of the architects in the United States were women. In 1984, that figure rose to 10.8 percent. Changes *are* occurring, and in the right direction! In 1983, 27 percent of the people graduating from medical school were women, compared to 9 percent in 1972. In 1975, women represented 22 percent of executive, administrative, and managerial occupations. By 1984, the female share had risen to 34 percent. The number of women senior administrators at colleges and universities increased 90 percent between 1975 and 1983. Women represented 47 percent of pharmacy school graduates in 1982, while in 1971 they made up only 25 percent of the first-year students. In 1984, 41 percent of all accountants and auditors were women, 6 percent of engineers, 16 percent of lawyers, 31 percent of mathematical and computer scientists, 35 percent of computer programmers, 40 percent of economists, 55 percent of psychologists, and 49 percent of public relations specialists.

In the field of engineering, the percentage of women looks alarmingly low, but it needs to be viewed in context. The share of women earning bachelor's degrees in engineering has grown from less than 1 percent in 1970 to 13.2 percent in 1983, from less than

1 percent to 9 percent at the master's level, and from .9 percent to 4.7 percent at the doctoral level. Seventeen percent of the freshman engineering students in 1983 were women.

STARTING SALARIES

There is a wide discrepancy in starting salaries for the various careers and professions, of which you should be aware.

The following is a sampling of national average monthly salary offers made to women with bachelor's degrees during the 1984–85 school year. These figures were taken from the *College Placement Council's Salary Survey* published in July 1985:*

Electrical engineering	$2,294
Computer science	$2,055
Mathematics	$2,032
Chemistry	$1,848
Physical and earth sciences	$1,776
Health (medical professions)	$1,722
Accounting	$1,698
Economics	$1,689
Business—including management	$1,592
Marketing and distribution	$1,486
Social sciences	$1,443
Humanities	$1,424
Agricultural sciences	$1,409
Biological sciences	$1,371

The *Catalyst Career Opportunity Series* booklets discuss the status of women in each of the occupations. For instance, the booklet on bank management points out that the field of banking has improved tremendously since 1960, when only 9 percent of bank managers and officers were women. In 1980, women made up 36.5 percent of this group. Nevertheless, there are still very few women in the very top management levels.

The Catalyst publication states that banks are presently one of the three most actively hiring industries, and that jobs will increase by 45 percent between 1982 and 1995. A bachelor's degree in business administration is an excellent preparation for officer training

---

*The beginning salary data reported are based on offers (not acceptances) to graduating students in selected curricula and graduate programs during the normal college recruiting period, September to June.

positions, and a master's degree in this area would lead to a higher starting salary. Many people who go into bank management continue with their M.B.A. degrees at night.

According to the Catalyst publication, willingness to participate in management-training programs once you are on the job means more opportunity for advancement. Likewise, those bankers who will consider relocation have more options in the field.

The publication refers women interested in careers in bank management to the American Bankers Association, the Financial Women's Association of New York, and the National Association of Bank Women, as well as to selected books, pamphlets, and periodicals.

KEEP ASSESSING YOUR PLANS

Questioning whether or not you are on the right career path and if school is the best way for you to get there is part of the whole reentry process.

It is important to keep assessing how your own particular blend of skills, interests, and needs fits in with what you have learned about the job or career that interests you. Does it still seem appealing as you become more familiar with it? Is there a quicker or different way to get there that might be better fitted to your lifestyle?

You may discover that the route you have chosen isn't at all what you had in mind—once you have taken a good look at the map! If this happens, you'll need to begin systematically exploring the alternatives. Is there another program that would suit you better? Ought you to consider leaving school and entering the working world sooner rather than later? What about on-the-job training or an apprenticeship?

If a particular program turns out not to fit your needs, don't waste your time bemoaning it as a personal failure! The whole process of finding out what you want to do is, can be, a growing experience. In the words of e.e. cummings,

> *the goal of living is to grow)*
> *forgetting why, remember how**

---

* From "in time of daffodils" in *Complete Poems 1913–1962* by e.e. cummings. Reprinted by permission of Harcourt Brace Jovanovich, Inc.

You should be careful not to get caught up in the everyday hassles and distractions that are part of student life, forgetting about your long-range goals. Your days as a student *will* come to an end— all too quickly or all too slowly, depending on how you feel about it. If one of your main reasons for being in school is to acquire working skills, keep your eyes open and make sure you are, in fact, getting the right ones for you.

THE BIG *IF*— WHAT IF YOU DON'T KNOW WHAT YOU WANT TO DO?

Intensive self-exploration time! The best way to decide what kind of work you would like to do is to make a careful examination of your past for clues. What activities have given you the most and the least pleasure? In what setting do you feel most comfortable, least comfortable? What was the worst/best job you ever had? What was so awful/wonderful about it?

If you allow yourself enough time to do a thorough self-investigation, you will end up with a current picture of your skills, interests, and values. If you combine this with extensive research into the world of work, you can then match what you have to offer with whoever or whatever could best make use of your talents.

As you go about this process of self-exploration, probably the most supportive atmosphere will be in a group of other people who are also involved with major life-planning decisions. Most colleges offer at least one career and life-planning class each quarter. Inquire of the Career Development Center, Continuing Education Division, or Women's Studies Department whether such a course exists on a campus near you. If there is a women's resource center or a counseling organization in your community, it, too, will be likely to offer workshops or courses.

The very best resource in the area of career planning and for the subsequent job hunt process is *What Color Is Your Parachute?: A Practical Manual for Job Hunters & Career Changers* by Richard Bolles, published by Ten Speed Press. If *anyone* can convince you that career planning is an exciting and productive way to spend your time, *plus* show you how to do it, it's Richard Bolles. The book provides not only the information—the "how-to's"—but also the inspiration to propel you from point A to point B. The latest editions of the book include *The New Quick Job-Hunting Map*. This is a self-paced series of exercises and self-evaluations that will help you identify what your skills are, where you might want to use them, and how to get to where you want to go. Considering that jobs in this country last an average of 3.6 years, *Parachute* is a book that you should be sure to have on your bookshelf.

Chapter 20

Finding a Job

Did you know that the average college graduate changes jobs *three* times in the first two years out of school? Do *you* have the time for that much trial-and-error? By combining self-knowledge, knowledge of what is available, and good job-hunting techniques, you should be able to avoid losing valuable working time.

To track down leads, try the following:

1. *Read the newspapers.* Sunday is usually the best day to look at the classified ads. Be sure to scan *all* of them since you can't assume that the editor categorizes jobs the same way you would. Don't rely very heavily on the classified ads, however. Richard Bolles reports a study showing that 85 percent of the employers in San Francisco and 75 percent in Salt Lake City did not hire *any* employees through want ads in a typical year!

It's very important not to limit yourself to the classified section of the newspaper either. For example, jobs in market research, finance, and engineering might be listed in the Business and Finance section. Also, an article on your field of interest could tip you off about positions that have not yet opened up. You may find out, for example, that a commercial bank is planning to open two new branches in your community three months hence. If you hope to find a job in banking, that announcement could be your clue to put yourself in touch with the main office of the bank right away.

Don't wait until the month before graduation to consider the newspaper as a resource. As soon as your career goals are fairly well focused, make a habit of clipping ads and articles that might provide you with clues as your job-hunt process gets closer. Start a special file or notebook on job hunting, with a section for potential resources of this sort.

2. *Read professional journals.* Don't just look at the help-wanted ads in professional journals, but take note of the authors of each article, where they are employed, and what their positions are. You might start a correspondence with any of these writers if there is a potential mutual interest.

All interviewers are impressed when you can demonstrate that you know something about the organizations they represent, and about the latest events and trends in the field in general. Professional journals can provide you with current material of this kind. You may not find a job as a direct result of reading journals, but it can give you important contacts and information that may lead to a job. Be sure to look for meetings, conventions, or workshops where you can meet other people in your field.

3. *Register with your college placement office.* Some or all of the following services might be available to you here:

• job-vacancy announcements, nationwide

• a special telephone number you can call which has a recording of job announcements of interest to college seniors

• access to recruiters

• applications for state and federal positions

• seminars and workshops on various aspects of the job-hunting process, including interviewing techniques and resume writing

• personal assistance from career counselors with resumes, cover letters, and the whole basic approach to finding a job

• professional file services for credential and master's degree candidates

• a listing of people in your field, local or nationwide, who might be good contacts.

4. *Think of your entire university or college as a resource.* Fellow students, professors, and alumni all have the potential to be important to your job search. On many campuses, the alumni office keeps an active file of graduates, listed by various job categories, who are interested in serving as contacts for new graduates. Faculty members often are actively involved with community organizations and industries, and can also provide you with local contacts. Where were your favorite professors before they came to your campus? Faculty contacts can cover wide geographical areas. Be sure to network with your student friends as well. Colleagues may have contacts at organizations that do not interest them but may interest you.

5. *Register with private employment agencies.* But be careful! Richard Bolles points out that in 1968, the average placement rate for employment agencies was only 5 percent of its clients. If you plan to use a private employment agency, find one that specializes in your particular field. You can call some of the organizations that interest you and ask them which agencies they use most frequently.

When you fill out an application form with one of these agencies, you should be aware that it is a *contract*. Be absolutely sure you know what you are signing. What is the fee for finding you a job? Who pays the fee and when? What services are covered? What happens if you leave the position or get fired? Are you free to use other agencies? Find out!

6. *Register with your state employment office.* These offices, in most states, have set up a computerized job bank to provide daily listings of job openings in their area. However, Bolles mentions that employers prefer to fill jobs that pay an annual salary above $11,000 in more informal ways.

7. *Register with a United States Employment Service (USES) office.* There are approximately 2,600 such offices, and they serve both entry-level workers and professionals. You should be able to find out about positions in your local area as well as nationally. However, of the 15+ million who registered with USES in 1979, only 30 percent were placed in jobs, and over half of these placements were in blue-collar positions. In one area, 57 percent of the people placed by USES were no longer at their jobs only 30 days later!

8. *Apply directly to the personnel department of organizations that interest you.* Probably this won't produce an immediate result unless you just happen to hit the company at the right moment. If possible, arrange an interview with a personnel worker then and there, so that someone will have a face to connect with the pieces

of paper you leave behind. Remember that the main function of a personnel department is to screen prospective employees, and that your chances of actually being hired tend to be better if you're able to bypass this step completely. Establishing your own chain of contacts is one way of doing this.

9. *Establish a chain of contacts.* Bolles says that only two out of every ten job openings above entry level are listed in any conventional way! To find out about the remaining 80 percent, talk to everybody from your Aunt Tillie to the grocery store clerk. Tell absolutely everyone, as far in advance as possible, that you will be looking for a certain kind of position, and ask for suggestions about people to talk to. Don't forget: (1) relatives; (2) friends of relatives; (3) people you have worked with; (4) your dentist and gynecologist; (5) friends and neighbors and the parents of your children's friends; and (6) people you do business with—bank tellers, the florist, your accountant, and so on.

10. *Do a personal survey of the organization that interests you.* It is much easier to approach a potential employer if you can say that a mutual friend or acquaintance has sent you, and if you can think of the purpose of the interview not as job-hunting but rather as a fact-finding session. You *do* have certain skills that you want to put to good use—would this be an appropriate place? If so, an alert organization will be as much interested in knowing about you, for future reference, as you are in knowing about it.

Before you conduct this kind of interview, find out as much as you can about the organization and the person you will be talking to. Your aim during the interview will be to learn all that you can about the place and the people who work there. Find out, especially, who is the top person dealing with workers with similar qualifications. You may want to call on that person next. After any interviews that you do, send a thank-you note and your resume. It would be very surprising if you weren't invited to apply the next time a position came up.

This kind of research interview is most effective when it is done *well in advance* of your "active" job-hunting days. Richard Bolles's *What Color Is Your Parachute?* explains how to—and how *not* to—conduct these valuable interviews.

HOW TO GET THE MOST OUT OF A JOB INTERVIEW

The key to a good job interview is willingness to spend a lot of time preparing for it. Each interview is an opportunity for you to try matching your unique set of interests and skills with a particular way of utilizing them. Doesn't that sound like a positive experience? To prepare for it, you need to know a lot about yourself and a lot about the organization that is in a position to hire you.

Spend time assessing yourself. If you were an employer, what would *you* want to know about a job candidate? To begin with, you'd want to know why this person is interested in working for your organization, what she has to offer, and just what sort of person is now sitting in your office. If you have skills that would be beneficial to the organization, you should be prepared to talk about your past work (both paid and unpaid) and your personal experiences in a way that demonstrates you have these skills. In order to get yourself into the proper frame of mind, think of your five strongest assets and how they could benefit the organization. Either write them down or keep them listed mentally, being sure to let them surface during the actual interview.

Are you taking your most valuable skills for granted? A music major hesitated to apply for a job that involved arranging speaking engagements for a women's center because she felt she had no related experience—until a friend reminded her that she had been solely responsible for setting up a university concert series. By discussing what was involved in that, she was able to convince the hiring committee that she was the best qualified of all the applicants for the position.

So be sure to spend a considerable amount of time thinking about your past accomplishments and what skills they entail. (Bolles's *The New Quick Job-Hunting Map* is extremely helpful for this process.) Don't limit yourself to paid work experience! Explore the skills you've acquired through daily living, in volunteer work, through hobbies, your activities as a student, your involvement in the community, and so on. These skills come with you to any task that you approach. If most of your work experience has been unpaid, refer to the competency lists in *How to Get College Credit for What You Have Learned As a Homemaker and Volunteer* (Ekstrom, Harris, and Lockheed, Educational Testing Service).

The following resume has been used by a career counseling center in Arcata, California, to show the kinds of valuable skills that can come from working in a variety of unpaid settings.

RESUME

Patricia Woodstock
431 Elm Street
Arcata, CA 95521
707-524-3478

Skills Summary

PROGRAM PLANNING	Planned and coordinated a public information series which included funding, scheduling, promoting, and evaluation. Acted as chairperson for nine-month concert series which successfully funded a community service. Codesigned and implemented a three-year Sunday school curriculum involving eight teachers and 40 children. Assisted with grant proposal development for special experimental community projects.
ADMINISTRATION	Organized and maintained referral and information files. Edited and did layout for newsletters and brochures. Established and maintained accounting system, including preparation of federal and state taxes. Helped establish nonprofit status for new nonprofit organization. Trained and supervised volunteer staff of 20. Acted as chairperson, board member, and member of various task forces over 12-year period.
PUBLIC SPEAKING	Have addressed groups of 6 to 400, including city council, official city and county commissions regarding community and school projects. Participated in television and radio interview shows. Wrote and distributed press releases to newspapers, radio, and television. Spokesperson for children's rights groups.
SPECIAL SKILLS	Bilingual in Spanish CPR Short story writer

INTERESTS	Chamber music Community involvement Backpacking
REFERENCES	Available on request

Spend time researching the organization. Find out as much as you can about the organization itself and the actual position for which you are being considered. How large is the organization? What kind of corporate structure does it have? What are its problems, its strengths? What is its projected growth? How can you make a significant contribution here?

Read recruitment brochures, promotional pamphlets, and annual reports. Talk with anyone who knows anything about the company. Your research should definitely turn up some unanswered questions for you, and good questions will be welcomed by your interviewer.

Be prepared to answer a lot of questions. The interviewer is going to try to find out all he or she can about you in a relatively short period of time (usually 20 or 30 minutes). This means that there will be lots of questions directed at you. Some of them may surprise you:

• What are your short-term and long-term career plans?

• What have you enjoyed most about jobs you have had? What have you enjoyed least? Why did you leave your last job?

• What do you consider to be your major strengths? What are your weaknesses?

• From a look at your resume, you don't seem as qualified as some of the other candidates. What made you apply for the job?

As long as you've spent time beforehand thinking about the potential match between you and this particular job, "surprise" questions shouldn't throw you.

Think carefully about the kind of impression you want to give. The interviewer will want to know what kind of person you are, on the basis of the interview. In a research project at California State University, Sacramento, interviewers were asked to rank in importance the items they watched for in an interview. The top 10 were:

APPLIED ARTS GRADUATES	LIBERAL ARTS GRADUATES
1. motivation	1. ability to take directions
2. dependability	2. initiative
3. enthusiasm	3. motivation
4. willingness to learn	4. verbal ability—articulate
5. sincerity	5. concern for people
6. initiative	6. dependability
7. confidence	7. willingness to learn
8. verbal ability—articulate	8. adaptability
9. ability to take directions	9. punctuality
10. dedication	10. flexibility

Some placement offices offer to videotape a mock interview so that you can actually *see* the impression you are making. Your nonverbal behavior, you will discover, says *so* much about you! If videotaping is unavailable, why not ask someone close to you to clue you in on your habits that make him or her most uncomfortable. Do you squirm a lot when you talk? Eat the tops off all your pens? Squint when you are preoccupied? Get a good friend to tell you about it!

Try to judge when the interview has gone on long enough. When the interviewer begins to wrap it up, don't bring up another long topic of discussion. Be absolutely sure you know what the next step in the hiring selection process will be. When and how will the interviewer be in touch with you? Do you need to send any additional material? A thank-you note reaffirming your interest and adding any relevant information is usually a good idea.

RESUME WRITING

A resume is most effective when you leave it behind you *after* an interview. Many job announcements require, however, that you submit one in advance, so you should take the time to produce a good one. Think of resume writing as a golden opportunity to organize your thoughts, to focus on what it is you have to offer. Richard Bolles points out that when an employer looks at your resume, he or she is trying to guess about your future potential by reading about your past. (See his *Tea Leaves: A New Look at Resumes.*)

One problem with resumes is that employers read them *very* quickly. "Tell me in fifteen seconds or less what you can do for me" is bound to be the approach of someone who has to shuffle all these pieces of paper that resemble each other so closely. If your resume is neat and coherent, concise and interesting, you will be that much ahead.

You should have one or two copies of a basic resume on hand to send out or leave behind you. At the same time, you should be willing to tailor your resume so that it responds to specific job announcements. When you find an announcement that really interests you, read it through word for word. Then try to use the language of the announcement in your tailored resume. Does it say the employer wants someone who can "coordinate," "supervise," "develop," "promote"? Think back on your experiences, either paid or unpaid, to find instances where you coordinated, promoted, supervised, or developed something. Then use *those* words in your resume specifically to describe what you did. "This sounds exactly like the person we've been looking for!" would be a not unlikely reaction from an employer.

If you hear about a job verbally, you can still listen carefully for the action words that are used to describe the responsibilities involved. Using these same words in your resume will improve your chances of getting a personal interview—and the face-to-face contact is your aim.

Another approach is to ask yourself what five or six skills would be most important for this job. If "ability to work with a wide variety of people," "able to work overtime," "willing to be self-motivating" come up, for example, think of instances that demonstrate *you* have those qualities.

What should you include in your standard resume?

- your name and where you can be reached

- educational experience

- work experience: paid, unpaid, volunteer

- special skills and/or interests (optional): foreign language fluency, travel, awards, hobbies, community involvement, things that give a picture of who you are when you're not working

- statement of professional goals and objectives (optional)

- information about available references

Try to limit your resume to one page. There's a very good chance that the information on page two or three will not be read, and superfluous information will dilute your strong points. Begin your descriptive phrases with action words such as *designed, organized, responsible for.* Underscore major headings such as job titles, since your underlinings may be all that the employer will look at in a first reading of your resume. The point is to organize it so that the major points stand out or can be zeroed in on quickly.

Avoid listing the following information on your resume: salary information, reasons for leaving a previous job, narrow geographic preferences, specific references, and your philosophy and values. Leave out everything that is not absolutely relevant or of exceptional interest.

There are two widely accepted formats for resumes. A chronological one lists your educational and work experience beginning with what you have done most recently. With this kind of resume, any interruption in your work or education sticks out like a sore thumb. A skills or functional resume presents your experience in categories such as public relations, administration, research, and community organization. Dates are basically unimportant with this kind of resume. Large gaps in an employment or academic record become invisible, and whether your experience was paid or unpaid is not made into an issue. The resume on pages 220-221 is an example of the functional type. With a functional resume, be sure to include *all* the skills that you have gathered from any volunteer or unpaid work experience. Looking at other people's skills resumes can help you think of your own unpaid experience in terms of the skills you have acquired.

Always send a cover letter with your resume, stating why you are interested in a specific position and *briefly* summarizing the qualifications that apply to it most directly. You may also need to suggest the next step in the employment process, that you'll call on such and such a date about setting up an interview, and so on.

Whenever possible, the letter should be addressed to a specific person; be sure you have the correct job title. A telephone call to the receptionist can help eliminate embarrassing errors of this kind.

Catalyst has an excellent booklet about resume writing, *Resume Preparation Manual: A Step-By-Step Guide For Women* ($5.95).

KEEPING CURRENT

People change jobs on an average of once every three and a half years. In fact, a study published by Future Directions for a

Learning Society indicates that in any given year, more than 40 million Americans are in some stage of career transition or job change! So the point is not to land yourself a job once and for all, but to acquire the tools it takes to hunt for jobs effectively throughout your life.

Finding a job that appeals to you now is no reason to close down all your options. Your needs, interests, skills, and values will all go on changing—*that* you can count on. The career you have chosen today may not suit you at all next year. Or even if you still find it stimulating, you will most likely outgrow the specific job you were hired to do. So it's important to keep your job-hunting techniques current.

Any time you discover a job or career that intrigues you, begin to look into it. Set up a file on it, and find out what you can through reading and talking with as many people as possible. Being already employed puts you in an ideal situation to conduct personal surveys of the kind that have been described.

To get yourself into gear for thinking about the job-hunt process as a fascinating and ongoing part of your life, be sure to read Richard Bolles's *What Color Is Your Parachute?: A Practical Manual for Job Hunters & Career Changers* (Ten Speed Press). Whatever color your parachute is today, it will probably be slightly different tomorrow! With growth comes new options.

Epilogue

Seven years after the women and members of their families were interviewed for this book, I wrote to those who were featured in Chapter 2 for a brief update on events in their lives, and I received the following replies:

• Anna is still in charge of the operating rooms at a major teaching hospital. She has recently begun to do consulting work, which adds nicely to her income. She finds her work tremendously satisfying.

• Gloria really enjoyed being a community organizer at a free clinic. She then went on to work at a community college as a counselor for older adults, and this led to an interest in gerontology. So it was back to school, this time in a graduate certificate program called "Specialist in Aging." Gloria now does workshops relative to the elderly and sits on the local Council of Aging. She and her husband, who is now almost 75 years old, are enjoying their time together, and Gloria takes great pride in "helping out with the dual career households of my kids and their kids."

• Lorraine got a marvelous job as a coordinator for a community action agency that serves the elderly. However, since her mother and mother-in-law both needed a great deal of medical attention, she decided to work part-time. For four and a half years, she was an interviewer with the United States Bureau of the Census. The flexible hours allowed her to help care for both parents. Future plans include going back to school for a master's degree in Marriage and Family Counseling.

• Judith is exactly ten units away from graduating with a degree in interdisciplinary studies, with a 3.86 average! She has already been offered a paid position doing research at her university. Being an on-again/off-again student for over eleven years was what worked best for Judith and her family. She is *very* excited about the research position.

• Florence found quite a glamorous job doing public relations and promotion for a major tourist attraction in New England. She got married in 1979 and became a full-time mother several years ago. She is enjoying this role very much and plans to stay home until both children are in school.

• Susan graduated with honors from the community college in 1983. She and her husband were divorced shortly thereafter. She was accepted at a state university, where she is majoring in both home economics and education, as well as getting a teaching credential. Susan plans to be employed as a teacher in fall 1986. She has just been invited to join the Honor Society of Phi Kappa Phi.

• Carla graduated from college and found a paid position as an aide in a third grade classroom. She went on to work as a Learning Disabilities teacher, returning to school to earn graduate credits in special education. She has also been involved with teaching educable developmentally disabled children. Now retired, Carla takes great pleasure in the volunteer work she does with a youth group. Her husband died in 1981. The son whom Carla commuted to college with is now a sixth grade teacher; he just completed a master's degree in school administration. Her daughter, age 41, has just decided to go back to school for a degree in nursing.

• Donna received her master's degree in architecture with an unexpected area of interest: set design. While a student, she and a partner bought a house to remodel and sell. Remarrying in 1980, Donna and her husband work for her parents' business: Donna as operations manager and her husband as chief engineer. The couple has been involved with several major renovations, and Donna has done a number of set designs on a freelance basis. Donna has also expanded on her interest in costume design.

• Tracy was salutatorian of her community college graduating class. She had a second child several months later and decided to take a year off from full-time studies. One year later, she received a full scholarship to an Ivy League college, where she graduated cum laude in 1982 with a bachelor's degree in sociology. Tracy then went on to law school. Her marriage ended shortly thereafter. She graduated in 1985, and has just passed the bar. She is now employed as a corporate attorney.

• Tamara received her master's degree in psychology in 1982. For her master's project, she produced a handbook providing guidelines for other counselors to assist Native American students with their college adjustment. Tamara left her community college counseling job of nearly 15 years to move closer to her fiancé. She just got a job as a mental health counselor and will be team counseling referred offenders. She is very pleased to be taking on this type of counseling and thrilled about the new commitment in her personal life.

• Connie graduated with a degree in nursing and worked part-time for four years as a medical surgical nurse in a community hospital. She left her job because it required her to be at the hospital every other weekend, and she wanted to be home with her family. She has been a hospice nurse for the past three years, working about 20 hours a week. The work is very satisfying to her, and the flexible hours integrate well with her lifestyle. She thinks that she will soon be at another career crossroads. She is becoming more and more interested in the field of nutrition, and may return to school to pursue a career in that field.

• Ruth found a part-time job doing therapeutic recreation in a nursing home. She managed to develop the position into full-time employment. After seven years, she decided to retire. Her husband is cutting back on his work, and they anticipate doing some traveling in the next few years. Although Ruth is "in her retirement years," she is taking stock of her interests in order to pursue other work.

• Cathy was not available to give a recent update. Five years ago, she received her master's degree in psychology. She also did a one-year internship, which qualified her as a school psychologist. Degree in hand, she and her son moved from California to New

York, where she married a man she had known since childhood. She was feeling very optimistic about her training and her potential in the job market.

• Mary, also unavailable to give a recent update, took a semester off from school, "accepting the reality that I was not—and did not want to be—'Wonder Woman.'" Encouraged by a professor-friend, she switched her goal of a bachelor's degree in accounting to a master's degree in business. Instead of trying to plow through the courses as quickly as possible, she decided to take her time. She hoped to finish in two or two and a half years, and then planned to do financial or managerial consulting.

Several of the women had additional comments they wanted to share with the readers of this book. Here are Susan's:

> Eight years ago, when I went back to school, it saved my life. My spirit was dying. Going back to school also turned my life upside down. Nevertheless, I do not regret going back to school for one minute. It was an excellent decision, for I am finally on my way to a place where I know I can shine! It is one of the best things that I have ever done for myself and for my children. I would say to anyone that if going back to school is important to them, then do it and not to let anything deter them.

Mary offered some advice to the initially overzealous returnee:

> Next to fear of failure, burning out is the biggest pitfall women returning to school face. When women like myself, who have domestic responsibilities, return to school with a career in mind, they are ravenous for the whole experience. And, feeling this way, I did not plan as carefully and methodically as I needed, and hence the burn-out. Like the child learning to walk, I needed to slow down and appreciate each step I took before trying to climb every mountain in sight.

Florence deftly described the kind of tightrope many women have to walk when they apply for high-powered positions:

> It's a catch-22 as far as certain interviews go, because you must appear very capable and at the same time, act cooperative, sweet, sensitive, docile, and nonthreatening to others.

Connie warns about some of the tensions that can accompany

entering the work force in middle age:

> People thought I had been working for many years when I first started
> nursing at the age of 37. They figured I knew it all, but I felt like I
> didn't know a thing. Actually, it's a lot easier to say "I don't know"
> when you're 37 than it is when you're 18.

Many of the women who were interviewed for this book are
thinking about going back to school yet *again*—to get additional
training in their field, gather different skills, or simply to develop a
new interest. As Donna comments: "I loved being in an academic
environment where experimentation was encouraged. It was deeply
rewarding. If there were half an excuse, I'd go back again. I'd like
to take more art courses, study theatre arts, anthropology. . . ."
Connie adds: "I'll probably still be going back to school when I'm
80. Getting old doesn't mean that you've stopped dreaming, that
you've stopped wanting to learn."

Gloria feels that her experiences in school and as an employee
have made her better prepared in her personal life:

> I am very well aware that my going back to school as a middle-aged
> adult—both times—and handling the jobs I had did much for further
> developing my self-esteem and self-management skills. I realize this
> especially when I am with my peers who did not have these kinds of
> experiences. As I look ahead, I believe that learning more about set-
> ting priorities, diving into unknown stressful situations, being more
> assertive, and generally taking more control of my life—all of which
> came with my later school and work experiences—are invaluable. I
> look forward to getting older and feel kind of toughened up for the
> losses and adjustments that are likely to be out there.

Self-doubt *can* and usually does appear during a stint as a reentry student, but most reentry students believe that the anxieties
they experienced were worth it in the end. Tracy comments:

> During law school, there were times when I wondered whether I
> would make it. Now that it's over, I look back and wonder how I did.
> I was a single parent at the same time I was taking a full load of
> courses, plus working 15 to 20 hours a week! *It's worth it!* I'm *finally*
> self-sufficient. My children are very proud of my achievements and
> have developed high motivation of their own.

What's in it for *you*? What are the odds? Am I doing the right thing? Anyone who returns to school will find herself asking this question—again and again—all along the reentry route. For reassurance when you are plagued by doubts, remember that 96 percent of the graduated reentry women students in one survey felt their college experience had been worthwhile in terms of their own personal development, and over three-quarters of them felt that school had expanded their employment opportunities. So the odds are definitely in your favor.

You won't find a more enthusiastic group of students on campus than the returnees who have been there long enough to get their academic feet wet. They will tell you that working through the practical problems and psychological hassles is a major opportunity for professional and personal growth and change.

I hope that you have found a good supply of encouragement, moral support, and practical advice in this book. Want some more? Go to a campus near your home and ask a slightly overtired-looking student who is about your age why she's there. Happy landings!

Appendix A

How to Find Career and Educational Counseling

If you decide to return to school, you will be making an impressive number of major decisions. For one thing, you will need to figure out what focus you want your studies to take. If you are going to college in order to prepare for employment, make sure that your studies are either preparing you for employment in your chosen field or, at the very least, giving you a solid educational background.

Many resources for educational and career counseling are available to you. College continuing education departments hold weekend and evening workshops on the various aspects of finding or changing careers. Get onto the mailing list for the bulletins put out by nearby campus continuing education departments (they may also be called "extension" or "community relations" departments.) Also, call the college career development center to see if they are holding any workshops that might be of special interest to you. And be sure to check out the junior colleges in your area.

Workshops are also put on by special interest groups such as the YWCA. Libraries sometimes hold information fairs about the educational opportunities in their area.

Ask friends and relatives to recommend resources. As you gather information, keep a file of programs so that you can compare types of services and costs.

Two organizations can be helpful to you in your search for career and educational counseling:

Catalyst
250 Park Avenue South
New York, NY 10003

The National Center for Educational Brokering
325 Ninth Street
San Francisco, CA 94103

Catalyst has organized The Catalyst Network, a group of independent resource centers that provide career and educational counseling and programs for individuals who wish to advance their careers, change fields, or reenter the job market. According to their free pamphlet, which lists over 170 centers, "these centers represent a wide range of groups, including profit and nonprofit organizations, college and university programs, and individual career consultants. All have a particular commitment to meeting the career needs of women." Affiliation with Catalyst does *not* represent formal accreditation or regulation, but it does mean that these centers are expected to meet certain established criteria. Get a copy of the free listing of those who are involved with the Catalyst Network— it's a very good first step in locating educational and career counseling opportunities near you. See Chapter 19 for other Catalyst resources.

The National Center for Educational Brokering puts out a listing of over 1,100 educational brokering-type programs in its *Educational and Career Information Services for Adults Directory*. The most recent edition is 1985. Educational brokers can serve as important mediators between adult learners and the enormous array of educational resources they confront. These impartial brokers can help you make educational and career decisions and select appropriate educational resources. Brokers do *not* recruit students for individual institutions. To find out what programs are in your area, call NCEB, 415-626-2378, or send $4.00 to the above address for a copy of the directory.

Appendix B

A Selected Listing of Financial Resources for Women

Altrusa International Founders Fund Vocational Aid

Chairman, Founders Fund Vocational Aid Committee
Altrusa International Foundation, Inc.
8 South Michigan Avenue
Chicago, IL 60603

Maximum awards of $800 are given for training or retraining that will lead to employment. The emphasis is on vocational education. Women participating in two-year technology programs are eligible during the last half of their studies. Awards are not given to students pursuing a four-year college degree. Selection is based on aptitude and need; older women are preferred. Approximately 175 awards are given. Apply to the national office, although screening is done through the nearly 600 local clubs.

Amelia Earhart Fellowship Awards

Zonta International
35 East Wacker Drive
Chicago, IL 60601

These $6,000 awards are for women demonstrating a superior academic record, a bachelor's degree in a related science, and graduate school acceptance. Applicants should be entering or continuing full-time graduate study in aerospace-related fields. The fellowships are open to women of all ages. In 1985, 28 fellowships were awarded. Recipients may reapply. The funds may be used in any way, and in combination with other financial aid.

American Association of University Women—Project Renew Grants, scholarships, fellowships.

> *AAUW Educational Foundation Programs*
> *2401 Virginia Avenue NW*
> *Washington, DC 20037*

Project Renew Grants are for women who received a bachelor's degree at least five years prior to applying for this grant. Grants ranging from $500 to $3,500 are for the purpose of financially assisting women who are returning to school in order to begin or further a career. AAUW members are given preference. In 1984, 14 out of 150 applicants were awarded grants; in 1985, there were 27 out of 150. The Educational Foundation also sponsors generous fellowships for those in the advanced years of a professional or doctoral degree and postdoctoral research. In addition, contact local AAUW chapters about possible reentry scholarships awarded at the local level.

American Business Women's Association scholarships, grants, and loans

> *American Business Women's Association*
> *National Headquarters*
> *P.O. Box 8728*
> *Kansas City, MO 64114-0728*

ABWA offers scholarships through local chapters. During the past several years, the chapters have awarded over $2 million annually for local scholarships to women of all ages. Contact the national association for the name of the chapter nearest you. Grants and interest-free loans, sponsored by the local chapters, are offered through the Stephen Bufton Memorial Educational Fund. For these, students must be at least a junior in college, a U.S. citizen, and attending a college or university in the USA. Grants for as much as $800 and interest-free loans for a maximum of $1,500 are available. For further information about the grants and loans, contact the national headquarters.

The BPW/Sears-Roebuck Loan Fund for Women in Graduate Business Studies

Business and Professional Women's Foundation
2012 Massachusetts Avenue NW
Washington, DC 20036

Providing $75,000 annually, this loan fund is directed toward American women seeking their master's in business administration. Study may be full- or part-time. Women must already be: accepted into a degree program; able to demonstrate career motivation and ability to complete the course of study; and able to demonstrate financial need. Loans range from $500 to $2,500 per year, with the maximum of $5,000. The interest rate is 7 percent per annum, in five installments, with repayment beginning 12 months after completion of the program.

The Business and Professional Women's Foundation Loan Fund for Women in Engineering Studies

Business and Professional Women's Foundation
2012 Massachusetts Avenue NW
Washington, DC 20036

This fund is designed to assist American women in their final two years of any accredited engineering program, including undergraduate, refresher, and conversion programs, as well as graduate studies. Study may be full-time or part-time. Applicants must be able to demonstrate their financial need and show their career motivation and technical ability to complete the course of study. Approximately $50,000 is distributed annually. A maximum of $5,000 is lent to any one person for an academic year. Additional loans may be applied for up to $10,000. The interest rate is currently 7 percent, with repayment beginning 12 months after completion of the educational program.

Career Advancement Scholarship

> *Business and Professional Women's Foundation*
> *2012 Massachusetts Avenue NW*
> *Washington, DC 20036*

These scholarships are awarded to American women age 25 years and older for full- or part-time study. They cover academic, vocational, or paraprofessional courses. Applicants must demonstrate financial need in order to update skills or complete their education for career advancement, be within 24 months of completing the program of study, and be officially accepted into an accredited institution. In addition, applicants must have a definite plan to use the training to improve chances for advancement, train for a new career field, or enter or reenter the job market. Scholarships range from $200 to $1,000 for one year, with an average award of $750. Approximately $50,000 was distributed in 1985.

Clairol Scholarship Program

> *Business and Professional Women's Foundation*
> *2012 Massachusetts Avenue NW*
> *Washington, DC 20036*

These scholarships are awarded to American women age 30 years and older who are in school full- or part-time pursuing academic, vocational, and paraprofessional coursework. Applicants must be able to demonstrate financial need in order to upgrade skills or complete education for career advancement, be within 24 months of completing the program of study, and be officially accepted into an accredited institution. In addition, applicants must have a definite plan to use the training to improve chances for advancement, train for a new career field, or enter or reenter the job market. Scholarships range from $200 to $1,000 for one year, and the average award is $750. Approximately $50,000 is distributed yearly. (An additional $25,000 will be distributed to women who have graduated from college who can now serve as role models for other reentry women. Grants are $1,000 each. For further information, contact: Clairol Scholarship Program, 345 Park Avenue, New York, NY 10154.)

Jean Arnot Reid Scholarship Program

National Association of Bank Women, Inc.
500 North Michigan Avenue, Suite 1400
Chicago, IL 60611

Applicants must be members of NABW and demonstrate a need for further education to achieve their career goals. There are six scholarships: $5,000 (1); $4,000 (1); $3,000 (1); and $2,000 (3). Funds awarded are to be used for tuition, room, and board at the banking or financial educational program of the recipient's choice, including the NABW Bachelor's Degree Program. The awards can be used for undergraduate or graduate study.

Junior League of Northern Virginia scholarships

Junior League of Northern Virginia
400 North Washington Street, Suite 110
Falls Church, VA 22046

Applicants must be American women at least 30 years old and able to demonstrate clear financial need in order to either pursue the development of a career, upgrade their career potential, or change career direction. Applicants must live in northern Virginia. Approximately $10,000 is distributed yearly.

Mary McEwen Schimke Scholarship

Secretary to the Committee, Graduate Fellowships
Office of Financial Aid
Wellesley College
Wellesley, MA 02181

This supplemental award, ranging from $500 to $1,000, is designed to give students relief from household and child care expenses while pursuing graduate study at any accredited American academic institution. The award is made on the basis of scholarly expectation and identified need. The candidate must be at least 30 years old and currently engaged in graduate study in literature and/ or history. Preference is given to students of American Studies.

New York Life Foundation Scholarship Program for Women in the Health Professions

> *Business and Professional Women's Foundation*
> *2012 Massachusetts Avenue NW*
> *Washington, DC 20036*

Scholarships ranging from $250 to $1,000 are awarded for full- or part-time study to American women, age 25 years and older, who are seeking the education necessary to enter into or advance within a career in the health-care field. Applicants must be officially accepted by an accredited institution and be within 24 months of completing the program. Applicants must be able to demonstrate financial need in order to upgrade skills or complete their education for career advancement, and training must lead to entry or reentry into the job market or improve their chances for advancement. Approximately $50,000 is distributed annually.

Soroptomist Training Awards Program

> *Soroptomist International of the Americas, Inc.*
> *1616 Walnut Street*
> *Philadelphia, PA 19103*

The Training Award Program gives cash awards of $1,500 each to 43 women. The awards are designed to assist the mature woman who, as head of household, must enter or reenter the job market or further her skills and training in order to upgrade her employment status. Recipients are chosen on the basis of financial need as well as their statement of clear career goals. Primary consideration is given to women entering vocational or technical training, or completing an undergraduate degree. Competition for the Training Awards Program begins at the local Soroptomist Club level. Local clubs choose recipients at their own discretion, and these recipients become eligible for the award of $1,500. Contact your local Soroptomist Club.

USEFUL REFERENCES

Better Late Than Never: Financial Aid for Older Women Seeking Education and Training. This booklet includes: programs offering financial aid and counseling; federal financial aid programs; and non-governmental sources of scholarships, fellowships, grants, and loans. It is specifically geared for the woman who needs to train or retrain for reentry into the job market. Send a check for $8.00 to Women's Equity Action League, 1250 I Street NW, Suite 305, Washington, DC 20005.

Directory of Financial Aids for Women, 1987–1988, Gail Ann Schlachter, Los Angeles: Reference Service Press, 1986. This 400-page book provides the most comprehensive and up-to-date listing of financial aid programs for women: in all, there are over 1,500 references and cross-references to scholarships, loans, fellowships, grants, internships, awards, and prizes set aside primarily or exclusively for women. The directory sells for $37.50, and it should be available in the reference section of your local library.

Educational Financial Aids. This guide, specifically geared toward women, includes fellowships, scholarships, and internships in higher education. Send a check for $6.00 to Sales Office, American Association of University Women, 2401 Virginia Avenue NW, Washington, DC 20037.

Educational Financial Aid Sources for Women. This free pamphlet is prepared by the Clairol Scholarship Program. It provides information about the major sources of financial aid for women seeking to further their education. Write to Clairol Scholarship Program, 345 Park Avenue, New York, NY 10154.

Financial Aid: A Partial List of Resources for Women. This booklet describes scholarships, grants, and loans available to high school students applying to college as well as to older women, minority women, women considering nontraditional careers, and others at all levels of postsecondary education. Send a check for $2.50 to Project on the Status and Education of Women, Association of American Colleges, 1818 R Street NW, Washington, DC 20009.

Higher Education Opportunities for Minorities and Women: Annotated Selections. This 75-page booklet includes opportunities for women and minorities, arranged by various fields of study. Sources of general information and a student's guide to federal financial aid programs are included. Send a check for $3.00 to Superintendent of Documents, Government Printing Office, Washington, DC 20401.

Paying for Your Education: A Guide for Adult Learners. This book, put out by The College Board, discusses aid opportunities for 12 special categories of adult learners, a description of federal aid programs, and a listing of state and local funding sources. The book costs $7.95 and is available at bookstores.

Scholarship Guide, The Women's Sports Foundation. This directory lists athletic scholarships for women at over 800 schools. Send a check for $2.00 to The Women's Sports Foundation, 195 Moulton Street, San Francisco, CA 94123.

Also: See Appendix D, Section 4 of this book for a listing of general financial aid directories and resources. And see Chapters 12 and 13 for advice on how to find and apply for financial aid.

Appendix C

Accrediting Associations —and Why They are Important to You

Once you make a commitment to getting a college degree or credential, you want to make sure that it is a "good" one when all is said and done. If you want a bona fide college degree and the school you choose isn't accredited by a reputable agency, you will be deeply disappointed over precious time lost. The solution is to find out whether the school you are looking at is accredited—*and by whom!*

There are accrediting associations, recognized by The Council on Postsecondary Accreditation in Washington, DC, that evaluate entire colleges and universities. In addition, there are professional accrediting associations, also recognized by COPA, that evaluate either specialized schools or specific departments or programs within a school.

The Council on Postsecondary Accreditation's *Accredited Institutions of Postsecondary Education*, published by the Macmillan Publishing Company, lists all the institutions that are accredited by any of the 14 recognized accrediting bodies. In addition, it lists all programs that are accredited by a professional or specialized accrediting agency. You should be able to get this book at your local library. If not, ask them to borrow it for you through an interlibrary loan.

The first question to ask is: Is this school accredited by one of the associations recognized by the Council on Postsecondary Accreditation? If the answer is no, then the next question is: Has the program I am interested in been accredited by a relevant professional association?

It is hard to believe that an academic institution would fudge on its accreditation status, but it happens. Remember, just because a school is accredited does *not* mean that a reputable agency has done the accrediting. Take time to check it out.

Appendix D

Selected Bibliography

The following listing is designed to guide you to other resources that can help throughout the reentry process. It is labeled a "selected" bibliography because it does not include all the many articles and books that exist on the subject, only those that I view as most useful. A * appears next to those publications that might be useful to people working with reentry students. I have included several excellent books that are now out of print, designated by the initials "O.P." You might be able to find these books at used book stores and at your library. If your library does not have the book you want, ask if they can get it for you through an interlibrary loan.

I am constantly accumulating material concerning the topics involved with reentry. If you find something that you think might be of interest to me, please send me a note about it c/o Ten Speed Press, P.O. Box 7123, Berkeley, CA 94707.

1. SOURCES OF INFORMATION
ABOUT REENTRY STUDENTS

ADELSTEIN, DIANE, et al. "Dimensions Underlying the Characteristics and Needs of Returning Women Students," *Journal of the National Association for Women Deans, Administrators, and Counselors* 46:4 (Summer 1983), pp. 32–37.*

"Applying the Gray Matter: A Boom in Adult Courses Proves You Are Never Too Old to Learn." *Time*, October 3, 1977, p. 92.

ASLANIAN, CAROL, and BRICKELL, HENRY. *Americans in Transition: Life Changes as Reasons for Adult Learning.* New York: College Entrance Examination Board, 1980.

ASTIN, HELEN S., ed. *Some Action of Her Own: The Adult Woman and Higher Education.* Lexington, Mass.: D.C. Heath & Company, 1976. O.P.*

BERKOVE, GAIL. "Returning Women Students: A Study of Stress and Success." Abstract of research in progress with excerpts from a panel discussion called "Problems of Women's Continuing Education," March 1977. In Dorothy McGuigan, ed., *Newsletter*, Center for Continuing Education of Women, University of Michigan, 10:1 (Summer 1977), pp. 1–5.*

BRANDENBURG, JUDITH B. "The Needs of Women Returning to School." *Personnel and Guidance Journal* 53:1 (September 1974), pp. 11–18.*

BRENDON, MARY ANN. "Retention of Undergraduate Women of Nontraditional Age: Patterns, Strategies, and Services," *Journal of the National Association for Women Deans, Administrators, and Counselors* 48:3 (Spring 1985), pp. 22–27.*

CAMPBELL, JEAN W. "The Nontraditional Student in Academe." In W. Todd Furniss and Patricia Albjerg Graham, eds., *Women in Higher Education.* Washington, D.C.: American Council on Education, 1974, pp. 192–99.* O.P.

————. "Women Drop Back In: Educational Innovation in the Sixties." In Alice S. Rossi and Ann Calderwood, eds., *Academic Women on the Move.* New York: Russell Sage Foundation, 1973, pp. 93–124.*

CLEMENTS, K. "Emotional Characteristics of Mature Women Students in Education." Paper presented at meeting of the American Research Association, Chicago, 1974. (ERIC Document Reproduction Service No. ED 087 980.)*

COPAS, ERNESTINE, and DWINELL, PATRICIA. "Women's Opportunities Network: An Entity for Initiating Programs and Services for Nontraditional Women Students," *Journal of the National Association for Women Deans, Administrators, and Counselors* 46:3 (Spring 1983), pp. 23–37.*

DI NUZZO, THERESA, and TOLBERT, E. L. "Promoting the Personal Growth and Vocational Maturity of the Re-entry Woman: A Group Approach," *Journal of the National Association for Women Deans, Administrators, and Counselors* 45:1 (Fall 1981), pp. 26–31.*

DOTY, BARBARA A. "Why Do Women Return to College?" *Journal of the National Association of Women Deans and Counselors* 29:4 (Summer 1966), pp. 171–74.*

DURCHHOLZ, PAT, and O'CONNOR, JANET. "Why Women Go Back to College." In *Women on Campus: The Unfinished Liberation.* New Rochelle, NY: *Change* Magazine, 1975, pp. 236–41.*

EMERSON, SHIRLEY. "Guilt in Mature Women Students." Abstract of research in progress plus excerpts from a panel discussion called "Problems of Women's Continuing Education," March 1977. In Dorothy McGuigan, ed., *Newsletter*, Center for Continuing Education of Women, University of Michigan, 10:1 (Summer 1977), pp. 1–5.*

EWING, GLEASON. "Employment Opportunities of Mature Women Graduates of California State University, Hayward." Unpublished survey for University Reentry Program, 1978.*

GEISLER, MARGARET P., and THRUSH, RANDOLPH S. "Counseling Experiences and Needs of Older Women Students." *Journal of the National Association for Women Deans, Administrators, and Counselors* 39:1 (Fall 1975), pp. 3–8.*

GRAY, EILEEN. *Everywoman's Guide to College.* Millbrae, CA: Les Femmes Publishing, 1975. O.P.

GREENFEIG, BEVERLY, and GOLDBERG, BARBARA. "Orienting Returning Adult Students." In M. L. Upcraft, ed., *Orienting Students to College.* San Francisco: Jossey-Bass, 1984.*

HALFTER, IRMA T. "The Comparative Academic Achievement of Young and Old." *Journal of the National Association of Women Deans and Counselors* 25:2 (January 1962), pp. 60–67.*

HAPONSKI, WILLIAM, and MCCABE, CHARLES. *New Horizons: The Education and Career-Planning Guide for Adults.* Princeton, NJ: Peterson's Guides, 1985.

HAWES, GENE. *The College Board Guide to Going to College While Working: Strategies for Success.* New York: College Entrance Examination Board, 1985.

HENDEL, DARWIN. "Adult Women's Perceptions of Continuing Education for Women," *Journal of the National Association for Women Deans, Administrators, and Counselors* 46:4 (Summer 1983), pp. 38–42.*

HILTUNEN, WANDALYN A. "A Counseling Course for the Mature Woman." *Journal of the National Association of Women Deans and Counselors* 31:2 (Winter 1968), pp. 93–96.*

HOWARD, TONI A. "Reentry Programs." In Clare Rose, ed., *New Directions for Higher Education: Meeting Women's New Educational Needs.* San Francisco: Jossey-Bass, Inc., Publishers, Autumn 1975 (11), pp. 43–59.* O.P.

KAPLAN, SUSAN ROMER. "A Feminist Cinderella Tale: Women Over Thirty in Graduate and Professional School," *Journal of the National Association for Women Deans, Administrators, and Counselors* (Spring 1982) 45:3, pp. 9–15.*

KARELIUS-SCHUMACHER, KAREN L. "Designing a Counseling Program for the Mature Woman Student." *Journal of the National Association for Women Deans, Administrators, and Counselors* 41:1 (Fall 1977), pp. 28–31.*

KEEGAN, LYNN, and PATTILLO, MARILYN. *Survival!: The Busy Woman's Guide for Returning to School.* Temple, TX: Datalife Resources, 1984.

KOLAR, ANNE, and HILLS, BARBARA. "Stress and Incentive in Female Social Work Students." Abstract of research in progress with excerpts
from a panel discussion called "Problems of Women's Continuing Education," March 1977. In Dorothy McGuigan, ed., *Newsletter*, Center
for Continuing Education of Women, University of Michigan 10:1
(Summer 1977), pp. 1–6.*

LENZ, ELINOR, and SHAEVITZ, MARJORIE HANSEN. *So You Want to Go
Back to School: Facing the Realities of Reentry*. New York: McGraw-
Hill Book Company, 1977. O.P.; possible reprint.

MANHEIMER, JOAN. "Thoughts on Continuing Education," *Journal of the
National Association for Women Deans, Administrators, and Counselors* 46:4 (Summer 1983), pp. 11–14.*

MANIS, LAURA G., and MOCHIZUKI, JUNE. "Search for Fulfillment: A Program for Adult Women." *Personnel and Guidance Journal* 50:7 (March
1972), pp. 594–99.*

MARGOLIS, DIANE ROTHBARD. "A Fair Return." In *Women on Campus: The
Unfinished Liberation*. New Rochelle, NY: *Change* Magazine, 1975,
pp. 249–56.

MARKUS, HELEN. "Characteristics and Experiences of Returning Women
Students at the University of Michigan." Report on research with excerpts from a panel discussion called "Problems of Women's Continuing Education," March 1977. In Dorothy McGuigan, ed., *Newsletter*, Center for Continuing Education of Women, University of
Michigan, 10:1 (Summer 1977), pp. 1–8.*

————. "Continuing Education of Women: Factors Influencing a Return
to School and the School Experience." Unpublished paper, University
of Michigan, 1972.*

MARPLE, BETTY LOU N. "Adult Women Students Compared With Younger
Students on Selected Personality Variables." *Journal of the National
Association for Women Deans, Administrators, and Counselors* 40:1
(Fall 1976), pp. 11–15.*

MATTHEWS, ESTHER E. "The Counselor and the Adult Woman." *Journal
of the National Association of Women Deans and Counselors* 32:3
(Spring 1969), pp. 115–22.*

MCGUIGAN, DOROTHY, ed. *The University of Michigan Center for Continuing Education of Women 1964–1977: A Report*. Ann Arbor: University of Michigan, 1978.*

MENDELSOHN, PAMELA. "Positive and Negative Effects from Returning to
School as Perceived by Reentry Women and Their Mates." Master's
project, Humboldt State University, Arcata, CA, 1978.*

MISHLER, CAROL. "From Adult Learner to Wage Earner: What Happens
to Homemakers after College Graduation," *Journal of the National
Association for Women Deans, Administrators, and Counselors* 46:4
(Summer 1983), pp. 15–21.*

MITCHELL, S. B. "Women and the Doctorate." Ph.D. dissertation, Oklahoma State University, 1969.*

MOMMA women, University of California, Santa Barbara. "Going Back to School." In Karol Hope and Nancy Young, eds., *MOMMA: The Sourcebook for Single Mothers*. New York: The New American Library, 1976, pp. 175–88. O.P.

NICHOLS, C. G. "A Seminar in Personality Development for Mature Women." *Journal of the National Association for Women Deans, Administrators, and Counselors* 37:3 (Spring 1974), pp. 123–27.*

PALMER, STACY. "Congress Showing More than Usual Concern about the Needs of Non-Traditional Students," *Chronicle of Higher Education* 30:18 (July 3, 1985), pp. 15–16.*

PIRNOT, KAREN, and DUNN, WENDY. "Value Priorities of Adult Students," *Journal of the National Association for Women Deans, Administrators, and Counselors* 46:4 (Summer 1983), pp. 22–25.*

PROJECT ON THE STATUS AND EDUCATION OF WOMEN. Three packets, five papers each, focusing on reentry women. Intended for institutional use. $5.00 per packet. Project on the Status and Education of Women, Association of American Colleges, 1818 R Street, NW, Washington, DC 20009.*

Review Article: Barriers to Academic Re-entry Women and How to Overcome Them. The Program on Women, Northwestern University, 617 Noyes Street, Evanston, IL 60201.*

RICE, JOY. "Operation Second Chance," *Journal of the National Association for Women Deans, Administrators, and Counselors* 46:4 (Summer 1983), pp. 3–10.*

————, and GOERING, MARGARET L. "Women in Transition: A Life-Planning Model." *Journal of the National Association for Women Deans, Administrators, and Counselors* 40:2 (Winter 1977), pp. 57–61.*

ROACH, R. M. "'Honey, Won't You Please Stay Home?'" *Personnel and Guidance Journal* 55:2 (October 1976), pp. 86–89.*

Second Wind: A Program for Returning Women Students, University of Maryland at College Park. EDC/WEEA Publishing Center Order Department, 55 Chapel Street, Newton, MA 02160.*

SPREADBURY, CONNIE. "Family Adjustment When Adult Women Return to School," *Journal of the National Association for Women Deans, Administrators, and Counselors* 46:4 (Summer 1983), pp. 26–31.*

STONE, ELIZABETH. "The New Kid in Class Is Your Mother." *Ms.*, September 1979, pp. 46–50.

TITTLE, CAROL KEHR, and DENKER, ELENOR RUBIN. "Reentry Women: A Selective Review of the Educational Process, Career Choice, and Interest Measurement." *Review of Educational Research* 47:4 (Fall 1977), pp. 531–84.*

VAN METER, M. J. S. "Role Strain Among Married College Women." Report on research with excerpts from a panel discussion called "Problems of Women's Continuing Education," March 1977. In Dorothy McGuigan, ed., *Newsletter*, Center for Continuing Education of Women, University of Michigan, 10:1 (Summer 1977), pp. 1–7.*

VAN'T HUL, NELVIA, ed. *The University of Michigan Center for Continuing Education of Women 1964–1984: A Report*. Ann Arbor: University of Michigan, 1984.*

WESTERVELT, ESTHER MANNING, and FIXTER, DEBORAH A. *Women's Higher and Continuing Education: An Annotated Bibliography with Selected References of Related Aspects of Women's Lives*. New York: College Entrance Examination Board, 1971.* O.P.

2. SOURCES OF INFORMATION ABOUT TWO-YEAR AND FOUR-YEAR COLLEGES AND UNIVERSITIES

AMERICAN COLLEGE TESTING PROGRAM. 1985–1986 *College Planning/ Search Book: Steps for Successful College Planning*. Iowa City, IA: The American College Testing Program, 1985.

AMERICAN COUNCIL ON EDUCATION, ed. *American Universities and Colleges*. 12th ed. New York: Walter de Gruyter, 1983.

Barron's Guide to the Two-Year Colleges. Vol. 1. New York: Barron's Educational Series, 1981.

Barron's Profiles of American Colleges. Vols. 1–2. 13th ed. New York: Barron's Educational Series, 1982.

CARRIS, JOAN, and CRYSTAL, MICHAEL. *SAT Success*. Princeton, NJ: Peterson's Guides, 1985.

CASS, JAMES, and BIRNBAUM, MAX. *Comparative Guide to American Colleges: For Students, Parents, and Counselors*. 12th ed. New York: Harper & Row, Publishers, 1985.

—————. *Comparative Guide to Two-Year Colleges and Career Programs*. New York: Harper & Row, Publishers, 1976. O.P.

The College Board Achievement Tests: 14 Tests in 13 Subjects. New York: College Board, 1983.

The College Handbook, 1985–86. 23rd ed. New York: College Entrance Examination Board, 1985.

Directory of Graduate Programs: 1986 & 1987. Vol. A–D. Princeton, NJ: Educational Testing Service, 1985.

GOLDSTEIN, AMY, ed. *Peterson's Annual Guides to Graduate Study 1986*. 20th ed. Books 1–5. Princeton, NJ: Peterson's Guides, 1986.

GRAY, EILEEN. *Everywoman's Guide to College*. Millbrae, CA: Les Femmes Publishing, 1975. (Chaps. 6–8: on choosing a school.) O.P.

GRE Information Bulletin 1985–86. Includes registration material for the Minority Graduate Student Locater Service. Princeton, NJ: Educational Testing Service. Graduate Record Exams, CN6000, Princeton, NJ 08541-6000. (Free.)

HARRIS, SHERRY. *1985–86 Accredited Institutions of Postsecondary Education.* New York: Macmillan Publishing Company, 1986.

HOWE, FLORENCE, et al. *Everywoman's Guide to Colleges and Universities: An Educational Project of The Feminist Press.* Old Westbury, NY: 1982.

LEHMAN, ANDREA, ed. *Peterson's Annual Guide to Undergraduate Study: Four-Year Colleges 1986.* 16th ed. Princeton, NJ: Peterson's Guides, 1985.

————. *Peterson's Annual Guide to Undergraduate Study: Two-Year Colleges 1986.* 16th ed. Princeton, NJ: Peterson's Guides, 1985.

LENZ, ELINOR, and SHAEVITZ, MARJORIE HANSEN. *So You Want to Go Back to School: Facing the Realities of Reentry.* New York: McGraw-Hill Book Company, 1977. (Chaps. 3–4: on choosing a school.) O.P.; possible reprint.

Practicing to take the GRE General Test. Practicing to Take the GRE Subject Tests. 6 practice books. Princeton, NJ: Educational Testing Service, 1985.

Preparing for the ACT Assessment. (Bulletin.) Iowa City: ACT Registration Department, PO Box 414, Iowa City, IA 52243. (Free.)

Registration Bulletin 1985–86: SAT and Achievement Tests. Princeton, NJ: College Board ATP, CN6200, Princeton, NJ 08541-6200. (Free.)

Registering for the ACT Assessment 1985–86. (Bulletin.) Iowa City ACT Registration Department, PO Box 414, Iowa City, IA 52243. (Free.)

10 SATs: Scholastic Aptitude Tests of the College Board. New York: College Board, 1983.

STRANGE, MARLISS, and BENNETT, JACK. *Applying to Graduate School: A Student's Guide.* New York: Arco Publishing Company, 1985.

STRAUGHN, CHARLES II, and STRAUGHN, BARBARASUE, eds. *Lovejoy's College Guide.* 17th ed. New York: Monarch Press, 1985.

3. SOURCES OF INFORMATION ABOUT INNOVATIVE ACCESS ROUTES TO A COLLEGE DEGREE

BEAR, JOHN. *Bear's Guide to Non-Traditional College Degrees.* 9th ed. Berkeley, CA: Ten Speed Press, 1985.

CLEP Colleges: Test Centers and Other Participating Institutions. CLEP Publications, CN6600, Princeton, NJ 08541-6600. (Free.)

DUFFY, JAMES. *How to Earn a College Degree without Going to College.* New York: Stein and Day, 1982.

EISENBERG, GERSON. *Learning Vacations: Mind-Expanding Recreation for Every Interest, Age, and Budget.* 4th ed. Princeton, NJ: Peterson's Guides, 1982.

EKSTROM, RUTH B., HARRIS, ABIGAIL M., and LOCKHEED, MARLAINE E. *How to Get College Credit for What You Have Learned As a Home-maker and Volunteer.* Princeton, NJ: Educational Testing Service, 1977. ($5.00.)

GROSS, RONALD. *New Paths to Learning: College Education for Adults* (Public Affairs Pamphlet No. 546). Public Affairs Committee, 381 Park Avenue South, New York, NY 10016. ($1.00.)

Guide to the CLEP Examinations. New York: College Board, 1984. College Board Publications, Department B10, Box 886, New York, NY 10101. ($5.00.)

HEGENER, KAREN, ed. *Who Offers Part-Time Degree Programs?* 2nd ed. Princeton, NJ: Peterson's Guides, 1985.

LEVIN, FELICE MICHAELS. "Old Roots, New Branches: An Update on CLEP," *The College Board Review,* 131 (Spring 1984), pp. 2–6.*

MEYER, PETER. *Awarding College Credit for Non-College Learning.* San Francisco: Jossey-Bass Publishers, 1975.

MODOC PRESS, INC., ed. *The Macmillan Guide to Correspondence Study.* New York: Macmillan Publishing Company, 1983.

Moving Ahead With CLEP. CLEP Publications, CN6600, Princeton, NJ 08541-6600. (Free.)

MUNZERT, ALFRED W. *National Directory of External Degree Programs.* New York: Hemisphere Publications, 1977.

READY, BARBARA. *The Independent Study Catalog: NUCEA's Guide to In-dependent Study Through Correspondence Instruction 1986–1988.* Princeton, NJ: Peterson's Guides, 1986.

Regents College Degrees: General Information (catalog). The University of the State of New York, Cultural Education Center, Albany, NY 12230. (Free.)

Regents College Degrees (view book). The University of the State of New York, Cultural Education Center, Albany, NY 12230. (Free.)

SIMOSKO, SUSAN. *Earn College Credit for What You Know.* Washington, DC: Acropolis Books Ltd., 1985.

SULLIVAN, EUGENE, ed. *Guide to External Degree Programs in the United States.* 2d ed. New York: Macmillan Publishing Company, 1983.

THALER, PAT, and SHAPIRO, SONYA. "New Routes to a College Degree: Nontraditional College Education in New York and New Jersey." *New York Magazine,* August 29, 1977, pp. 33–44.

4. SOURCES OF INFORMATION ABOUT FINANCIAL AID FOR STUDENTS

BEAR, JOHN. *Bear's Guide to Finding Money for College.* Berkeley, CA: Ten Speed Press, 1984.

CASSIDY, DANIEL, and ALVES, MICHAEL. *The Scholarship Book: The Com-*

plete Guide to Private-Sector Scholarships, Grants, and Loans for Undergraduates. Englewood Cliffs, NJ: Prentice-Hall, Inc., 1984.

The College Blue Book: Scholarships, Fellowships, Grants, and Loans. 19th ed. New York: Macmillan Publishing Company, 1983.

The College Cost Book, 1985–86. 6th ed. New York: College Entrance Examination Board, 1985.

EVANGELAUF, JEAN. "Forty Percent of Adults want more education, but most say they would need student aid," *Chronicle of Higher Education* 31:8 (October 23, 1985), p. 17.

FEINGOLD, S. NORMAN, and FEINGOLD, MARIE. *Scholarships, Fellowships, and Loans.* Vol. 7. Arlington, MA: Bellman Publishing Co., 1982.

JOHNSON, WILLIS L., ed. *Directory of Special Programs for Minority Group Members: Career Information Services, Employment Skills Banks, Financial Aid Sources.* Garrett Park, MD: Garrett Park Press, 1980.

KEESLAR, OREON. *Financial Aids for Higher Education: A Catalog for Undergraduates.* 11th ed. Dubuque, IA: William C. Brown Company, Publishers, 1984.

LEHMAN, ANDREA, ed. *The 1986 College Money Handbook.* Princeton, NJ: Peterson's Guides, 1985.

LEIDER, ROBERT. *Your Own Financial Aid Factory: The Guide to Locating College Money.* Alexandria, VA: Octameron Press, 1983.

Need A Lift? 35th ed., 1985. The American Legion, National Emblem Sales, PO Box 1055, Indianapolis, IN 46206. ($1.00.)

U.S. Department of Education. *The Student's Guide: Five Federal Financial Aid Programs, 1985–86.* (Booklet.) Consumer Information Center-V, PO Box 100, Pueblo, CO, 81002. (Free.)

5. SOURCES OF INFORMATION ABOUT IMPROVING STUDY HABITS, TAKING EXAMS, AND WRITING TERM PAPERS

BROWN, WILLIAM F., and HOLTZMAN, WAYNE H. "Organizing for Effective Study," "Passing Exams." In Kathryn Paulsen and Ryan A. Kuhn, eds., *Woman's Almanac: 12 How-to Handbooks in One.* Philadelphia: J.B. Lippincott Company, 1976, pp. 249–52. O.P.

EHRLICK, EUGENE H. *How to Study Better and Get Higher Marks.* Rev. ed. New York: Thomas Y. Crowell, 1976.

LENZ, ELINOR, and SHAEVITZ, MARJORIE HANSEN. *So You Want to Go Back to School: Facing the Realities of Reentry.* New York: McGraw-Hill Book Company, 1977. (Chap. 8: "How to Study and Make the Grades.") O.P.; possible reprint.

PAUK, WALTER. *How to Study in College.* 3rd ed. Boston: Houghton Mifflin Company, 1983.

RAYGOR, ALTON L., and WARK, DAVID M. *Systems for Study.* New York: McGraw-Hill Book Company, 1979.

SPACHE, GEORGE D., and BERG, PAUL C. *The Art of Efficient Reading.* New York: Macmillan Publishing Co., 1984.

STRUNK, WILLIAM, JR., and WHITE, E. B. *The Elements of Style.* New York: Macmillan Publishing Co., 1979.

THATCHER, REBECCA. *Academic Skills: A Handbook for Working Adults Returning to School.* (Booklet.) Ithaca, NY: Industrial and Labor Relations Press, 1980. ILR Press, New York State School of Industrial and Labor Relations, Cornell University, Ithaca, NY 14851-0952. ($2.00.)

YAGGY, ELINOR. *How to Write Your Term Paper.* 5th ed. New York: Harper & Row, Publishers, 1984.

6. SOURCES OF INFORMATION ABOUT CHILD CARE

AUERBACH, STEVANNE. *Choosing Child Care: A Guide for Parents.* New York: E. P. Dutton, 1981. O.P.

BARKO, NAOMI. "One-on-One Child Care: The Options and Costs," *Working Mother,* August 1985, pp. 35–38, 95–98.

DELATINER, BARBARA, and others. "Who Takes Care of the Children?" *McCall's Working Mother,* October 1978, pp. 40-48.

EVANS, E. BELLE, et al. *Designing a Day Care Center: How to Select, Design, and Develop a Day Care Center.* Boston: Beacon Press, 1975. O.P.

Guide for the First-time Babysitter. Johnson & Johnson Baby Products Company, Consumer & Professional Services, Grandview Road, Skillman, NJ 08558. (Free.)

GULLEY, BEVERLY, et al. "A Profile of Campus Child Care Services in the United States," *Journal of the National Association for Women Deans, Administrators, and Counselors* 48:3 (Spring 1985), pp. 8–13.*

KELLY, MARGUERITE, and PARSONS, ELIA S. *The Mother's Almanac.* New York: Doubleday & Co., 1975.

MEYERS, CAROLE. *How to Organize a Babysitting Cooperative and Get Some Free Time Away from the Kids.* Albany, CA: Carousel Press, 1976.

NEWMAN, BETSY. "In Search of Mary Poppins," *Working Woman,* August 1985, pp. 92–93.

ROBERTS, FRANCES. "A Great Nursery School for Your Terrific Kid," *Parents,* September 1985, pp. 85–88.

SCHMIDT, LISA. "Help For Working Parents: San Francisco's Trend-Setting Law Makes Developers Chip in for Child Care," *Image,* November 17, 1985, pp. 9–10.

SEEFELDT, CAROL, and DITTMAN, LAURA L. "Choosing a Day Care Home for Your Child." In Kathryn Paulsen and Ryan A. Kuhn, eds., *Woman's*

Almanac: 12 How-to Handbooks in One. Philadelphia: J. B. Lippincott Company, 1976, pp. 220–21. O.P.

SHAPIRO, CAROL. "How to Organize a Day Care Center." In Kathryn Paulsen and Ryan A. Kuhn, eds., *Woman's Almanac: 12 How-to Handbooks in One.* Philadelphia: J. B. Lippincott Company, 1976, pp. 222–27. O.P.

Some Ways of Distinguishing a Good Early Childhood Program. (Brochure.) National Association for the Education of Young Children, 1834 Connecticut Avenue NW, Washington, DC 20009. (Free.)

U.S. Department of Agriculture, Agricultural Research Unit. *USDA Estimates of the Cost of Raising a Child: A Guide to Their Use and Interpretation.* Misc. publication number 1411. Washington, DC: U.S. Department of Agriculture, 1981.

U.S. Department of Labor, Women's Bureau. *Employers and Child Care: Establishing Services through the Workplace.* Pamphlet 23. Washington, DC: U.S. Department of Labor Women's Bureau, revised, 1982.*

————. *Facts on U.S. Working Women.* Fact Sheet No. 85–4, July 1985: "Working Mothers and Their Children," and Fact Sheet No. 85-2, July 1985: "Women Who Maintain Families." Washington, DC: U.S. Department of Labor, Women's Bureau.*

WEINSTEIN, FRAN. "Start a Day-Care Center." *Working Woman,* August 1978, pp. 24–25.

7. SOURCES OF INFORMATION ABOUT SEX-ROLE SOCIALIZATION AND DISCRIMINATION AGAINST WOMEN IN THE ACADEMIC AND WORKING WORLDS

ANDREWS, LORI. "Myths & Facts About Working Women: A Woman's Career May Suffer Because of Her Employer's Misguided Beliefs," *Parents,* July 1983, pp. 26–30.

ASTIN, HELEN. "Achieving Educational Equity for Women," *National Association of Student Personnel Administrators Journal* 14:1 (Summer 1976), pp. 15–24.*

COX, SUE. *Female Psychology: The Emerging Self.* New York: St. Martin's Press, 1981.

CROSS, K. PATRICIA. "The Woman Student." In FURNISS, W. TODD, and GRAHAM, PATRICIA ALBJERG, eds. *Women in Higher Education.* Washington, D.C.: American Council on Education, 1974, pp. 29–50.* O.P.

DOWD, MAUREEN. "Where Do Women Belong?: Poll Shows They Think Their Place Is on the Job;" *San Francisco Chronicle,* December 12, 1983, p. 24.

ELIAS, MARILYN. "Do You Get Your Share of Financial Aid?" *Ms.,* October 1984, pp. 87–88.

ETAUGH, CLAIRE. "Women Faculty and Administrators in Higher Education: Changes in their Status Since 1972," *Journal of the National Association for Women Deans, Administrators, and Counselors.* 48:1 (Fall 1984), pp. 21–25.*

EVANGELAUF, JEAN. "Women Earned More Doctorates in Education," *Chronicle of Higher Education* 29:3 (September 12, 1984), p. 20.

FIELDS, CHERYL. "High Court Refuses To Review Comparable Worth Claims," *Chronicle of Higher Education* 29:31 (December 5, 1984).*

FORTENBAUGH, JENNIFER. "Hard Facts: The World of Work," *Working Woman,* September 1983, p. 81.

FREEMAN, JO, ed. *Women: A Feminist Perspective.* Palo Alto, CA: Mayfield Publishing Co., 1984.

GERSON, KATHLEEN. *Hard Choices: How Women Decide about Work, Career, and Motherhood.* Berkeley, CA: University of California Press, 1985.

GORNICK, VIVIAN, and MORAN, BARBARA K., eds. *Woman in Sexist Society: Studies in Power and Powerlessness.* New York: New American Library, 1972.

GRAY, EILEEN. *Everywoman's Guide to College.* Millbrae, CA: Les Femmes Publishing, 1975. Chap. 4, "How Women Have Been Socialized to Fail." O.P.

HACKER, ANDREW. "Why Women Still Earn Less than Men," *Working Mother,* October 1983, pp. 25–36.

HARRIS, ANN SUTHERLAND. "The Second Sex in Academe." *American Association of University Professors (AAUP) Bulletin* 56:3 (September 1970), pp. 283–95.*

HARRIS, MICHAEL. "Women May Gain Soon in Earnings Race," *San Francisco Chronicle,* August 31, 1985, p. 5.

HORNER, MARTINA S. "Fail: Bright Women." *Psychology Today.* November 1969, pp. 36–38.

MACCOBY, ELEANOR EMMONS, and JACKLIN, CAROL NAGY. *The Psychology of Sex Differences.* Stanford, CA: Stanford University Press, 1974.

Ms. Magazine, November 1978.

BERNAY, ELAYN. "Affirmative Inaction," pp. 87–90.

CRAWFORD, MARY. "Climbing the Ivy-Covered Walls," pp. 61–63.

On Campus With Women. A quarterly publication of the Project on the Status and Education of Women, $15/year for individuals, $25/year for institutions. Includes occasional topical papers. Project on the Status and Education of Women, Association of American Colleges, 1818 R Street NW, Washington, DC 20009.*

PEAR, ROBERT. "Women Continue to Earn Less: Despite Improvements, Annual Income Only 62% of Men's," *New York Times News Service,* January 9, 1984.

ROSSI, ALICE S., and CALDERWOOD, ANN. *Academic Women on the Move.*

New York: Russell Sage Foundation, 1973:

HUBER, JOAN. "From Sugar and Spice to Professor," pp. 125–35.

ROBY, PAMELA. "Institutional Barriers to Woman Students in Higher Education," pp. 93–124.

STEPHEN, BEVERLY. "Disapproval of Working Moms," *San Francisco Chronicle*, August 29, 1983, p. 15.

WATKINS, BEVERLY. "Number of Women College Presidents Has Doubled in Decade, Study Finds," *Chronicle of Higher Education* 31:3 (September 18, 1985), p. 1.*

8. SOURCES OF INFORMATION ABOUT CAREERS AND FINDING WORK

BARUCH, GRACE, et al. *Lifeprints: New Patterns of Love and Work for Today's Women*. New York: McGraw-Hill Book Company, 1983.

BERNARD, SUSAN, and THOMPSON, GRETCHEN. *Job Search Strategy for College Grads: The Ten Step Plan for Career Success*. Boston: Bob Adams, Inc., 1984.

BODGER, CAROLE, "The *Working Woman* Sixth Annual Salary Survey," *Working Woman*, January 1985, pp. 65–74.

BOLLES, RICHARD. *Tea-Leaves: A New Look at Resumes*. Berkeley, CA: Ten Speed Press, 1979. (50 cents.)

————. *The 1986 What Color Is Your Parachute?: A Practical Guide for Job Hunters & Career Changers*. Berkeley, CA: Ten Speed Press, 1986.

————. *The New Quick Job-Hunting Map*. Berkeley, CA: Ten Speed Press, 1985. ($1.95.)

CATALYST, 250 Park Avenue South, New York, NY 10003. Titles include: *Catalyst Career Opportunity Series for Women*, 40 booklets; two career-planning booklets; the Catalyst Network listing (free); and *Resume Preparation Manual: A Step-by-Step Guide for Women*.

CETRON, MARVIN, and APPEL, MARCIA. *Jobs of the Future: the 500 Best Jobs—Where They'll Be and How to Get Them*. New York: McGraw-Hill Book Company, 1984.

College Placement Council Survey. Bethlehem, PA: The College Placement Council, Inc., July 1985.

Directory: Educational and Career Information Services for Adults, 1985. (Booklet.) San Francisco, CA: The National Center for Educational Brokering, 325 Ninth Street, San Francisco, CA 94103. ($4.00.)

FEINGOLD, S. NORMAN, and MILLER, NORMA. *Emerging Careers: New Occupations for the Year 2000 and Beyond*. Garrett Park, MD: Garrett Park Press, 1983.

"From Surplus to Shortage of Teachers," *U.S. News and World Report*, November 27, 1978, p. 68.

258 / Happier By Degrees

GATES, ANITA. *Ninety Most Promising Careers for the 80's.* New York: Monarch Press, 1982.

GOOD, C. EDWARD. *Does Your Resume Wear Blue Jeans?: The Book on Resume Preparation.* Charlottesville, VA: Word Store, 1985.

HACKER, ANDREW. "Why Families Need Two Incomes," *San Francisco Chronicle,* March 5, 1984, p. 14.

HARDY, CHARLES. "Teacher Shortage Worsens," *San Francisco Examiner,* October 20, 1985, p. A-1.

"'Hidden Subculture' of Unskilled Women," *San Francisco Chronicle,* October 11, 1978, p. 12.

MEDLEY, H. ANTHONY. *Sweaty Palms: The Neglected Art of Being Interviewed.* Berkeley, CA: Ten Speed Press, 1984.

MICHELOZZI, BETTY. *Coming Alive From Nine to Five: The Career Search Handbook.* 2d ed. Palo Alto, CA: Mayfield Publishing Company, 1984. (*This book has an instructor's manual.)

MIRANKER, C. W. "Women Struggle to Climb High-Tech Ladder," *San Francisco Chronicle,* September 1, 1985, p. D-1.

MOORE, SANDRA, et al. *The Turning Point: A Program for Women in Transition.* Workshop outlines, readings, and exercises for program directors and counselors involved with displaced homemakers. Trainer's manual and participant packet. The University of Kansas Division of Continuing Education's Adult Life Resource Center, Continuing Education Building, Lawrence, KS 66045-2610. 1982.*

PIFER, ALAN. "Women Working Toward a New Society," *The Urban and Social Change Review* 11:1 (1978), pp. 3–11.*

Recruiting '86. Bethlehem, PA: The College Placement Council, Inc., October 1985.

SARGENT, JON. "The Job Outlook for College Graduates through the Mid-1990's," *Occupational Outlook Quarterly* 28:2 (Summer 1984), pp. 2–7.

U.S. Department of Commerce, Bureau of the Census. *Money Income and Poverty Status of Families and Persons in the United States: 1984.* Series P-60, No. 149, August 1985.

U.S. Department of Labor, Bureau of Labor Statistics. *Employment and Earnings.* January 1985.

————. *Occupational Outlook Handbook, 1984–85 Edition.* Bulletin 2205. Washington, D.C.: U.S. Government Printing Office, 1984.

————. Women's Bureau. *The United Nations Decade for Women, 1976–1985: Employment in the United States.* Washington, DC: Women's Bureau, 1985. (Free.)

————. *Job Options for Women in the 80's.* Pamphlet 18. 1980. U.S. Department of Labor, Women's Bureau, Washington, D.C. 20210. (Free.)

9. OTHER RESOURCES

BERNARD, JESSIE. *The Future of Marriage.* New Haven, CT: Yale University Press, 1982.

BLUMSTEIN, PHILIP, and SCHWARTZ, PEPPER. "What Makes Today's Marriages Last," *Family Weekly*, November 13, 1983, pp. 4–6.

FELDMAN, SAUL. "Impediment or Stimulant? Marital Status and Graduate Education." In Joan Huber, ed., *Changing Women in a Changing Society.* Chicago: University of Chicago Press, 1973, pp. 220–232.

GROSS, RONALD. *Invitation to Lifelong Learning.* New York: Cambridge Press, 1982.

HOFFMAN, LOIS. "Effects of Maternal Employment on the Child—A Review of the Research," *Developmental Psychology* 10:2 (March 1974), pp. 204–28.

KOON, BRUCE. "Housing Prices Increase," *San Francisco Examiner*, October 27, 1985, p. H-1.

PATTERSON, GERALD. *Families: Applications of Social Learning to Family Life.* Champaign, IL: Research Press, 1975.

ROBBINS, MICHAEL. "Adult Education: Using Your Head," *New York*, August 19, 1985, pp. 50–60.

SMITH, SALLIE, ed. *A Directory of Research on Women: 1980.* Center for Continuing Education of Women, University of Michigan, 350 South Thayer Street, Ann Arbor, MI 48104-1608. ($2.50.)*

STEINMANN, ANNE, and FOX, DANIEL. "Male-Female Perceptions of the Female Role in the United States," *The Journal of Psychology* 64 (1966), pp. 265–276.*

WASOWICZ, LIDIA. "American Family 'Resilient,'" *United Press International*, September 22, 1985.

350 Ways Colleges Are Serving Adult Learners. New York: College Board, 1979.*

Index